Guernsey Memorial Library
3 Court Street, Norwich, NY 13815
(607) 334-4034
www.guernseylibrary.org

Women
Tennis Stars

Women Tennis Stars

Biographies and Records of Champions, 1800s to Today

DENNIS J. PHILLIPS

Foreword by Bud Collins

McFarland & Company, Inc., Publishers

Jefferson, North Carolina, and London

LIBRARY OF CONGRESS CATALOGUING-IN-PUBLICATION DATA

Phillips, Dennis J., 1947–
Women tennis stars : biographies and records
of champions, 1800s to today / Dennis J. Phillips ;
foreword by Bud Collins.
p.   cm.
Includes bibliographical references and index.

ISBN 978-0-7864-3528-9
illustrated case binding : 50# alkaline paper ∞

1. Women tennis players — Biography.   I. Title.
GV994.A1P55   2009   796.3420922 — dc22 [B]   2008049016

British Library cataloguing data are available

On the cover, from the top: Evonne Goolagong stretching for a backhand
while playing on the Virginia Slims Tour (Carol L. Newson);
Steffi Graf celebrating her 6th French Open singles title in 1999
after beating Martina Hingis in three sets (Carol L. Newson);
Monica Seles playing her baseline game while hitting her
two-handed forehand at the US Open (Mark M. Mayers);
Venus Williams prepares to hit a topspin forehand at the
Wimbledon Championships in 2002 (Carol L. Newsom).
Background ©2009 Shutterstock

Manufactured in the United States of America

*McFarland & Company, Inc., Publishers
Box 611, Jefferson, North Carolina 28640
www.mcfarlandpub.com*

For those who made tennis a significant part of my life —

Jerome H. Lipson, who always believed in me; Irene Lipson, without whose genetic blueprint I wouldn't be able to strike a tennis ball properly; Denis Ross, my first tennis buddy; Edgar Levy, who taught me how to hit a backhand groundstroke without slice; my favorite doubles partner, Chuck Lumia who never quit on the court and always gave me a ride home when I needed one; Nancy Rosenthal, who was my one and only mixed doubles partner; Coach Bernie Forer, who showed me the geometry of a tennis court; Coach Bob Kilgus, who offered me a tennis scholarship to Rider University; Coach Ken Webb, who opened the door to coaching for me; Dr. Gene Slaski, who was responsible for having the tennis facility built at Penn State Lehigh Valley; and Jim Brown, who introduced me to a whole other dimension of the game. Also, for my worthy opponents over the years, my college teams, the hundreds of kinesiology students who taught me as much about human nature as I taught them about tennis, my sons Brian and Dennis, who continue to allow me to share with them my passion for the sport, my grandson, Gage, who has great instincts on the tennis court, my granddaughter, Callie, who I'm sure will be equally instinctive, and my wife, Susan, who knows how to play the game.

Acknowledgments

Many people and organizations contributed to this book. The magnificent photos of Carol Newsom grace several pages between its covers. They appear through the generosity of her estate and the cooperation of her husband, David Newsom, and his assistant, Carmita Baker. Carol Newsom, who passed away from breast cancer in 2004, was the first female photographer to be granted press credentials for Centre Court at Wimbledon. In her memory, the author's royalties are being donated to Susan G. Komen for the Cure. Others who contributed photographs are www.sporting-heroes.net, the Prints and Photographs Division of the Library of Congress, the ITA Women's Hall of Fame, Kenneth Ritchie Wimbledon Library, International Tennis Hall of Fame and Museum, and Mark M. Mayers.

Thanks to the Sony Ericsson WTA Tour and, in particular, Gina Clement, for providing statistical help. Gratitude to Bud Collins, who generously shared information from his popular tennis encyclopedia with the author. As usual, Frank Phelps was there for me when I needed his historical expertise. A thank you to Penn State University for providing me with the scholarly environment, colleagues, friends, and financial support necessary to complete the book. In particular, I want to thank several Nittany Lions — Judy Sandt, Kathy Romig, Steph Derstine, Roger Egolf, Barbara Cantalupo, and Kenneth Thigpen. Others who helped along the way were Millie West, Kat Anderson, Audrey Snell, Pat Yeomans, Joanie Agler, and Jeanne Cherry. Special thanks for the research and writing contributions of Susan Phillips and Shali Rego, associated with "A Brief History of Women's Tennis Fashion," which appears as Appendix F of this book.

Contents

II — Records

III — Rankings

Foreword
by Bud Collins

The gang's all here, and what a collection of varied personalities and extraordinary skills Dennis Phillips has corralled between covers in his monumental book.

They came from across the globe, grasping their moments of fame, these women making indelible marks as they battled for championships and places in history in a very competitive game called lawn tennis. Several leap out at you, captured in brilliant photos — some of them, I'm happy to say, by my friend Carol Newsom. Determined, talented Carol, the first woman to be permitted a place in photographers' row at Wimbledon's Centre Court, sadly is no longer with us. But her striking work is, and a portion of the proceeds from this book will go in Carol's name to Susan G. Komen for the Cure.

The women's journey from the earliest tournaments in the 1880s to the present day hasn't been easy. In the upper reaches of the game they generally played second racket to the men, receiving less attention in the press and inferior prize money when open tennis — the integration of amateurs and professionals — dawned in 1968.

But Dennis's recognition of and devotion to the female game brought forth this remarkable book that belongs to the women alone, a parade of all-time champs accompanied by their accomplishments, particularly in the four major champi-onships: the Australian, French, and U.S. Opens, and Wimbledon.

Starting with Lottie Dod, the English child prodigy who won Wimbledon at fifteen in 1887, he has tracked down such champs of the early twentieth century — in corsets and ankle-length gowns — as England's Dorothea Douglass Chambers and the first American great, May Sutton Bundy. Then on to France's invincible Suzanne Lenglen after World War I, who shortened her skirts, introducing sex appeal, and Americans Helen Wills Moody, who almost never lost, and Alice Marble, boldly attacking at the net. After World War II, a period of American domination, Althea Gibson leaped the color bar to become the initial black champ, and "Little Mo" Connolly achieved the first female Grand Slam. Then in 1968 peppery Californian Billie Jean King led the way into professionalism, cheering the U.S. Open's paying equal prize money to men and women in 1973. By 2007, as long-limbed Venus Williams won the fourth of her five Wimbledon prizes, all four majors were paying the same money to both sexes, and lady millionaires were popping up all over. In fact, first prize in the 2008 U.S. Open was $1.6 million.

Dennis tells you all about them. Moreover, he gets into fashion, a some-times magnetic feature ever since Mlle. Lenglen showed calves, chasing petticoats and whalebone corsets to the attic. But compared to Serena Williams's latter-day, skimpy "cat suit," Lenglen would have seemed overdressed.

I congratulate Dennis Phillips on his research and dedication to the women and their progress, and am glad to have his work in my library.

Bud Collins is a journalist and commentator with the *Boston Globe*, ESPN, and the Tennis Channel. He is also the author of several books including *My Life with the Pros, The Education of a Tennis Player* with Rod Laver, and *The Bud Collins History of Tennis: An Authoritative Encyclopedia and Record Book.*

Preface

On September 20, 1973, a tennis match was played in the Houston Astrodome with more than 30,000 spectators in attendance. Fifty million curious fans watched on prime time television. The participants in this historic match were 29-year-old Billie Jean King and 55-year-old Bobby Riggs. King beat Riggs rather convincingly: 6–4, 6–3, 6–3. King's victory was noteworthy in two ways — it enhanced dramatically the image of women's tennis around the world, and it accelerated the broader women's movement in the United States and internationally. Today, women's professional tennis is exploding with new stars and record prize money. In 2007, the All England Lawn Tennis Club at Wimbledon announced that equal prize money would be awarded to both men and women players for the first time in the history of the esteemed Grand Slam tournament. It was the last of the Grand Slam venues to establish gender parity as it applied to prize money. The impact on sports and society of many of the game's stars continues to be significant. Venus and Serena Williams have shown young women, regardless of their backgrounds, how dreams can come true on and off the tennis court. The popularity of these two sisters, along with the influx of Russian and Eastern European players, is carving the future of women's tennis in the 21st century.

Women Tennis Stars contains biographical and statistical information about the most prominent players the game has known. It summarizes the careers of 35 great players who made important contributions to the game — Suzanne Lenglen, Helen Wills, Maureen Connolly, Billie Jean King, Chris Evert, Martina Navratilova, Steffi Graf, Monica Seles, and many more. Looking into the future, the sport patiently awaits how history will judge today's stars, such as the Williams sisters, Lindsay Davenport, Justine Henin and a host of young players from around the world, some of whom have already made an impact on the sport.

Professional women's tennis is currently played in a style unlike any in the past. With an emphasis on extreme physical conditioning, high tech rackets, and powerful shots, the game has captured the attention of sports fans around the world. Readers looking for factual information about female champions will find it here. The Records section is a source for the results of major competitions in women's tennis. It comprehensively covers the final outcome of major events, including Fed Cup, Olympic Games, Wightman Cup, Hopman Cup, and Grand Slam tournaments. Yearly rankings, career earnings, and other statistics are also included.

The accuracy and reliability of information on the individuals who've made it such a popular and entertaining game have been of paramount importance to the author. The most reliable sources were consulted when gathering data. Information was obtained from publications issued by sanctioned tennis organizations, including the United States Tennis Association (USTA), the Women's Tennis Association (WTA), and the International Tennis Federation (ITF). Other sources consulted are highly regarded and well-known within the field.

Players in the Profiles of Champions section are listed chronologically according to the year of their birth. Such an arrangement adds a refreshing historical perspective to the book. Each player's full name is listed in this section. A different form of a player's name may appear in other sections of the book depending on her marital status, her preferred name at the time of the event, or the name the player uses today.

A number of acronyms have been used throughout the book. They are as follows:

ATA— American Tennis Association

DNP— Did not play

ESPY— Excellence in Sports Performance Yearly

ILTF— International Lawn Tennis Federation

ITF— International Tennis Federation

ITA— Intercollegiate Tennis Association

NCAA— National Collegiate Athletic Association

RSHE Club de Campo— Real Sociedad Hípica Española Club de Campo

USLTA— United States Lawn Tennis Association

USTA— United States Tennis Association

WTA— Women's Tennis Association

UNESCO— United Nations Educational, Scientific and Cultural Organization

I

PROFILES OF CHAMPIONS

LOTTIE DOD

Charlotte Dod

b. September 24, 1871, Bebington, England / *d.* June 27, 1960, Sway, England
Right-handed; "Lottie," "The Little Wonder"

Grand Slam Highlights

Wimbledon

Year	Result
1893	Winner, Singles
1892	Winner, Singles
1891	Winner, Singles
1888	Winner, Singles
1887	Winner, Singles

Honors

- Inducted into the International Women's Sports Hall of Fame in 1986
- Inducted into the International Tennis Hall of Fame in 1983

About Lottie Dod

Lottie Dod, the youngest of four children, was the daughter of a wealthy cotton broker. All four of the Dod children shared a passion for sports and games of all kinds. When her family was struck with the lawn tennis mania that was spreading through the leisure classes, Lottie started playing tennis on the two courts located in her family's garden. When she was 11 she won her first tournament, a consolation doubles title at the Northern Championships in Manchester. In 1886, she beat the invincible Maud Watson in the singles finals at a tournament in Bath. A year later she won her first Wimbledon title at the age of 15. She went on to win 5 Wimbledon singles titles from 1887 to 1893 without losing a match. In 1890, she skipped the tournament to go yachting with her sister.

After winning Wimbledon in 1893, Dod retired from tennis at the age of 21. Having exhausted her love for tennis, she quickly moved on to other sports. She showed her natural athletic ability, speed, and coordination by excelling in whatever she attempted. She won the British Ladies' Golf Championship at Troon in 1904. At the 1908 Olympic Games, she won a silver medal in archery. She enjoyed winter sports by participating in hockey, ice skating, and bobsledding. She also enjoyed cycling, mountaineering, and playing the piano.

Many consider Dod to be the first real female athlete to play tennis. Her level of athleticism was compared to that of the men who played the game. In a handicapped exhibition match against the reigning men's Wimbledon champion, Ernest Renshaw, she lost in three hard fought sets 2–6, 7–7, 7–5. Later that year in a similar exhibition match, she played William Renshaw, a 6-time Wimbledon champion, and beat him 6–2, 6–4. The teenage prodigy dominated her female competitors. She combined her powerful forehand and reliable backhand with a fine overhead and an outstanding volley to produce an almost unbeatable style of play. She was an all-court player with no obvious weakness. Her serve, however, was struck under-handed because she believed that the over arm serve was a waste of energy and had

no compensating advantages. Like many champions who followed her, she had the ability to hit risky shots under pressure to win important points in a match. The most notable woman champion of the 19th century, Lottie Dod transformed the image of a genteel Victorian woman into an aggressive, physically fit, competitive athlete.

At the time of her death at age 88, Lottie Dod was reputed to be a competitive bridge player. She never married.

Lottie Dod, 19th century Wimbledon champion (courtesy Kenneth Ritchie Wimbledon Library).

Notable Quote About Lottie Dod

"A player of carefully-cultivated skills, split-second reactions, and relentless determination, her manner in the arena was invariably businesslike." Jeffrey Pearson, sports journalist

Writings About Lottie Dod

Little, Alan. *Lottie Dod: Wimbledon Champion and All-Rounder Extraordinary*. London: Wimbledon Lawn Tennis Museum, 1983.

Pearson, Jeffrey. *Lottie Dod, Champion of Champions: The Story of an Athlete*. Birkenhead, England: Countyvise, 1988.

DOROTHEA DOUGLASS

Dorothea Katherine Douglass Lambert Chambers

b. September 3, 1878, Ealing, England / *d.* January 7, 1960, London, England
Right-handed; "Dolly"

Career Rankings

World Top 10 Singles

Year	Ranking
1925	7

Wightman Cup Record

Year	Record
1926	Singles: DNP, Doubles: 0–1
1925	Singles: 1–0, Doubles: 1–0

Olympic Tennis Medals

Year	Medal
1908	Singles: Gold

Grand Slam Highlights

Tournament	Year	Result
Wimbledon	1920	Finalist, Singles
Wimbledon	1920	Finalist, Doubles
Wimbledon	1919	Finalist, Singles
Wimbledon	1919	Finalist, Doubles
Wimbledon	1919	Finalist, Mixed Doubles
Wimbledon	1914	Winner, Singles
Wimbledon	1913	Winner, Singles
Wimbledon	1913	Finalist, Doubles
Wimbledon	1911	Winner, Singles
Wimbledon	1910	Winner, Singles
Wimbledon	1907	Finalist, Singles
Wimbledon	1906	Winner, Singles
Wimbledon	1905	Finalist, Singles
Wimbledon	1904	Winner, Singles
Wimbledon	1903	Winner, Singles

Honors

- Inducted into the International Tennis Hall of Fame in 1981

About Dorothea Douglass

Dorothea Douglass, seven-time Wimbledon singles champion, played her most memorable match in 1919 at the age of 40. When the Wimbledon Championships resumed after World War I there was an unprecedented demand for tickets in anticipation of the match between Dorothea Douglass and Suzanne Lenglen. Some 8,000 spectators, including King George V and Queen Mary, were in attendance to watch the finals match. The drama-filled match lived up to fan expectations. After losing the first set 10–8, Douglass came back to take the second set 6–4. Lenglen darted to a 4–1 lead in the third set. Douglass once again came back to take a 6–5, 40–15 lead, but could not hold on for the victory. Lenglen eventually won the decisive set 9–7. Douglass' loss, however, did not diminish her brilliant career.

Born the daughter of the vicar of St. Matthews in Ealing, she began playing tennis against a wall. Always present were her dolls, teddy bears, and other nursery animals lined up to watch her play. She

9

won her first tournament at the Ealing Club when she was only 8 years old. She played in her first Wimbledon match in 1900 at the age of 19. She won her first Wimbledon singles title three years later. One of her fiercest rivals was May Sutton, whom she played in the finals from 1905 to 1907. Douglass played in a total of 11 Wimbledon finals, winning 7 of them. Despite a chronic wrist injury, she dominated the game until the outbreak of the war.

Douglass' game centered around a flexible forehand and a fine drop shot. She often hit a short angled, cross court forehand shot for a winner. A capable volleyer and shrewd tactician, she advocated baseline play for women.

Douglass extended her competitive tennis career by helping Great Britain win the Wightman Cup in 1925. She won both her singles and doubles matches to capture a 4–3 win over the United States. At the

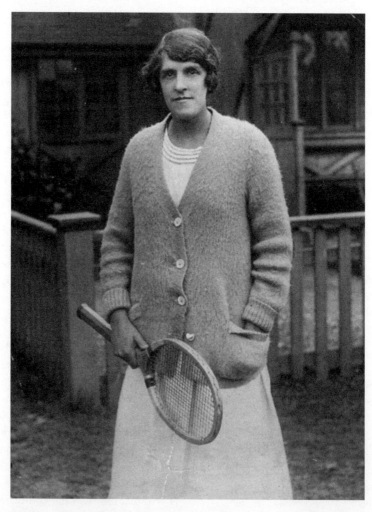

Dorothea Douglass, 7-time Wimbledon champion, led Britain to a Wightman Cup victory over the United States in 1925 (courtesy International Tennis Hall of Fame and Museum, Newport, RI).

time she was 46 years old. She played in her last Wimbledon doubles match at the age of 48. She later became a professional coach and remained fanatically keen on tennis until her death in 1960 at the age of 81.

Notable Quote About Dorothea Douglass

"In 1911 she achieved the most one sided success in the history of lawn tennis. She became Wimbledon champion without losing a game." Alan Little, tennis historian

Writings By and About Dorothea Douglass

Chambers, Dorothea Katherine Lambert. *Lawn Tennis for Ladies*. London: Methuen, 1910.

Davidson, Owen, and C.M. Jones. *Great Women Tennis Players*. London: Pelham Books, 1971, pp. 10–13.

Little, Alan. *Dorothea Chambers: Wimbledon Champion Seven Times*. London: Wimbledon Lawn Tennis Museum, 1985.

Little, Alan, and Lance Tingay. *Wimbledon Ladies: A Centenary Record 1884–1984; The Single Champions*. London: Wimbledon Lawn Tennis Museum, 1984, pp. 18–19.

MOLLA MALLORY

Anna Margarethe Bjurstedt Mallory

b. March 6, 1884, Oslo, Norway / *d.* November 22, 1959, Stockholm, Sweden
Right-handed; "Molla"

Career Rankings

USTA Top 10 Singles

Year	Ranking
1928	4
1927	2
1926	1
1925	3
1924	3
1923	2
1922	1
1921	1
1920	1
1919	3
1918	1
1916	1

World Top 10 Singles

Year	Ranking
1927	4
1926	4
1925	5
1924	4
1923	5
1922	2
1921	2

Wightman Cup Record

Year	Record
1928	Singles: 0–2, Doubles: DNP
1927	Singles: 2–0, Doubles: DNP
1925	Singles: 1–1, Doubles: 0–1
1924	Singles: 0–2, Doubles: DNP
1923	Singles: 2–0, Doubles: 1–0

Olympic Tennis Medals

Year	Medal
1912	Singles: Bronze

Grand Slam Highlights

Tournament	Year	Result
Wimbledon	1922	Finalist, Singles
United States	1926	Winner, Singles
United States	1924	Finalist, Singles
United States	1924	Finalist, Mixed Doubles
United States	1923	Finalist, Singles
United States	1923	Winner, Mixed Doubles
United States	1922	Winner, Singles
United States	1922	Finalist, Doubles
United States	1922	Winner, Mixed Doubles
United States	1921	Winner, Singles
United States	1921	Finalist, Mixed Doubles
United States	1920	Winner, Singles
United States	1920	Finalist, Mixed Doubles
United States	1918	Winner, Singles
United States	1918	Finalist, Doubles
United States	1918	Finalist, Mixed Doubles
United States	1917	Winner, Singles
United States	1917	Winner, Doubles
United States	1917	Winner, Mixed Doubles
United States	1916	Winner, Singles

Tournament	Year	Result
United States	1916	Winner, Doubles
United States	1915	Winner, Singles
United States	1915	Finalist, Mixed Doubles

Honors

• Inducted into the International Tennis Hall of Fame in 1958

About Molla Mallory

Best known for her indomitable fighting spirit, Mallory grew up in Nor-

Molla Mallory, 8-time United States singles champion, hitting a forehand drive at Forest Hills (courtesy Prints and Photographs Division, Library of Congress).

way playing tennis at the Christiana Lawn Tennis Club. She won the Norwegian national championship ten times and was a bronze medal winner at the 1912 Olympics before coming to the United States in 1914. She burst upon the American scene by winning the United States national singles title in 1915. It was the first of eight national titles she won between the years 1915 and 1926. Her most remarkable victory came at the age of 40 when she beat Elizabeth Ryan after trailing 1–5 and 15–40 in the third set. She also won several national doubles and mixed doubles titles during her rein as one of the top women players of her time.

Recognized as one of America's pioneer women tennis champions, Mallory never won an international title outside of the United States after leaving Norway in 1914. She was a singles finalist at Wimbledon in 1922, losing to Suzanne Lenglen in straight sets. A year earlier, she beat Lenglen in the semi-finals of the U.S. Championships when the French woman defaulted the match after double faulting in the first game of the second set. It was the only post–World War I defeat that Lenglen suffered as an amateur. Molla played on five Wightman Cup teams from 1923 to 1928 when she compiled a 5–5 record in singles and a 1–1 record in doubles. She married Franklin I. Mallory in 1919. After suffering a knee injury in 1929, she retired from tournament competition. Fluent in several languages, she worked in the U.S.

Office of Censorship during the Second World War. Later, she worked as a sales associate for Lord and Taylor. She passed away in 1959 after a long illness.

Although Mallory was generous and friendly toward her competitors, she was a fierce opponent. She was once described by a reporter as a panther stalking its victim, ready to spring at any time. She revolutionized the women's game with her powerful forehand ground stroke. Her steady backhand lacked power and she was not a strong net player. Her will to win and extremely competitive spirit overcame her weaknesses. She was to women's tennis what Bill Tilden was to the men's game — but unlike Tilden, she never questioned a line call and was never involved in a dispute on or off the court. With her great sportsmanship, she always brought out the best in her opponents. The Norwegian always kept the game in perspective, never letting it become the be-all and end-all of her existence.

Notable Quote About Molla Mallory

"No woman can beat Molla." Bill Tilden, tennis champion

Writings By and About Molla Mallory

Bjurstedt, Molla, and Samuel Crowther. *Tennis for Women*. New York: Doubleday, Page, 1916.

Jacobs, Helen Hull. *Gallery of Champions*. New York: A.S. Barnes, 1949. pp. 86–102.

MAY SUTTON

May Godfray Sutton Bundy

b. September 25, 1886, Plymouth, England /
d. October 4, 1975, Santa Monica, California
Right-handed

Career Rankings

USTA Top 10 Singles

Year	Ranking
1928	5
1925	8
1922	5
1921	4

World Top 10 Singles

Year	Ranking
1922	9
1921	6

Wightman Cup Record

Year	Record
1925	Singles: DNP, Doubles: 0–1

Grand Slam Highlights

Tournament	Year	Result
Wimbledon	1907	Winner, Singles
Wimbledon	1906	Finalist, Singles
Wimbledon	1905	Winner, Singles
United States	1925	Finalist, Doubles
United States	1904	Winner, Singles
United States	1904	Winner, Doubles
United States	1904	Finalist, Mixed Doubles

Honors

• Inducted into the International Tennis Hall of Fame in 1956

About May Sutton

Although she was of British heritage, May Sutton was the first American to win Wimbledon. Born in England, her family moved to a 10 acre ranch outside of Pasadena, California, when she was six. May learned to play tennis when she was 10 years old on a clay court built by her brother on the ranch. She shared the court with her four sisters, who also played tennis. Three of her sisters, Violet, Ethel, and Florence, played competitively. As the youngest daughter, May had to fight for time on the family tennis court. Finally, in 1900, after beating her sister Violet in a minor tournament, she earned the respect of her siblings. At age 12, she beat Violet in the finals of the Southern California Championships. She went on to win the Pacific Coast Championships in that same year. In 1904, her brother took her east to play in the National Championships, where she won the singles and doubles titles. Although she did not compete in many tournaments, she was considered the top-ranked woman player in the United States for several years.

Before traveling abroad and playing at Wimbledon, May Sutton won several tournaments in California and the U.S. national championship. May played in three consecutive singles finals on the grass in London, winning the title in 1905 and 1907. She utilized her speed, a powerful serve, a driving forehand, and aggressive net game to win her titles on grass. She was a pioneer in tennis fashion. She wore shorter skirts than other women players of her day and rolled up her sleeves while playing to gain more freedom of movement.

Sutton embodied the California tennis style as well as its lifestyle. During a match against Hazel Wightman in 1910, after splitting sets, Sutton sat down in a wicker chair and asked for a cup of tea. A waiter from the nearby hotel delivered her tea on a tray; she drank it and 20 minutes later resumed the tennis match. She won the third set 6–4. Although she was criticized for exhibiting "shocking gamesmanship" at the time, California tennis players and California itself turned out to be winners.

May Sutton was married to Thomas Bundy in 1912. She played competitive tennis through the 1920s. In 1929, she reached the quarterfinals at Wimbledon at the age

May Sutton's exaggerated follow-through while hitting a backhand during the challenge round at Coronado Country Club in 1908 (courtesy Prints and Photographs Division, Library of Congress).

of 41. Sutton remained active in tennis throughout her lifetime. She was a tennis instructor during the 1930s, 1940s, and 1950s, and continued playing until age 85. Her daughter, Dorothy Bundy Cheney, became the first American to win the women's singles title at the Australian Open in 1938. May died of cancer at age 88.

Notable Quote About May Sutton

"Her main weapon was the forehand drive which she wielded with power and precision. Her temperament was ideal and her enthusiasm boundless." Alan Little, tennis historian

Writings By and About May Sutton

Little, Alan. *May Sutton: The First Overseas Wimbledon Champion.* London: The Wimbledon Lawn Tennis Museum, 1984.

Sutton, May. "My Career as a Lawn Tennis Player." *American Lawn Tennis* May 5, 1912: 40–41.

HAZEL HOTCHKISS WIGHTMAN

Hazel Virginia Hotchkiss Wightman

b. December 20, 1886, Healdsburg, California /
d. December 5, 1974, Chestnut Hill, Massachusetts
Right-handed; "Lady Tennis," "Queen Mother of Tennis"

Career Rankings

USTA Top 10 Singles

Year	Ranking
1919	1
1918	2
1915	2

Wightman Cup Record

Year	Record
1931	Singles: DNP, Doubles: 0–1
1929	Singles: DNP, Doubles: 0–1
1927	Singles: DNP, Doubles: 1–0
1924	Singles: DNP, Doubles: 1–0
1923	Singles: DNP, Doubles: 1–0

Olympic Tennis Medals

Year	Medal
1924	Doubles: Gold, Mixed Doubles: Gold

Grand Slam Highlights

Tournament	Year	Result
Wimbledon	1924	Winner, Doubles
United States	1928	Winner, Doubles
United States	1926	Finalist, Mixed Doubles
United States	1924	Winner, Doubles
United States	1923	Finalist, Doubles

Tournament	Year	Result
United States	1920	Winner, Mixed Doubles
United States	1919	Winner, Singles
United States	1919	Finalist, Doubles
United States	1918	Winner, Mixed Doubles
United States	1915	Finalist, Singles
United States	1915	Winner, Doubles
United States	1915	Winner, Mixed Doubles
United States	1911	Winner, Singles
United States	1911	Winner, Doubles
United States	1911	Winner, Mixed Doubles
United States	1910	Winner, Singles
United States	1910	Winner, Doubles
United States	1910	Winner, Mixed Doubles
United States	1909	Winner, Singles
United States	1909	Winner, Doubles
United States	1909	Winner, Mixed Doubles

Honors

- Inducted into the ITA Women's Collegiate Tennis Hall of Fame in 1995
- Selected for the International Women's Sports Hall of Fame in 1986
- Received the Order of Honorary Commander of the British Empire in 1973

• Inducted into the International Tennis Hall of Fame in 1957

About Hazel Hotchkiss Wightman

In her lifetime, Hazel Hotchkiss Wightman made several significant contributions to the game of tennis. She introduced net play to the women's game, reformed tennis fashion, founded international women's tennis competition, and organized teaching programs for young-

sters. In 1912, she married George William Wightman of Boston and eventually had five children.

She learned the fundamentals of tennis in her graveled back yard playing with her brothers over a rope strung across the yard. Not wanting to get a bad bounce off the unpredictable gravel surface, she always tried to hit the ball before it bounced. She became the first woman tennis player to rely heavily on the volley in tournament competition. Her strong net game permitted her to play doubles into her 40s. She won her last doubles title at the age

Hazel Hotchkiss playing in a 1910 exhibition match against May Sutton at Mt. Washington in Los Angeles before 3000 spectators (courtesy Prints and Photographs Division, Library of Congress).

of 56. Her darting movements at the net required less restrictive clothing and she often wore sleeveless dresses. This was revolutionary for a turn-of-the-century American woman.

In 1919, Wightman envisioned a women's tournament similar to the Davis Cup. She even donated a silver vase to the United States Lawn Tennis Association to promote competition among women from different countries. The first Wightman Cup match took place four years later when the United States played Great Britain at the West Side Tennis Club at Forest Hills. Wightman represented the United States as a player in 1923, 1924, 1927, 1929, and 1931. She also coached the team for thirteen years. In honor of the 50th anniversary of the Wightman Cup in 1973, Queen Elizabeth II made Wightman an honorary Commander of the British Empire.

Wightman's accomplishments on the court were incomparable. She won the U.S. national titles in singles, doubles, and mixed doubles in 1909, 1910, and 1911. In 1911, she won all three of her finals matches on the same day. She won the women's doubles title at Wimbledon in 1924, and "double" gold at the 1924 Summer Olympics by winning the women's doubles and the mixed doubles titles in Paris. Wightman was a self-taught tennis player. Her unique style emphasized the volley and half-volley and a variety of spins and chops. Her success in doubles is attributed to her extraordinary volleying skills.

Her teaching career began in the 1920s. She conducted free clinics at the Longwood Cricket Club and held tournaments for players of all skill levels for more than 50 years. Her enthusiasm for tennis was contagious. She inspired hundreds of young girls to participate in the sport. She single-handedly turned a "genteel" game into what has become one of the most popular individual sports for women in the world. Her most famous pupils included Helen Wills Moody (Roark) and Helen Hull Jacobs. Until her death in 1974, she continued to teach tennis.

Notable Quote About Hazel Hotchkiss Wightman

"She had obviously been a fierce competitor, yet her code of behavior was firmly old-fashioned. She spoke emphatically about proper manners — about grace, femininity, and good sportsmanship — on and off the court among women players." Barbara Klaw, sports journalist

Writings By and About Hazel Hotchkiss Wightman

Carter, Tom. *First Lady of Tennis: Hazel Hotchkiss Wightman.* Berkley, Calif.: Creative Arts Book Co., 2001.

Klaw, Barbara. "Queen Mother of Tennis: An Interview with Hazel Hotchkiss Wightman." *American Heritage* August 1975: 16–24ff.

Maddocks, Melvin. "The Original Little Old Lady in Tennis Shoes." *Sports Illustrated* April 10, 1972: 36–38ff.

Wightman, Hazel Hotchkiss. *Better Tennis.* Boston: Houghton Mifflin, 1933.

Wind, Herbert Warren. "Profiles: Hazel Hotchkiss Wightman." *New Yorker* 30 August 1952: 31–32ff.

SUZANNE LENGLEN

Suzanne Rachel Flore Lenglen

b. May 24, 1899, Paris, France / d. July 4, 1938, Paris, France
Right-handed; "The Divine One"

Career Rankings

World Top 10 Singles

Year	Ranking
1926	1
1925	1
1924	1
1923	1
1922	1
1921	1

Olympic Tennis Medals

Year	Medal
1920	Singles: Gold
	Doubles: Bronze
	Mixed Doubles: Gold

Grand Slam Highlights

Tournament	Year	Result
French	1926	Winner, Singles
French	1926	Winner, Doubles
French	1926	Winner, Mixed Doubles
French	1925	Winner, Singles
French	1925	Winner, Doubles
French	1925	Winner, Mixed Doubles
Wimbledon	1925	Winner, Singles
Wimbledon	1925	Winner, Doubles
Wimbledon	1925	Winner, Mixed Doubles
Wimbledon	1923	Winner, Singles
Wimbledon	1923	Winner, Doubles
Wimbledon	1922	Winner, Singles
Wimbledon	1922	Winner, Doubles
Wimbledon	1922	Winner, Mixed Doubles
Wimbledon	1921	Winner, Singles
Wimbledon	1921	Winner, Doubles
Wimbledon	1920	Winner, Singles
Wimbledon	1920	Winner, Doubles
Wimbledon	1920	Winner, Mixed Doubles
Wimbledon	1919	Winner, Singles
Wimbledon	1919	Winner, Doubles

Honors

- In 2000, ranked number 33 in *Sports Illustrated for Women*'s "100 Greatest Female Athletes of the 20th Century"
- Selected for the International Women's Sports Hall of Fame in 1984
- Inducted into the International Tennis Hall of Fame in 1978

About Suzanne Lenglen

Of all her appearances on the tennis court, the most talked about and watched tennis match Lenglen played was in a minor tournament at the Carlton Club in Cannes, France, in 1926. It was here where the two best women tennis players of their day met for the first and only time in their careers. Helen Wills, the young rising American star, was playing the Riviera circuit in hopes of forcing the long-awaited showdown. Hundreds of reporters and cameramen were present. Distinguished guests included royalty, literary personalities, and world renowned businessmen. Many spectators watched from the tops of cars, trees, and roofs — all hoping for just a glimpse of the players in action. Lenglen, fighting off fatigue, coughing spells, and a bizarre ending to the match, prevailed in straight sets 6–3, 8–6.

At an early age, Suzanne showed unusual athletic ability. She was a large-boned girl with outstanding coordination. She became a skilled cyclist and strong swimmer at a very young age. While vacationing on the Riviera, her father became fascinated with tennis. Although not a player, he was mesmerized by the tactical aspects of the game. Eventually, Suzanne shared her father's interest in the game. After presenting his daughter with her first racket, Papa Lenglen outlined a tennis court on a nearby lawn. Suzanne loved playing the game. She quickly mastered the skills of striking the ball and understood the tactical part of the game. In 1914, at the age of 15, she won the World Hard Court Championships at Saint-Cloud, France. Her triumph marked the beginning of an extraordinary tennis career. Papa Lenglen was Suzanne's teacher, trainer, coach, agent, manager, and oftentimes her most severe critic, until his death in 1929.

Lenglen won her first Grand Slam tournament at Wimbledon in 1919 and lost just one match until her retirement from amateur tennis in 1926. Her only singles defeat was suffered at the hands of Molla Mallory at Forest Hills in 1921. Losing the first set and trailing 2–1 in the second, she defaulted the match, resulting in a storm of criticism. It was the last time she played on U.S. soil until she joined the pro tour in 1926 with Mary K. Browne. She won Wimbledon each year from 1919 through 1925, except 1924, when illness forced her to withdraw after the fourth round. In 1926, her last Wimbledon appearance resulted in disaster. Following a misunderstanding about her match start time, she fainted and withdrew from the tournament. During her illustrious career she won a total of 81 singles titles, 73 doubles, and 8 mixed doubles. She won 21 Grand Slam titles.

Lenglen was perceived by her fans and the press as a tennis goddess. She was an invincible sports figure of her era. She revolutionized women's tennis fashion by wearing a skirt that provocatively exposed her thighs, a low-cut blouse, and her brightly colored bandeau. She sipped brandy and reapplied her make-up between sets. She was expected to win all of her matches. She had extraordinary strokes, mobility, and a strong competitive spirit on the court. She played with the grace of a ballerina and the skill of an artist. Her judgment was faultless and she possessed instinctive strategy. There was no chink in her armor.

In 1927, Suzanne retired from her short-lived appearance on the professional tour and founded the Lenglen Tennis School in Paris. Suzanne Lenglen never married and had no children. She died of pernicious anemia at the age of 39. To honor one of the greatest ladies of tennis, the Federation Francaise de Tennis named one of the major venues at Roland Garros, site of the French Open, Court Suzanne Lenglen.

Suzanne Lenglen executing her glamorous style of play during a singles match at Wimbledon in 1925 (courtesy Prints and Photographs Division, Library of Congress).

Notable Quotes About Suzanne Lenglen

"She was so good that her opponents counted the points, not the games that they won from her." Charlotte Cooper Sterry, tennis champion

"You couldn't really win points against her — she had to make an error. And Suzanne Lenglen rarely, rarely made a mistake." Helen Jacobs, tennis champion

Writings By and About Suzanne Lenglen

Engelmann, Larry. *The Goddess and the American Girl: The Story of Suzanne Lenglen and Helen Wills.* New York: Oxford University Press, 1988.

Gardiner, A.G. "Suzanne Lenglen." In *Certain People of Importance.* London: Jonathan Cape, 1926, pp. 139–147.

Jacobs, Helen Hull. *Gallery of Champions.* New York: A.S. Barnes, 1949, pp. 1–17.

Lenglen, Suzanne. *Lawn Tennis: The Game of Nations.* New York: Dodd, Mead, 1925.

Lenglen, Suzanne, and Margaret Morris. *Tennis by Simple Exercises.* London: William Heinemann Ltd., 1937.

Lidz, Franz. "Tennis Everyone? When Helen Wills and Suzanne Lenglen Clashed on the Riviera in 1926, the Whole World Awaited the News." *Sports Illustrated* Fall 1991: 89–94ff.

Little, Alan. *Suzanne Lenglen, Tennis Idol of the Twenties.* London: Wimbledon Lawn Tennis Museum, 1988.

Pileggi, Sarah. "The Lady in the White Silk Dress." *Sports Illustrated* 13 September 1982: 62–66ff.

HELEN WILLS

Helen Newington Wills Moody Roark

b. October 6, 1905, Centerville, California /
d. January 1, 1998, Carmel, California
Right-handed; "Little Miss Poker Face," "Queen Helen"

Career Rankings

USTA Top 10 Singles

Year	Ranking
1933	2
1931	1
1929	1
1928	1
1927	1
1925	1
1924	1
1923	1

World Top 10 Singles

Year	Ranking
1938	1
1935	1
1933	1
1932	1
1931	1
1930	1
1929	1
1928	1
1927	1
1925	2
1924	3
1923	3
1922	3

Wightman Cup Record

Year	Record
1938	Singles: 2–0, Doubles: 0–1
1932	Singles: 2–0, Doubles: 0–1
1931	Singles: 2–0, Doubles: 0–1
1930	Singles: 2–0, Doubles: 0–1
1929	Singles: 2–0, Doubles: 1–0
1928	Singles: 2–0, Doubles: 0–1
1927	Singles: 2–0, Doubles: 1–0
1925	Singles: 2–0, Doubles: 0–1
1924	Singles: 0–2, Doubles: 1–0
1923	Singles: 2–0, Doubles: 1–0

Olympic Tennis Medals

Year	Medal
1924	Singles: Gold, Doubles: Gold

Grand Slam Highlights

Tournament	Year	Result
French	1932	Winner, Singles
French	1932	Winner, Doubles
French	1932	Finalist, Mixed Doubles
French	1930	Winner, Singles
French	1930	Winner, Doubles
French	1929	Winner, Singles
French	1929	Finalist, Mixed Doubles
French	1928	Winner, Singles
French	1928	Finalist, Mixed Doubles
Wimbledon	1938	Winner, Singles
Wimbledon	1935	Winner, Singles
Wimbledon	1933	Winner, Singles
Wimbledon	1932	Winner, Singles
Wimbledon	1930	Winner, Singles
Wimbledon	1930	Winner, Doubles

Helen Wills focusing on the ball as she prepares to hit a backhand during competition (courtesy International Tennis Hall of Fame and Museum, Newport, Rhode Island).

Tournament	Year	Result	Tournament	Year	Result
Wimbledon	1929	Winner, Singles	United States	1933	Finalist, Doubles
Wimbledon	1929	Winner, Mixed Doubles	United States	1931	Winner, Singles
			United States	1929	Winner, Singles
Wimbledon	1928	Winner, Singles	United States	1928	Winner, Singles
Wimbledon	1927	Winner, Singles	United States	1928	Winner, Doubles
Wimbledon	1927	Winner, Doubles	United States	1928	Winner, Mixed Doubles
Wimbledon	1924	Finalist, Singles			
Wimbledon	1924	Winner, Doubles	United States	1927	Winner, Singles
United States	1933	Finalist, Singles	United States	1925	Winner, Singles

Tournament	Year	Result
United States	1925	Winner, Doubles
United States	1924	Winner, Singles
United States	1924	Winner, Doubles
United States	1924	Winner, Mixed Doubles
United States	1923	Winner, Singles
United States	1922	Finalist, Singles
United States	1922	Winner, Doubles
United States	1922	Finalist, Mixed Doubles

Honors

- In 2000, ranked number 52 in *Sports Illustrated for Women*'s "100 Greatest Female Athletes of the 20th Century"
- Selected for the ITA Women's Collegiate Tennis Hall of Fame in 1996
- Inducted into the International Tennis Hall of Fame in 1969
- Named the Associated Press Female Athlete of the Year in 1935

About Helen Wills

Helen Wills grew up playing tennis mostly against men in Berkeley, California. Under the guidance of her father, who was a physician, she enjoyed good health and was physically fit throughout her tennis career. Beginning tournament play at an early age, she won the U.S. Girls' singles and doubles titles in 1921. By 1923, Wills was at the top of American women's tennis after winning the U.S. Championships. She went on to win 19 Grand Slam singles titles, 9 doubles titles, and 3 mixed doubles titles. Remarkably, she did not lose a set in singles from 1927 to 1932. She won Olympic gold medals in women's singles and doubles in 1924. The most memorable match she played was on the French Riviera in 1926 when she met Suzanne Lenglen in a minor tournament. Although Lenglen won the closely contested match 6–3, 8–6, Wills showed the world that she had the skills to become the dominant figure in international tennis.

Wills was not particularly quick on the court, but possessed powerful ground strokes and a hard serve, along with patience and an unprecedented level of concentration. In fact, her ability to completely focus on her play while on the court was one of her main weapons. She played entire matches without a change of expression. She had a reserved, unemotional demeanor which earned her the nickname "Little Miss Poker Face." Many journalists described her in one word: "imperturbable." She constantly put pressure on her opponents. She relentlessly hit low, powerful ground strokes into the back corners. She had a distinctive body rotation which was synchronized with the swing of her racket that resulted in tremendous power. When her opponents charged the net she responded with deep lobs. Many times her matches ended before her opponents could find their rhythm. Although her powerful ground strokes were infallible, she could serve and volley effectively if she was forced. Her major victories were won almost entirely from the backcourt, as she relied on her retrieving ability, power, and the accuracy of her ground strokes.

Usually dressed in a school-girlish white middy blouse, pleated skirt, and her trademark white eyeshade, Helen Wills always strove to be the best and expected the same in others. She had complete confidence in herself on and off the tennis court, and was impervious to the attitudes of and criticisms from others. One of the few times she showed emotion on the court was after she won her 8th Wimbledon singles title in 1938.

Although tennis played a central role in her life, Helen Wills had a fulfilling life off the court. She was a featured syndicated writer for United Press, a novelist, and a fine painter who exhibited her work in New York and London. She married Frederick Moody, a stockbroker, whom she met at the Lenglen match in 1926. After divorcing Moody in 1937, she married Aidan Roark in 1939. She remained an avid tennis player into her 80s. The Southern California resident, who graduated from the University of California at Berkeley with a degree in fine arts, died in 1998.

Notable Quotes About Helen Wills

"She is powerful, repressed and imperturbable. She plays her game with a silent, deadly earnestness, concentrated on her work." W. O. McGeehan, writer, *New York Herald Tribune*

"When she steps on a tennis court, all but the game ceases to exist." William "Pop" Fuller, her early tennis coach

Writings By and About Helen Wills

Engelmann, Larry. *The Goddess and the American Girl: The Story of Suzanne Lenglen and Helen Wills.* New York: Oxford University Press, 1988.

Jacobs, Helen Hull. *Gallery of Champions.* New York: A.S. Barnes, 1949, pp. 18–38.

Lidz, Franz. "Tennis Everyone? When Helen Wills and Suzanne Lenglen Clashed on the Riviera in 1926, the Whole World Awaited the News." *Sports Illustrated* Fall 1991: 89–94ff.

Wills, Helen. *Fifteen-Thirty: The Story of a Tennis Player.* New York: Scribner's, 1937.

Wills, Helen. *Tennis.* New York: Scribner's, 1928.

HELEN JACOBS
Helen Hull Jacobs

b. August 6, 1908, Globe, Arizona /
d. June 2, 1997, East Hampton, New York
Right-handed; "Little Helen," "Helen the Second"

Career Rankings

USTA Top 10 Singles

Year	Ranking
1941	5
1940	2
1939	2
1937	2
1936	2
1935	1
1934	1
1933	1
1932	1
1931	2
1929	2
1928	2
1927	4

World Top 10 Singles

Year	Ranking
1939	3
1938	2
1937	6
1936	1
1935	2
1934	2
1933	2
1932	2
1931	4
1930	6
1929	3
1928	9

Wightman Cup Record

Year	Record
1939	Singles: 1–1, Doubles: DNP
1937	Singles: 2–0, Doubles: DNP
1936	Singles: 0–2, Doubles: 1–0
1935	Singles: 1–1, Doubles: 1–0
1934	Singles: 2–0, Doubles: 1–0
1933	Singles: 2–0, Doubles: 1–0
1932	Singles: 1–1, Doubles: 1–0
1931	Singles: 2–0, Doubles: DNP
1930	Singles: 1–1, Doubles: 0–1
1929	Singles: 1–1, Doubles: 0–1
1928	Singles: 1–0, Doubles: 0–1
1927	Singles: 0–1, Doubles: DNP

Grand Slam Highlights

Tournament	Year	Result
French	1934	Finalist, Singles
French	1934	Finalist, Doubles
French	1930	Finalist, Singles
Wimbledon	1939	Finalist, Doubles
Wimbledon	1938	Finalist, Singles
Wimbledon	1936	Winner, Singles
Wimbledon	1936	Finalist, Doubles
Wimbledon	1935	Finalist, Singles
Wimbledon	1934	Finalist, Singles
Wimbledon	1932	Finalist, Singles
Wimbledon	1932	Finalist, Doubles
Wimbledon	1929	Finalist, Singles
United States	1940	Finalist, Singles
United States	1939	Finalist, Singles

Tournament	Year	Result
United States	1936	Finalist, Singles
United States	1936	Finalist, Doubles
United States	1935	Winner, Singles
United States	1935	Winner, Doubles
United States	1934	Winner, Singles
United States	1934	Winner, Doubles
United States	1934	Winner, Mixed Doubles
United States	1933	Winner, Singles
United States	1932	Winner, Singles
United States	1932	Winner, Doubles
United States	1932	Finalist, Mixed Doubles
United States	1931	Finalist, Doubles
United States	1928	Finalist, Singles

Honors

- Named the Associated Press Female Athlete of the Year in 1933
- Inducted into the International Tennis Hall of Fame in 1962
- Selected for the ITA Women's Collegiate Tennis Hall of Fame in 1996

About Helen Jacobs

Although Helen Jacobs had an impressive career record which included several Grand Slam singles, doubles, and mixed doubles titles, she is most remembered as the best runner-up in the history of women's tennis. Most notably was her losing rivalry against Helen Wills. The only time Jacobs won a tournament in which Wills participated was in 1933 at the U.S. Championships. Up to that time, Jacobs had lost to Wills seven times without winning a set. Even her lone victory, however, was bittersweet. Wills retired from the match while trailing 3–0 in the third set. Two years later the two met at Wimble-don. Jacobs had a match point while leading 5–3 in the third set but failed to successfully return a lob while at the net. Wills went on to win the next four games and the match. The Jacobs-Wills rivalry dominated women's tennis between 1928 and 1938. As youngsters, the two lived within a few blocks of each other and played at the same club, the Berkeley Lawn Tennis Club. Each received instruction from William "Pop" Fuller and Hazel Wightman. They both played the same tournament circuit. The Jacobs family even moved into a house previously occupied by the Wills family. Jacobs, the younger of the two by nearly 3 years, lived in the shadow of Wills for most of her career. Although Wills was the better player, Jacobs was the more popular. She was outgoing, pleasant, congenial, and always the crowd favorite.

During the 1930s Helen Jacobs dominated the competition on American soil. The tenacious competitor won four consecutive singles titles from 1932 to 1935 and was runner-up in '36, '39, and '40. Her winning streak at Forest Hills reached 28 consecutive matches before she lost to Alice Marble in the finals in 1936. In doubles competition, she captured three U.S. women's titles and a mixed doubles title in 1934 with George Lott. She won the Wimbledon singles crown in 1936 and finished runner-up four other times. In London, Jacobs made a fashion statement in 1933 when she became the first woman to wear shorts at Wimbledon. She participated in 13 consecutive Wightman Cups from 1927 to 1939, although she did not play in 1938.

Jacobs' game centered around a strong backhand drive which she developed early in her career. She was a fine volleyer, but lacked a powerful forehand. Instead, she used a chop shot most of the time when hitting the forehand, which remained a relatively weak shot throughout her career.

Helen Jacobs, winner of the Wimbledon singles title in 1936, was the first woman to wear shorts at the Championships (courtesy Prints and Photographs Division, Library of Congress).

She retired from competition in 1940. The modest yet highly intelligent Californian wrote 14 books on tennis, 3 historical novels, several juvenile novels for girls, and an autobiography. She entered Officer Train- ing School at William and Mary College in 1943 and served as an officer in the WAVES (Women Accepted for Volunteer Emergency Service) during World War II and the Korean War.

Notable Quote About Helen Jacobs

"Helen Jacobs was the most responsive and, in a way, the most satisfying pupil I've ever taught." Hazel Wightman, tennis champion

Writings By and About Helen Jacobs

Jacobs, Helen Hull. *Beyond the Game: An Autobiography*. Philadelphia: Lippincott, 1936.

Jacobs, Helen Hull. *By Your Leave Sir: The Story of a WAVE*. New York: Dodd, Mead, 1943.

Jacobs, Helen Hull. *Gallery of Champions*. New York: A.S. Barnes, 1949.

Jacobs, Helen Hull. *Improve Your Tennis*. London: Methuen, 1936.

Jabobs, Helen Hull. *Modern Tennis*. Indianapolis, Ind.: Bobbs-Merrill, 1933.

Jacobs, Helen Hull. *Proudly She Serves*. New York: Dodd, Mead, 1953.

Jacobs, Helen Hull. *Tennis*. New York: A.S. Barnes, 1941.

Jacobs, Helen Hull. *The Tennis Machine*. New York: Charles Scribner's Sons, 1972.

Messenger, Janet G. "Foremothers: Helen Hull Jacobs." *Womensports* April 1977: 14–16.

ALICE MARBLE

b. September 28, 1913, Beckwourth, California /
d. December 13, 1990, Palm Springs, California
Right-handed; "The Golden Girl"

Career Rankings

USTA Top 10 Singles

Year	Ranking
1940	1
1939	1
1938	1
1937	1
1936	1
1933	3
1932	7

World Top 10 Singles

Year	Ranking
1939	1
1938	3
1937	7
1936	4
1933	10

Wightman Cup Record

Year	Record
1939	Singles: 2–0, Doubles: 1–0
1938	Singles: 1–1, Doubles: 1–0
1937	Singles: 2–0, Doubles: 1–0
1933	Singles: DNP, Doubles: 0–1

Grand Slam Highlights

Tournament	Year	Result
Wimbledon	1939	Winner, Singles
Wimbledon	1939	Winner, Doubles
Wimbledon	1939	Winner, Mixed Doubles
Wimbledon	1938	Winner, Doubles
Wimbledon	1938	Winner, Mixed Doubles
Wimbledon	1937	Winner, Mixed Doubles
United States	1940	Winner, Singles
United States	1940	Winner, Doubles
United States	1940	Winner, Mixed Doubles
United States	1939	Winner, Singles
United States	1939	Winner, Doubles
United States	1939	Winner, Mixed Doubles
United States	1938	Winner, Singles
United States	1938	Winner, Doubles
United States	1938	Winner, Mixed Doubles
United States	1936	Winner, Singles
United States	1936	Winner, Mixed Doubles
United States	1932	Finalist, Doubles

Honors

- In 2000, ranked number 75 in *Sports Illustrated for Women*'s "100 Greatest Female Athletes of the 20th Century"
- Inducted into the International Tennis Hall of Fame in 1964
- Named Associated Press Female Athlete of the Year in 1939 and 1940

About Alice Marble

Alice Marble, despite her physical setbacks and the Second World War, ranks as one of the immortals of the game. She was the precursor of the post-war serve-volley style of women's tennis. Marble played the game more aggressively than any of her competitors. Her powerful American twist serve, driving volleys, and jumping overheads represented a style of play closer to the men's game of her day than to that of her female opponents. She added a fierce competitive spirit to her devastating strokes while dominating her sport for several years. Many attributed her aggressive tennis game to her tomboy days of baseball in Golden Gate Park.

Her first love was not tennis, but rather baseball. At age 13, the blonde Californian became the mascot of the San Francisco Seals, a local professional baseball team. Her strong throwing arm and enthusiasm for the game earned her the privilege of associating with the likes of Joe DiMaggio, Lefty Gomez, and even Babe Ruth in her role as the team's mascot. In her first year of high school Marble lettered in softball, basketball, and track. She was introduced to tennis by her brother, who presented her with a tennis racket for her 15th birthday. Within a week, Alice was hooked on the game.

She learned how to play the game at Golden Gate Park. The park became her favorite place. However, it soon became the site of a devastating event in her life. One evening while walking home from the tennis courts she was savagely attacked and raped. The traumatic incident psychologically scarred her for many years. "It was ten years before I could bring myself to have a physical relationship," she says in her autobiography, *Courting Danger*. She also admits, however, that the rape had

positive effects. She said years after the incident, "It made me tough, and made me turn all the more to tennis to counteract my low self-esteem."

In 1934, shortly after being chosen to represent the United States on the European touring team, she collapsed while playing at Stade Roland Garros. She was misdiagnosed as having tuberculosis and was told she would never play tennis again. The news devastated her. She was admitted into a sanatorium. Through the efforts of Eleanor Tennant, who became her teacher and coach, Alice returned to the courts. At the U.S. Championships in 1936 she won her first major singles title by beating Helen Jacobs. In 1939, she won the triple crown at Wimbledon, teaming up with the notorious Bobby Riggs to win the mixed doubles title. In an unprecedented performance she swept the U.S. titles in singles, doubles, and mixed doubles from 1938 to 1940. After relinquishing her amateur status in 1940, she toured as a professional player with Mary Hardwick, Don Budge, and Bill Tilden.

During World War II she took part in American espionage operations in Switzerland. She had strong connections in Hollywood with many actors, including Clark Gable, Caesar Romero, and Carole Lombard. She even had a brief singing career in 1937, making her debut at the Waldorf Astoria in New York. Back on the tennis court in 1959, she worked with another tomboyish player named Billie Jean King.

Determination to continue on in the face of adversity was the key to Marble's success. Although she was a born athlete, she needed to overcome personal tragedies as well as improve technical aspects of her tennis game. She was inconsistent and used too much topspin on her serve and forehand at the beginning of her career. She

Alice Marble, holder of 17 Grand Slam titles, showing her physical agility while jumping over the net (courtesy International Tennis Hall of Fame and Museum, Newport, Rhode Island).

went through a period of adjustment as she changed her racket grips. She was more interested in maximizing her own style of play in competition than in evaluating her opponent's weaknesses. The example she set for future players was unmistakable. The group of women players who immediately dominated the post war period —

including Pauline Betz, Margaret Osborne, Louise Brough, and Doris Hart — were greatly influenced by her style of play.

Notable Quote About Alice Marble

"Alice Marble is remembered as one of the greatest women to play the game because of her pioneering style in power tennis." Billie Jean King, tennis champion

Writings By and About Alice Marble

Davidson, Sue. *Changing the Game: The Stories of Tennis Champions Alice Marble and Althea Gibson.* Seattle, Wash.: Seal Press, 1997.

Jacobs, Helen Hull. *Gallery of Champions.* New York: A. S. Barnes, 1949, pp. 56–68.

Marble, Alice. *The Road to Wimbledon.* New York: Charles Scribner's Sons, 1946.

Marble, Alice, and Dale Leatherman. *Courting Danger.* New York: St. Martin's Press, 1991.

MARGARET OSBORNE DUPONT
Margaret Evelyn Osborne duPont

b. March 4, 1918, Joseph, Oregon
Right-handed; "Ozzie"

Career Rankings

USTA Top 10 Singles

Year	Ranking
1958	5
1956	4
1953	5
1950	1
1949	1
1948	1
1947	2
1946	2
1945	3
1944	2
1943	4
1942	3
1941	4
1938	7

World Top 10 Singles

Year	Ranking
1957	10
1956	10
1954	5
1953	5
1950	1
1949	1
1948	1
1947	1
1946	2

Wightman Cup Record

Year	Record
1962	Singles: DNP, Doubles: 1–0
1961	Singles: DNP, Doubles: 1–0
1957	Singles: DNP, Doubles: 1–0
1955	Singles: DNP, Doubles: 1–0
1954	Singles: DNP, Doubles: 1–0
1950	Singles: 2–0, Doubles: 1–0
1949	Singles: 2–0, Doubles: DNP
1948	Singles: 2–0, Doubles: 1–0
1947	Singles: 2–0, Doubles: 1–0
1946	Singles: 2–0, Doubles: 1–0

Grand Slam Highlights

Tournament	Year	Result
French	1950	Finalist, Doubles
French	1949	Winner, Singles
French	1949	Winner, Doubles
French	1947	Winner, Doubles
French	1946	Winner, Singles
French	1946	Winner, Doubles
Wimbledon	1962	Winner, Mixed Doubles
Wimbledon	1958	Finalist, Doubles
Wimbledon	1954	Winner, Doubles
Wimbledon	1954	Finalist, Mixed Doubles
Wimbledon	1954	Winner, Doubles
Wimbledon	1951	Finalist, Doubles
Wimbledon	1950	Finalist, Singles
Wimbledon	1950	Winner, Doubles
Wimbledon	1949	Finalist, Singles
Wimbledon	1949	Winner, Doubles

Tournament	Year	Result	Tournament	Year	Result
Wimbledon	1948	Winner, Doubles	United States	1950	Winner, Mixed Doubles
Wimbledon	1947	Winner, Singles			
Wimbledon	1947	Finalist, Doubles	United States	1949	Winner, Singles
Wimbledon	1946	Winner, Doubles	United States	1949	Winner, Doubles
United States	1960	Winner, Mixed Doubles	United States	1949	Finalist, Mixed Doubles
United States	1959	Winner, Mixed Doubles	United States	1948	Winner, Singles
			United States	1948	Winner, Doubles
United States	1958	Winner, Mixed Doubles	United States	1948	Finalist, Mixed Doubles
United States	1957	Winner, Doubles	United States	1947	Finalist, Singles
United States	1956	Winner, Doubles	United States	1947	Winner, Doubles
United States	1956	Winner, Mixed Doubles	United States	1946	Winner, Doubles
			United States	1946	Winner, Mixed Doubles
United States	1955	Winner, Doubles			
United States	1954	Finalist, Doubles	United States	1945	Winner, Doubles
United States	1954	Finalist, Mixed Doubles	United States	1945	Winner, Mixed Doubles
United States	1953	Finalist, Doubles	United States	1944	Finalist, Singles
United States	1950	Winner, Singles	United States	1944	Winner, Doubles
United States	1950	Winner, Doubles	United States	1944	Winner, Mixed Doubles

Margaret Osborne duPont on her way to the finals at Wimbledon in 1950 (courtesy International Tennis Hall of Fame and Museum, Newport, Rhode Island).

Tournament	Year	Result
United States	1943	Winner, Doubles
United States	1943	Winner, Mixed Doubles
United States	1942	Winner, Doubles
United States	1941	Winner, Doubles

Honors

- Selected for the International Women's Sports Hall of Fame in 1998
- Selected for the ITA Women's Collegiate Tennis Hall of Fame in 1996
- Recipient of the USTA Educational Merit Award in 1974
- Inducted into the International Tennis Hall of Fame in 1967
- Recipient of the USTA Service Bowl in 1945

About Margaret Osborne duPont

Margaret Osborne duPont started playing tennis in Spokane, Washington, when she was 9 years old. She developed her famous serve-and-volley style while playing on the hard courts at Golden Gate Park in San Francisco. Her fine American twist serve combined with her excellent volleying skills resulted in one of the most successful doubles records in women's tennis. In 1941, she won her first U.S. doubles championship with Sarah Palfrey Cooke. Margaret's incredible doubles record, however, was accomplished by partnering with Louise Brough. From 1942 to 1957, the duo won 12 U.S., 5 British, and 3 French doubles titles and lost only 8 matches. Although the two players frequently competed against each other in singles tournaments, they remained close friends

and superb teammates. duPont won the U.S. mixed doubles championship 11 times with four different partners, and in 1962 won the Wimbledon mixed doubles title with Neal Fraser.

duPont's superior tactical judgment, hard hitting style, and dogged determination led to a notable singles record as well. From 1948 to 1950, she won the U.S. singles championship at Forest Hills. She captured the Wimbledon singles title in 1947 and the French singles titles in 1946 and 1949. Earlier in her career, she became the first American woman to win the Canadian singles crown in 1935. All totaled, she won 25 national titles. If not for her vulnerable ground strokes, particularly her propensity to slice almost all of her backhands, duPont would have made an even stronger impact on the history of women's tennis.

Her Wightman Cup record was even more remarkable. From 1946 to 1957 and in 1961–1962, she was unbeaten while winning 10 singles and 9 doubles matches as the United States went undefeated against Great Britain. She later served as captain of the U.S. team which won 8 out of 9 matches. Much of duPont's success can be attributed to her very gracious manner, her sense of sportsmanship, friendly demeanor, and her appreciation of the skills of her opponents.

She married millionaire William du-Pont, Jr., of the notable Delaware family in 1947, but subsequently separated after having a son. More recently, she embarked upon a highly successful second career raising thoroughbred race horses in El Paso, Texas.

Notable Quote About Margaret Osborne duPont

"That a strong defense can be the best offense was a tennis axiom of which Margaret had apparently never heard." Helen Jacobs, tennis champion

Writings About Margaret Osborne duPont

Hart, Stan. *Once a Champion: Legendary Tennis Stars Revisited.* New York: Dodd, Mead and Co., 1985, pp. 390–406.

"An Interview with Margaret Osborne duPont." *World Tennis* January 1959: pp. 40–44.
Jacobs, Helen Hull. *Gallery of Champions.* New York: A. S. Barnes and Company, 1949, pp. 181–195.

PAULINE BETZ
Pauline May Betz Addie

b. August 6, 1919, Dayton, Ohio
Turned pro 1947; Right-handed; "Bobbie"

Career Rankings

USTA Top 10 Singles

Year	Ranking
1946	1
1945	2
1944	1
1943	1
1942	1
1941	2
1940	3
1939	8

Pauline Betz reaching for a forehand volley at mid-court during a match at Wimbledon in 1946 (courtesy the ITA Women's Hall of Fame).

World Top 10 Singles

Year	Ranking
1946	1

Wightman Cup Record

Year	Record
1946	Singles: 2–0, Doubles: 1–0

Grand Slam Highlights

Tournament	Year	Result
French	1946	Winner, Mixed Doubles
French	1946	Finalist, Doubles
French	1946	Finalist, Singles
Wimbledon	1946	Winner, Singles
Wimbledon	1946	Finalist, Doubles
United States	1946	Winner, Singles
United States	1945	Finalist, Singles
United States	1945	Finalist, Doubles
United States	1944	Winner, Singles
United States	1944	Finalist, Doubles
United States	1943	Winner, Singles
United States	1943	Finalist, Doubles
United States	1943	Finalist, Mixed Doubles
United States	1942	Winner, Singles
United States	1942	Finalist, Doubles
United States	1941	Finalist, Singles
United States	1941	Finalist, Mixed Doubles

Honors

- Selected for the ITA Women's Collegiate Tennis Hall of Fame in 1995
- Recipient of the USTA's Sarah Palfrey Danzig Award in 1990
- Inducted into the International Tennis Hall of Fame in 1965
- World Trophy for Outstanding Amateur Athlete of the Year in 1946

About Pauline Betz

Betz was introduced to tennis at the age of 9 by her mother, who was a high school physical education teacher. According to Pauline, her mother introduced her to tennis "to get me off the streets and doing something more ladylike." A graduate of Los Angeles High School at age 16, the red-haired Californian received a tennis scholarship to Rollins College in Florida. She played number 4 on the men's team. In 1942, while still a student at Rollins, she won the U.S. women's singles championship for the first time by defeating Louise Brough. Her three set comeback victory showed her persistent will to win and her lack of fear of defeat. She went on to win three more U.S. women's singles titles in 1943, 1944, and 1946. Her tournament victory run was temporarily halted in 1945 when she lost a heartbreaking finals match to Sarah Palfrey Cooke. She also won the Wimbledon singles championship in 1946 without losing a set.

Betz Addie possessed a strong, reliable backhand, but her style of play centered around her unrelenting ability to retrieve almost impossible shots. Although her forehand was vulnerable, with the help of Eleanor Tennant she overcame the weakness by improving her serve, strengthening her ground strokes, devising winning strategies, and possessing a "killer instinct." She often combined successful ball placement with unrestrained power during her matches. Noted for her competitiveness, she was friendly and well liked by many players.

Pauline ended her amateur career in 1946 by winning her last 27 matches. In 1947, she turned pro. She toured the country with Sarah Palfrey Cooke, playing exhibition matches several days a week. Later she joined another professional tour with

"Gussy" Moran, Jack Kramer, and Pancho Segura. In 1949, she married *Washington Post* sportswriter Bob Addie. After her competitive playing career ended, she became involved with community youth tennis programs and wrote about the sport for newspapers and magazines while raising her 5 children. Now a grandmother, she continues to play in a club league "with the kids."

Notable Quote About Pauline Betz

"...the fastest woman on foot ever to play the game." Jerome Scheuer, tennis historian

Writings By and About Pauline Betz

Addie, Pauline Betz. *Wings on My Tennis Shoes.* London: S. Low, Marston, 1949.

Jacobs, Helen Hull. *Gallery of Champions.* New York: A. S. Barnes and Company, 1949, pp. 103–117.

"The Way of a Champ." *Time.* Sept. 2, 1946: pp. 57–60.

LOUISE BROUGH

Althea Louise Brough Clapp

b. March 11, 1923, Oklahoma City, Oklahoma
Right-handed

Career Rankings

USTA Top 10 Singles

Year	Ranking
1957	2
1956	3
1955	3
1954	2
1953	4
1952	4
1950	3
1949	2
1948	2
1947	1
1946	3
1945	4
1944	3
1943	2
1942	2
1941	10

World Top 10 Singles

Year	Ranking
1957	4
1956	3
1955	1
1954	4
1953	3
1952	3
1951	7
1950	2
1949	2
1948	2
1947	2
1946	3

Wightman Cup Record

Year	Record
1957	Singles: DNP, Doubles: 1–0
1956	Singles: 2–0, Doubles: 1–0
1955	Singles: 2–0, Doubles: 1–0
1954	Singles: 1–0, Doubles: 1–0
1953	Singles: DNP, Doubles: 1–0
1952	Singles: DNP, Doubles: 1–0
1950	Singles: 2–0, Doubles: 1–0
1948	Singles: 2–0, Doubles: 1–0
1947	Singles: 2–0, Doubles: 1–0
1946	Singles: 1–0, Doubles: 1–0

Grand Slam Highlights

Tournament	Year	Result
Australian	1950	Winner, Singles
Australian	1950	Winner, Doubles
French	1950	Finalist, Doubles
French	1949	Winner, Doubles
French	1947	Winner, Doubles
French	1946	Winner, Doubles
Wimbledon	1955	Winner, Singles
Wimbledon	1955	Finalist, Mixed Doubles
Wimbledon	1954	Finalist, Singles
Wimbledon	1954	Winner, Doubles
Wimbledon	1952	Finalist, Singles
Wimbledon	1952	Finalist, Doubles
Wimbledon	1951	Finalist, Doubles
Wimbledon	1950	Winner, Singles
Wimbledon	1950	Winner, Doubles
Wimbledon	1950	Winner, Mixed Doubles

Wimbledon	1949	Winner, Singles
Wimbledon	1949	Winner, Doubles
Wimbledon	1949	Finalist, Mixed Doubles
Wimbledon	1948	Winner, Singles
Wimbledon	1948	Winner, Doubles
Wimbledon	1948	Winner, Mixed Doubles
Wimbledon	1947	Finalist, Doubles
Wimbledon	1947	Winner, Mixed Doubles
Wimbledon	1946	Finalist, Singles
Wimbledon	1946	Winner, Doubles
Wimbledon	1946	Winner, Mixed Doubles
United States	1957	Finalist, Singles
United States	1957	Winner, Doubles
United States	1956	Winner, Doubles
United States	1955	Winner, Doubles
United States	1954	Finalist, Singles
United States	1954	Finalist, Doubles
United States	1953	Finalist, Doubles
United States	1952	Finalist, Doubles
United States	1950	Winner, Doubles
United States	1949	Winner, Doubles
United States	1949	Winner, Mixed Doubles
United States	1948	Finalist, Singles
United States	1948	Winner, Doubles
United States	1948	Winner, Mixed Doubles
United States	1947	Winner, Singles
United States	1947	Winner, Doubles
United States	1947	Winner, Mixed Doubles
United States	1946	Winner, Doubles
United States	1946	Finalist, Mixed Doubles
United States	1945	Winner, Doubles
United States	1944	Winner, Doubles
United States	1943	Finalist, Singles
United States	1943	Winner, Doubles
United States	1942	Finalist, Singles
United States	1942	Winner, Doubles
United States	1942	Winner, Mixed Doubles

Honors

- Selected for the ITA Women's Collegiate Tennis Hall of Fame in 1996
- Inducted into the International Tennis Hall of Fame in 1967

About Louise Brough

Louise Brough learned how to play tennis on the public tennis courts in California. Although she started playing tennis at the early age of 4, she was a teenager when she began taking professional tennis lessons. At 17, she played in the national junior championships in Philadelphia and the national women's championships in New York at the same time. She won the national junior championships in 1940 and 1941.

Brough's high-kicking American twist serve, powerful net game, and heavy slice backhand helped her dominate Wimbledon during the decade following World War II. In her first postwar Wimbledon tournament in 1946, she almost won the triple crown, losing only to Pauline Betz in the singles finals. In 1948 and 1950 she won the triple at Wimbledon. In 1949, she played the singles, doubles, and mixed doubles finals on the same day, playing a total of 117 games in 8 sets. Brough went on to win 13 titles at Wimbledon, including 4 singles, 5 doubles, and 4 mixed doubles. Her favorite doubles partner was Margaret duPont, with whom she teamed up to win a total of 20 Grand Slam titles. Her attacking style of play permitted her to continue her dominance in doubles, winning 8 mixed doubles titles at Wimbledon and the U.S. Open. Her most amazing doubles accomplishment was the 9 straight titles she won at the U.S. Open between 1942 and 1950. In Wightman Cup competition

Louise Brough playing on Centre Court at Wimbledon during a Wightman Cup match in 1950 (courtesy International Tennis Hall of Fame and Museum, Newport, Rhode Island).

Louise Brough was perfect. From 1946 through 1957, she compiled a remarkable record of 22–0.

In 1958, Brough retired from amateur competition. She married Dr. A. T. Clapp and occasionally played in senior tournaments. She won the Over 40 U.S. Hardcourt Doubles Championship in 1971 and 1975. For many years after retiring she spent time on the tennis court teaching aspiring junior players.

Notable Quote About Louise Brough

"Louise had the nearest thing to a man's game that I had ever seen.... With the greatest of ease, she could serve a ball that was hard to follow in flight, and she volleyed with deftness and severity." Helen Hull Jacobs, tennis champion

Writings About Louise Brough

Biographical Dictionary of American Sports: Outdoor Sports. Ed. by David L. Porter. Westport, Conn.: Greenwood Press, 1988, pp. 337–338.

Jacobs, Helen Hull. *Gallery of Champions.* New York: A.S. Barnes and Company, 1949, pp. 169–180.

DORIS JANE HART

b. June 20, 1925, St. Louis, Missouri
Right-handed

Career Rankings

USTA Top 10 Singles

Year	Ranking
1955	1
1954	1
1953	2
1952	2
1951	2
1950	2
1949	3
1948	3
1947	3
1946	4
1945	6
1944	6
1943	3
1942	6

World Top 10 Singles

Year	Ranking
1955	2
1954	2
1953	2
1952	2
1950	3
1949	3
1948	3
1947	3
1946	4

Wightman Cup Record

Year	Record
1955	Singles: 1–1, Doubles: 1–0
1954	Singles: 2–0, Doubles: DNP
1953	Singles: 2–0, Doubles: 1–0

Year	Record
1952	Singles: 2–0, Doubles: 1–0
1951	Singles: 2–0, Doubles: 1–0
1950	Singles: 1–0, Doubles: 1–0
1949	Singles: 2–0, Doubles: 1–0
1948	Singles: 1–0, Doubles: 0–1
1947	Singles: 1–0, Doubles: 1–0
1946	Singles: DNP, Doubles: 1–0

Grand Slam Highlights

Tournament	Year	Result
Australian	1950	Finalist — Singles
Australian	1950	Winner — Doubles
Australian	1950	Winner — Mixed Doubles
Australian	1949	Winner — Singles
Australian	1949	Finalist — Doubles
Australian	1949	Winner — Mixed Doubles
French	1956	Finalist — Mixed Doubles
French	1953	Finalist — Singles
French	1953	Winner — Doubles
French	1953	Winner — Mixed Doubles
French	1952	Winner — Singles
French	1952	Winner — Doubles
French	1952	Winner — Mixed Doubles
French	1951	Finalist — Singles
French	1951	Winner — Doubles
French	1951	Winner — Mixed Doubles
French	1950	Winner — Singles
French	1950	Winner — Doubles
French	1948	Winner — Doubles

Doris Hart extending to hit a backhand volley while nearing the net in a match at Wimbledon in 1947 (courtesy International Tennis Hall of Fame and Museum, Newport, Rhode Island).

Tournament	Year	Result	Tournament	Year	Result
French	1948	Finalist — Mixed Doubles	Wimbledon	1955	Winner — Mixed Doubles
French	1947	Finalist — Singles	Wimbledon	1954	Finalist — Doubles
French	1947	Finalist — Doubles	Wimbledon	1954	Winner — Mixed Doubles
French	1946	Finalist — Doubles			

Tournament	Year	Result
Wimbledon	1953	Finalist — Singles
Wimbledon	1953	Winner — Doubles
Wimbledon	1953	Winner — Mixed Doubles
Wimbledon	1952	Winner — Doubles
Wimbledon	1952	Winner — Mixed Doubles
Wimbledon	1951	Winner — Singles
Wimbledon	1951	Winner — Doubles
Wimbledon	1951	Winner — Mixed Doubles
Wimbledon	1950	Finalist — Doubles
Wimbledon	1948	Finalist — Singles
Wimbledon	1948	Finalist — Doubles
Wimbledon	1948	Finalist — Mixed Doubles
Wimbledon	1947	Finalist — Singles
Wimbledon	1947	Winner — Doubles
Wimbledon	1946	Finalist — Doubles
United States	1955	Winner — Singles
United States	1955	Finalist — Doubles
United States	1955	Winner — Mixed Doubles
United States	1954	Winner — Singles
United States	1954	Winner — Doubles
United States	1954	Winner — Mixed Doubles
United States	1953	Finalist — Singles
United States	1953	Winner — Doubles
United States	1953	Winner — Mixed Doubles
United States	1952	Finalist — Singles
United States	1952	Winner — Doubles
United States	1952	Winner — Mixed Doubles
United States	1951	Winner — Doubles
United States	1951	Winner — Mixed Doubles
United States	1950	Finalist — Singles
United States	1950	Finalist — Doubles
United States	1950	Finalist — Mixed Doubles
United States	1949	Finalist — Singles
United States	1949	Finalist — Doubles
United States	1948	Finalist — Doubles
United States	1947	Finalist — Doubles
United States	1945	Finalist — Doubles
United States	1945	Finalist — Mixed Doubles
United States	1944	Finalist — Doubles
United States	1943	Finalist — Doubles
United States	1942	Finalist — Doubles
United States	1941	Finalist — Doubles

Honors

- Selected for the ITA Women's Collegiate Tennis Hall of Fame in 1995
- Inducted into the International Tennis Hall of Fame in 1969
- Recipient of the USTA Service Bowl in 1955

About Doris Hart

Doris Hart, winner of 35 Grand Slam titles, nearly had her leg amputated when she was 2 years old. Instead a doctor drained her infected right kneecap and her mother performed daily leg massages until Doris regained almost normal use of her leg. Several years later while in the hospital for an operation to straighten her leg, Hart observed people playing tennis nearby. She immediately became interested in learning the game. She and her brother practiced together and took lessons at public courts in Miami, Florida. Hart quickly developed an all-court game and won the USLTA girl's 18 singles championship in 1942 and 1943.

Born in St. Louis, Doris struggled in major tournament competition early in her career. Between the years 1941 and 1948, she lost an amazing 17 of 19 finals matches in grand slam play, winning only the doubles titles at Wimbledon in 1947 and at Paris in 1948, both with Patricia Canning Todd. Although Hart had beaten the likes of Margaret Osborne duPont and Louise Brough, she was not able to prevail against the top players in the final round of major championships. Many attribute her early failures to her relatively weak slice backhand. Doris Hart turned her career around, however, in Melborne, Australia, when in 1949 she won both the women's singles and mixed doubles titles. This marked the beginning of a highly successful run for the legendary doubles player. Her energetic, aggressive game, featuring superb racket control, became a favorite of fans around the world.

Hart is one of only a handful of women who have won all 12 of the major titles at least once — singles, doubles, and mixed doubles. She became the second woman after Maureen Connolly to win all four Grand Slam singles titles. To this day, only a handful of players have accomplished the feat. In 1951, she captured the triple championship at Wimbledon, and repeated the feat in 1954 at Forest Hills. Her doubles and mixed doubles records are extraordinary. She won the mixed doubles with Frank Sedgman in Australia in 1949 and 1950. Teamed with her favorite partner, Shirley Fry, she won in Paris from 1950 to 1953, Wimbledon from 1951 to 1953, and the U.S. Open from 1951 to 1954. She won the mixed doubles title at Roland Garros from 1951 to 1953, at Wimbledon from 1951–1955, and the U.S. title from 1951 to 1955.

During her illustrious playing career, Hart represented the United States in Wightman Cup competition for 10 consecutive years. From 1946 through 1955, Hart compiled a 22–2 record against Great Britain. During those years, the United States won all 10 matches. Hart retired from competition in 1956 and became a teaching professional. She lives in Coral Gables, Florida.

Notable Quote About Doris Hart

"She is a good-natured girl, full of fun, laughs easily and often, loves the gypsy life of a tennis player, has a repertoire of stories and songs and has a command of the latest jive and college talk and expressions." Alice Marble, tennis champion

Writings By and About Doris Hart

Collins, Bud. *Total Tennis: The Ultimate Tennis Encyclopedia.* Toronto: Sport Media Publishing, Inc., 2003, pp. 678–679.

Hart, Doris. *Tennis with Hart.* Philadelphia: Lippincott, 1955.

Marble, Alice. "Lesson in Courage — That's Doris Hart." *American Lawn Tennis* May 1948: p. 21.

SHIRLEY FRY

Shirley June Fry Irvin

b. June 30, 1927, Akron, Ohio
Right-handed

Career Rankings

USTA Top 10 Singles

Year	Ranking
1956	1
1955	2
1954	4
1953	3
1952	3
1951	3
1950	8
1949	6
1948	7
1947	5
1946	7
1945	7
1944	8

World Top 10 Singles

Year	Ranking
1956	1
1955	10
1954	6
1953	4
1952	4
1951	3
1950	8
1948	8
1946	9

Wightman Cup Record

Year	Record
1956	Singles: 1–1, Doubles: 1–0
1955	Singles: DNP, Doubles: 1–0
1954	Singles: DNP, Doubles: Not Played
1953	Singles: 1–0, Doubles: 1–0
1952	Singles: 1–0, Doubles: 1–0
1951	Singles: 1–1, Doubles: 1–0
1949	Singles: DNP, Doubles: 1–0

Grand Slam Highlights

Tournament	Year	Result
Australian	1957	Winner — Singles
Australian	1957	Winner — Doubles
French	1953	Winner — Doubles
French	1952	Finalist — Singles
French	1952	Winner — Doubles
French	1952	Finalist — Mixed Doubles
French	1951	Winner — Singles
French	1951	Winner — Doubles
French	1950	Winner — Doubles
French	1948	Finalist — Singles
French	1948	Finalist — Doubles
Wimbledon	1956	Winner — Singles
Wimbledon	1956	Winner — Mixed Doubles
Wimbledon	1954	Finalist — Doubles
Wimbledon	1953	Winner — Doubles
Wimbledon	1953	Finalist — Mixed Doubles
Wimbledon	1952	Winner — Doubles
Wimbledon	1951	Finalist — Singles
Wimbledon	1951	Winner — Doubles
Wimbledon	1950	Finalist — Doubles
United States	1956	Winner — Singles
United States	1956	Finalist — Doubles

Tournament	Year	Result
United States	1955	Finalist — Doubles
United States	1955	Finalist — Mixed Doubles
United States	1954	Winner — Doubles
United States	1953	Winner — Doubles
United States	1952	Winner — Doubles
United States	1951	Finalist — Singles
United States	1951	Winner — Doubles
United States	1951	Finalist — Mixed
United States	1950	Finalist — Doubles
United States	1949	Finalist — Doubles

Honors

- Selected for the ITA Women's Collegiate Tennis Hall of Fame in 1995
- Recipient of USTA Service Bowl Award in 1987
- Inducted into the International Tennis Hall of Fame in 1970

About Shirley Fry

Shirley Fry won her first tennis tournament at the age of 9 when she partnered with her sister to win a local doubles event. The victory was a prelude of what was to come from the gritty Fry, who also liked to hike, swim, and play basketball as a youngster. Although Shirley encountered difficulty in winning major singles titles, she became only the third woman player ever to win all 4 Grand Slam singles titles. She also achieved the distinction of a career Grand Slam in doubles with her long time partner Doris Hart (French, Wimbledon, U.S. Open), and Althea Gibson (Australian). Her doubles record with Doris Hart was particularly impressive, as the two combined for 11 Grand Slam titles from 1950 to 1954. In 1953, her doubles win with Hart over Brough and duPont ended the Brough-duPont record of 9 straight titles and 41 consecutive match wins at the U.S. Open.

Fry's style of play centered around her powerful ground strokes. Although her serve was adequate, her volleying skills were the reason for her outstanding results in doubles. She complemented her technical skills with tremendous concentration, stamina, steadiness, and mobility.

Considered the fastest player of her day, Fry suffered a sore elbow in 1954. She temporarily retired from the game, but returned during the winter of 1955. It didn't take her long to get back on the winning

Shirley Fry after winning the United States Championship at the West Side Tennis Club in 1956 (courtesy ITA Women's Collegiate Tennis Hall of Fame).

track, as she won the Wimbledon singles title the following year. In 1957, the Rollins College graduate married Karl Irvin, a tennis umpire, and the couple had four children. While living in Connecticut, Shirley stayed active in the sport by coaching tennis through the mid–1970s. Today, Fry enjoys her leisure days occasionally golfing in central Florida and spending time with her 12 grandchildren.

Notable Quote About Shirley Fry

"Shirley plays tennis with the zest and abandon of a 2-year-old filly sailing down the homestretch in the lead by a length." unknown source

Writings About Shirley Fry

Biographical Dictionary of American Sports: Outdoor Sports. Edited by David L. Porter. Westport, Conn.: Greenwood Press, 1988, pp. 359–360.

"Forty-Love Shirley." *American Magazine* August 1945: p. 115.

ALTHEA GIBSON

b. August 25, 1927, Silver, South Carolina
d. September 28, 2003, East Orange, New Jersey
Right-handed; "The Jackie Robinson of Tennis"

Career Rankings

USTA Top 10 Singles

Year	Ranking
1958	1
1957	1
1956	2
1955	8
1953	7
1952	9

World Top 10 Singles

Year	Ranking
1958	1
1957	1
1956	2

Wightman Cup Record

Year	Record
1958	Singles: 1–1, Doubles: 1–0
1957	Singles: 2–0, Doubles: 1–0

Grand Slam Highlights

Tournament	Year	Result
Australian	1957	Finalist — Singles
Australian	1957	Winner — Doubles
French	1956	Winner — Singles
French	1956	Winner — Doubles
Wimbledon	1958	Winner — Singles
Wimbledon	1958	Winner — Doubles
Wimbledon	1958	Finalist — Mixed Doubles
Wimbledon	1957	Winner — Singles
Wimbledon	1957	Winner — Doubles
Wimbledon	1957	Finalist — Mixed Doubles
Wimbledon	1956	Winner — Doubles
Wimbledon	1956	Finalist — Mixed Doubles
United States	1958	Winner — Singles
United States	1958	Finalist — Doubles
United States	1957	Winner — Singles
United States	1957	Finalist — Doubles
United States	1957	Winner — Mixed Doubles
United States	1956	Finalist — Singles

Honors

- Inducted into the U.S. Open Court of Champions in 2007
- In 2000, ranked number 30 in *Sports Illustrated for Women*'s "100 Greatest Female Athletes of the 20th Century"
- Selected for the ITA Women's Collegiate Tennis Hall of Fame in 1995
- Selected for the International Women's Sports Hall of Fame in 1980
- Inducted into the International Tennis Hall of Fame in 1971
- Named the Associated Press Female Athlete of the Year in 1957 and 1958

Althea Gibson stretching for a forehand during tournament play at the All England Lawn Tennis Club in 1957 (courtesy International Tennis Hall of Fame and Museum, Newport, Rhode Island).

About Althea Gibson

Born to sharecroppers on a cotton farm in Silver, South Carolina, Althea Gibson had few opportunities in life. At the age of three, Gibson's family moved to Harlem, where her life focused around her one passion — sports. She took a special liking to basketball while fitting the profile with her long, lean silhouette. Besides basketball, Gibson began playing paddle tennis, which eventually led her to a successful career in tennis.

Her dominating style in paddle tennis caught the attention of Buddy Walker, a coach at the New York Police Athletic League, who immediately took her under his wing. Using second-hand wooden tennis rackets, Gibson received instruction from Walker and played matches against teenage boys with considerably more experience than her. Gibson's strength, determination, and outstanding racket skills resulted in consistent victories against her male opponents.

From the time she learned the sport, Gibson loved to play tennis as much as she disliked school. She stopped playing hooky by quitting school altogether in order to focus on her tennis game. She eventually met Dr. Walter Johnson, a Lynchburg physician who was active in the black tennis community. Gibson received valuable instruction through Johnson and opportunities to compete in several tournaments. She trained full-time and won most of the tournaments she played within the American Tennis Association (ATA), a league primarily made up of black athletes. She won the New York State Championship from 1944 to 1950 and dominated the league. She became the number one player in the ATA. Gibson had risen as far as she could within the segregated league of the ATA. It was time for her to conquer another challenge — the color barrier.

After many failed attempts to enter all-white tournaments, a past champion and fan of Gibson's stood up in her defense. Alice Marble, a former U.S. Open champion, wrote a letter to the editor of *American Lawn Tennis* in July 1950 expressing her dismay over the situation. Marble's effort was not ignored. One week later Gibson received her first invitation to

the U.S. Open, where she proved her dominance and broke the tennis segregation barrier for black men and women. In 1957, she became the first African-American to win the U.S. Nationals, the precursor to the U.S. Open. She went on to win 11 major tournaments, including the singles titles in Paris in 1956 and at Wimbledon in 1957 and 1958.

Gibson, a right-handed player, was known for her "attacking serve-and-volley" playing style. When she added a consistent baseline game to her playing repertoire, she became an international champion. Her long, lean body fit perfectly into her playing style. Her ruthless attitude on court solidified her game. After a relatively short amateur tennis career, Gibson turned professional for a few years. She toured with the Harlem Globetrotters and played tennis matches before their basketball games.

Since there was no professional tennis tour at the time, Gibson turned to golf. In 1964, she became the only black American woman to play in the Ladies Professional Golf Association (LPGA). She played in the LPGA for a few years, but never made a name for herself, so she turned back to her favorite sport when open tennis began in 1968.

Gibson was faced with many challenges in her return to tennis. At the age of 40, her much younger opponents were too strong to conquer, so she decided to focus her efforts on teaching rather than competing. Gibson became the New Jersey State Commissioner of Athletics in 1975, a position she held for 10 years. She also served on the New Jersey State Athletic Control Board (1985–1988) and the New Jersey Governor's Council of Physical Fitness. She married William Darben of Montclair, New Jersey, in 1965, but shortly thereafter was divorced. In 2003, at the age of 76, Gibson died of respiratory failure.

Notable Quote About Althea Gibson

"She has humility and she also has pride — a rare combination, particularly amongst tennis players." Angela Buxton, Gibson's doubles partner

Writings By and About Althea Gibson

Davidson, Sue. *Changing the Game: The Stories of Tennis Champions Alice Marble and Althea Gibson*. Seattle, Wash.: Seal Press, 1997.

Gibson, Althea, and Ed Fitzgerald. *I Always Wanted to Be Somebody*. New York: Harper, 1958.

Gibson, Althea, and Richard Curtis. *So Much to Live For*. New York: Putnam's, 1968.

Gray, Frances Clayton, and Yanick Rice Lamb. *Born to Win: The Authorized Biography of Althea Gibson*. Hoboken, N.J.: John Wiley and Sons, 2004.

Munro, Christy. "Althea Gibson: Tragic Success Story." *Look* November 12, 1957: 132–36.

Reynolds, Quentin. "Long Road to Center Court." *Saturday Review* November 29, 1958: 16.

MAUREEN CONNOLLY
Maureen Catherine Connolly Brinker

b. September 17, 1934, San Diego, California / *d.* June 21, 1969, Dallas, Texas
Right-handed; "Little Mo," "Little Miss Poker Face"

Career Rankings

USTA Top 10 Singles

Year	Ranking
1953	1
1952	1
1951	1
1950	10

World Top 10 Singles

Year	Ranking
1954	1
1953	1
1952	1
1951	2

Wightman Cup Record

Year	Record
1954	Singles: 2–0, Doubles: DNP
1953	Singles: 2–0, Doubles: 1–0
1952	Singles: 2–0, Doubles: 1–0
1951	Singles: 1–0, Doubles: DNP

Grand Slam Highlights

Tournament	Year	Result
Australian	1953	Winner — Singles
Australian	1953	Winner — Doubles
Australian	1953	Finalist — Mixed Doubles
French	1954	Winner — Singles
French	1954	Winner — Doubles
French	1954	Winner — Mixed Doubles
French	1953	Winner — Singles
French	1953	Finalist — Doubles
French	1953	Finalist — Mixed Doubles
Wimbledon	1954	Winner — Singles
Wimbledon	1953	Winner — Singles
Wimbledon	1953	Finalist — Doubles
Wimbledon	1952	Winner — Singles
Wimbledon	1952	Finalist — Doubles
United States	1953	Winner — Singles
United States	1952	Winner — Singles
United States	1952	Finalist — Doubles
United States	1951	Winner — Singles

Honors

- In 2000, ranked number 28 in *Sports Illustrated for Women*'s "100 Greatest Female Athletes of the 20th Century"
- Elected to the International Women's Sports Hall of Fame in 1987
- Inducted into the International Tennis Hall of Fame in 1968
- Named the Associated Press Female Athlete of the Year in 1951, 1952, and 1953

About Maureen Connolly

Maureen Connolly was raised by her single mom in San Diego, where she was introduced to tennis at the age of nine by Wilbur Folsom, a local pro. He immediately was struck by her outstanding eye-hand coordination and burning inner drive. In her autobiography, *Forehand Drive*, she wrote, "By the time I was ten I had a goal and that was to be the best in the world." She followed through on her promise, becoming arguably the greatest, albeit fleeting, champion of all time.

Her style of play was characterized by powerful, yet consistent, ground strokes. Her one-handed backhand, in particular, was punishing yet uncannily accurate. It was not unusual for her to hit the lines of the court as many as twenty times or more during a match. Her timing and coordination were impeccable. She was nicknamed "Little Mo" because her fire power on the tennis court rivaled that of "Big Mo," the battleship USS *Missouri*. Since she seldom needed to advance to the net, she never developed a reliable volley. This was apparent in the 1953 when Connolly and her inexperienced partner, Julie Sampson, lost in the doubles final at Wimbledon to Shirley Fry and Doris Hart, 6–0, 6–0.

In 1953, Connolly became the first female player to win the Grand Slam, winning all four major singles championships in one calendar year. She lost only one set in the process. That same year, she won 10 of 12 tournaments and compiled an amazing 61–2 match record. Beginning in 1951, she won 9 consecutive major titles (3 U.S., 3 Wimbledon, 2 French, and 1 Australian) while remaining unbeaten in 50 matches. Connolly won every Grand Slam singles event she entered. She was a member of the Wightman Cup team from 1951 to 1954, winning all nine of her matches. Throughout her brief but illustrious tennis career she always treated her opponents with dignity and respect. Connolly believed that both winning and losing required the graciousness of humility and she, more than any other champion, embodied the quality.

Her playing career tragically ended in 1954 when, at only 19 years of age, she was in an unusual traffic accident while riding horseback. She was stuck by a concrete truck. Her right leg was crushed and her calf muscles were severed. Despite the freak accident, Maureen never lost her passion for riding. Following the accident, she became a coaching professional, but never played competitive tennis again. It was not unusual for promising junior tennis players as well as touring pros to spend a week or two at her home in Dallas receiving instruction and coaching advice from Connolly.

She married Norman Brinker and had two children before she died of cancer in 1969 at the age of 34. The year before she died, Connolly co–founded the Maureen Connolly Brinker Tennis Foundation, which is dedicated to developing promising young tennis players. Today, the foundation's namesake award is the most coveted one in junior girls' tennis.

Notable Quotes About Maureen Connolly

"She hits her forehand harder and better than any woman in history." Vinnie Richards, American tennis player

"Whenever a great player comes along you have to ask, 'Could she have beaten Maureen?' In every case the answer is, I think not." Lance Tingay, tennis journalist

Maureen Connolly showing the athleticism and form that made her one of the greatest champions of all time (courtesy International Tennis Hall of Fame and Museum, Newport, Rhode Island).

Writings By and About Maureen Connolly

Brinker, Maureen Connelly. *The Best of Brinker.* Highland Park, Ill.: Tennis Features, 1970.

Connolly, Maureen. *Championship Tennis.* London: Frederick Muller, 1954.

Connolly, Maureen. *Power Tennis.* New York: Barnes, 1954.

Connolly, Maureen, and Tom Gwynne. *Forehand Drive.* London: MacGibbon and Kee, 1957.

Simmons, Cindy Brinker, and Bob Darden. *Little Mo's Legacy: A Mother's Lessons, A Daughter's Story.* Irving, Texas: Tapestry Press, 2001.

DARLENE RUTH HARD

b. January 6, 1936, Los Angeles, California
Right-handed

Career Rankings

USTA Top 10 Singles

Year	Ranking
1963	1
1962	1
1961	1
1960	1
1959	2
1958	3
1957	4
1956	7
1955	9
1954	7

World Top 10 Singles

Year	Ranking
1963	6
1962	3
1961	2
1960	2
1959	3
1958	4
1957	2
1956	10
1955	7

Wightman Cup Record

Year	Record
1963	Singles: 1–1, Doubles: 1–0
1962	Singles: 2–0, Doubles: 0–1
1960	Singles: 2–0, Doubles: 1–0
1959	Singles: 1–1, Doubles: 1–0
1957	Singles: 0–1, Doubles: 1–0

Fed Cup

Career Record

Overall: 6–1
Singles: 3–1
Doubles: 3–0

World Group Finals Record

Year	Record
1963	Singles: 0–1, Doubles: 1–0

Grand Slam Highlights

Tournament	Year	Result
Australian	1962	Finalist — Doubles
Australian	1962	Finalist — Mixed Doubles
French	1961	Finalist — Doubles
French	1961	Winner — Mixed Doubles
French	1960	Winner — Singles
French	1960	Winner — Doubles
French	1957	Winner — Doubles
French	1956	Finalist — Doubles
French	1956	Finalist — Mixed Doubles
French	1955	Winner — Doubles
French	1955	Winner — Mixed Doubles
Wimbledon	1963	Winner — Doubles
Wimbledon	1963	Finalist — Mixed Doubles
Wimbledon	1960	Winner — Doubles
Wimbledon	1960	Winner — Mixed Doubles

Tournament	Year	Result
Wimbledon	1959	Finalist — Singles
Wimbledon	1959	Winner — Doubles
Wimbledon	1959	Winner — Mixed Doubles
Wimbledon	1957	Finalist — Singles
Wimbledon	1957	Winner — Doubles
Wimbledon	1957	Winner — Mixed Doubles
United States	1969	Winner — Doubles
United States	1963	Finalist — Doubles
United States	1962	Finalist — Singles
United States	1962	Winner — Doubles
United States	1961	Winner — Singles
United States	1961	Winner — Doubles
United States	1960	Winner — Singles
United States	1960	Winner — Doubles
United States	1959	Winner — Doubles
United States	1958	Finalist — Singles
United States	1958	Winner — Doubles
United States	1957	Finalist — Doubles
United States	1957	Finalist — Mixed Doubles
United States	1956	Finalist — Mixed Doubles

Honors

- Inducted into the ITA Women's Collegiate Tennis Hall of Fame in 1997
- Inducted into the Pomona College Athletic Hall of Fame in 1974
- Inducted into the International Tennis Hall of Fame in 1973

About Darlene Hard

Darlene Hard mowed lawns to help with family finances after her father died when she was 17 years old. Later during her tennis career she mowed down doubles teams on the grass at Wimbledon on her way to 4 doubles titles. In 1955, she teamed with Beverly Fleitz to win her first Grand Slam doubles championship in Paris. She went on to win a total of 21 Grand Slam tournaments, including 3 singles, 13 doubles, and 5 mixed doubles titles.

On Saturdays, as a youngster, Hard finished her chores at home, then rode a bus two hours to the Los Angeles Tennis Club to watch Louise Brough play. Usually Darlene just observed the action or served as a ball girl for those she wanted to emulate. Every so often she was permitted to hit some balls. Her tennis career had begun when she won her first trophy in a local doubles tournament. Tennis great Alice Marble coached Hard early in her career, but was suddenly dropped by the rising young star, who never received formal instruction thereafter.

She played tennis for Pomona College, where she majored in physical education. When she entered Pomona College in 1957, there were no athletic scholarships offered to women, so she received an academic scholarship. In 1958, she won the first women's national intercollegiate tennis title. Her off campus waitress jobs, however, caused her to miss several tournaments. After five semesters at Pomona, the lure of the tennis tour beckoned and she chose to return to the courts. While at Pomona, the tennis community disdained her waitress job because it was unbecoming for a lady tennis player. Hard's casual off-the-court attire as well as her propensity for playing in shorts alienated the tennis establishment even further. Throughout her career she cared little about her image or her ranking.

Hard's playing style was aggressive. Her big weapons were her backhand, serve, and volley. She was considered a complete all-court player. In particular, Darlene was an impressive doubles player. She won 18 Grand Slam women's and mixed doubles crowns. Her last doubles title came in 1969 at the U.S. Open, when she and her pupil

Darlene Hard playing with determination as she hits a slice forehand shot (courtesy International Tennis Hall of Fame and Museum, Newport, Rhode Island).

Francoise Durr surprisingly won the championship after Hard had retired from the game 5 years earlier. The improbable victory is Hard's signature moment, marking one of the most memorable matches in U.S. Open history. The duo lost the first eight games of the match before roaring back to win 0–6, 6–3, 6–4. In singles competition, she won the French in 1960 and captured the U.S. championship in 1960 and 1961. Her 1961 triumph came just months after recovering from hepatitis. Hard played on the Wightman Cup team for 5 years and amassed a 10–4 combined record. In 1963, she participated in the Fed Cup match against Australia. She lost her singles match against Margaret Smith, but came back to win in the doubles with Billie Jean King. The win sealed the United States' victory in the first ever Fed Cup.

Hard was one of the last great amateur players. She never regretted her amateur status. In her words, "We played for the love of the game. I loved it. I love tennis." In 1964, Hard became a teaching professional in California. In 1977, she married Richard Waggoner. She competed, taught, coached, and volunteered in the tennis community through the early 1980s. Today she is working as a computer systems supervisor at the University of Southern California.

Notable Quote About Darlene Hard

"She is regarded as one of the pioneers of women's tennis and the last great amateur player. Her doubles championships with 10 different partners are one of the reasons Hard's name is brought up in any conversation about the greatest doubles players in tennis history." SI.com

Writings About Darlene Hard

Biographical Dictionary of American Sports: Outdoor Sports. Edited by David L. Porter. Westport, Conn.: Greenwood Press, 1988, pp. 357–358.
"Darlene's Bluff." *Newsweek* September 18, 1961: p. 96.
Collins, Bud. *Total Tennis: The Ultimate Tennis Encyclopedia.* Toronto: Sport Media Publishing, Inc., 2003, p. 678.

MARIA BUENO

Maria Ester Andion Bueno

b. October 11, 1939, São Paulo, Brazil
Right-handed; "São Paulo Swallow"

Career Rankings

World Top 10 Singles

Year	Ranking
1968	5
1967	7
1966	3
1965	2
1964	2
1963	3
1962	2
1960	1
1959	1
1958	9

Fed Cup

Career Record

Overall: 3–3
Singles: 2–2
Doubles: 1–1

Grand Slam Highlights

Tournament	Year	Result
Australian	1965	Finalist — Singles
Australian	1960	Winner — Doubles
French	1965	Finalist — Mixed Doubles
French	1964	Finalist — Singles
French	1961	Finalist — Doubles
French	1960	Winner — Doubles
French	1960	Winner — Mixed Doubles
Wimbledon	1967	Finalist — Doubles
Wimbledon	1967	Finalist — Mixed Doubles
Wimbledon	1966	Finalist — Singles
Wimbledon	1966	Winner — Doubles
Wimbledon	1965	Finalist — Singles
Wimbledon	1965	Winner — Doubles
Wimbledon	1964	Winner — Singles
Wimbledon	1963	Winner — Doubles
Wimbledon	1960	Winner — Singles
Wimbledon	1960	Winner — Doubles
Wimbledon	1960	Finalist — Mixed Doubles
Wimbledon	1959	Winner — Singles
Wimbledon	1959	Finalist — Mixed Doubles
Wimbledon	1958	Winner — Doubles
United States	1968	Finalist — Singles (amateur)
United States	1968	Winner — Doubles (amateur)
United States	1968	Winner — Doubles (pro)
United States	1966	Winner — Singles
United States	1966	Winner — Doubles
United States	1964	Winner — Singles
United States	1963	Winner — Singles
United States	1963	Finalist — Doubles
United States	1962	Winner — Doubles
United States	1960	Finalist — Singles
United States	1960	Winner — Doubles
United States	1960	Finalist — Mixed Doubles
United States	1959	Winner — Singles
United States	1959	Finalist — Doubles

Maria Bueno at Wimbledon, ready to hit a return of serve near the baseline (courtesy sporting-heroes.net).

| United States | 1958 | Finalist — Doubles |
| United States | 1958 | Finalist — Mixed Doubles |

Honors

• Selected for the International Women's Sports Hall of Fame in 2004
• Inducted into the International Tennis Hall of Fame in 1978
• Named the Associated Press Female Athlete of the Year in 1959

About Maria Bueno

Maria Bueno contributed significantly to the popularity of tennis during the 1960s. Her flair, graceful movements on the court, and sense of fashion created a large international fan base and a seemingly omnipresent media corps. Her glittering arrival at Wimbledon in 1958 set the stage for a successful and memorable tennis career despite interruptions by illness and injury.

As a teenager Maria balanced her tennis tournaments with school. Although she never received formal instruction or coaching in tennis, eventually her commitment to the game won out over a career in teaching. Her family lived in an apartment across the street from the Sao Paulo tennis club. At the age of 5 she started playing with her brother, who became a United States intercollegiate champion and a Davis Cup player. She won the Brazilian women's championship at the age of 14 and the Italian women's singles title at 19. In 1959, she won her first singles Grand Slam title at Wimbledon and added the U.S. Championship in singles later that same year. Bueno repeated her win at Wimbledon in 1960, but was sidelined with hepatitis for

the next several years. It was 1963 when she regained her physical strength and exceptional playing skills and won the U.S. Open, the second of her four U.S. singles titles. She added another Wimbledon singles title in 1964. She won a total of 10 Grand Slam doubles titles, including both the amateur and professional crowns in 1968 in New York.

Bueno was noted for her powerful serves and ensuing volleys. Her shots were marked by impeccable timing and precise racket control. She had uncommon grace and fluidity in her game. She perceived tennis more as an artistic endeavor rather than a sport. Some writers contend that she enjoyed the beauty of the sport as much as the satisfaction of winning. Her tennis outfits attest to the contention. Many were designed by the famous designer Ted Tinling. In particular, the white dress with bright pink lining she wore at Wimbledon in 1964 caused a ruckus with British spectators. Many believe her game reached its pinnacle in power and beauty on the sacred grass growing near Church Road in London.

Today Maria travels around the world conducting tennis clinics for players of all ages. She continues to play three or four times a week despite several recent surgeries on her right arm and two hip replacements. Her sustained passion for the sport is evident by comments she made in a recent interview. "Tennis continues to be my life and I keep an active interest in everything that is going on. Above all, it is still a lot of fun."

Notable Quote About Maria Bueno

"Like Connolly, when the chips were down Maria rose like some Phoenix from the ashes of despair to hit with a bravery and decision which hammered hopelessness into her helpless opponents." From an article in *Lawn Tennis Magazine*

"Maria Bueno was probably the player with the most presence and grace on the court." Virginia Wade, tennis champion

Writings About Maria Bueno

Collins, Bud. *Total Tennis: The Ultimate Tennis Encyclopedia*. Toronto: Sport Media Publishing, Inc., 2003, pp. 651–652.

Moran, Sheila. "The Swan Song of the 'Sao Paulo Swallow.'" *Women Sports*. February 1977, 35–36.

Wancke, Henry. "Profile: Maria Bueno." *Tennis World* (Eng.) December 1985–January 1986: 21–23.

MARGARET SMITH

Margaret Smith Court

b. July 16, 1942, Albury, New South Wales, Australia
Right-handed; "The Arm," "Mighty Maggie"

Career Rankings

WTA Top 10 Singles

Year	Ranking
1975	6

World Top 10 Singles

Year	Ranking
1975	6
1973	1
1972	2
1971	3
1970	1
1969	1
1968	4
1966	2
1965	1
1964	1
1963	1
1962	1
1961	4

Fed Cup

Career Record

Overall: 35–5
Singles: 20–0
Doubles: 15–5

World Group Finals Record

Year	Record
1971	Singles: 1–0, Doubles: 1–0
1969	Singles: 1–0, Doubles: 0–1
1968	Singles: 1–0, Doubles: 1–0
1965	Singles: 1–0, Doubles: 0–1
1964	Singles: 1–0, Doubles: 0–1
1963	Singles: 1–0, Doubles: 0–1

Grand Slam Highlights

Tournament	Year	Result
Australian	1975	Finalist — Doubles
Australian	1973	Winner — Singles
Australian	1973	Winner — Doubles
Australian	1971	Winner — Singles
Australian	1971	Winner — Doubles
Australian	1970	Winner — Singles
Australian	1970	Winner — Doubles
Australian	1969	Winner — Singles
Australian	1969	Winner — Doubles
Australian	1969	Winner — Mixed Doubles
Australian	1968	Finalist — Singles
Australian	1968	Finalist — Mixed Doubles
Australian	1966	Winner — Singles
Australian	1966	Finalist — Doubles
Australian	1965	Winner — Singles
Australian	1965	Winner — Doubles
Australian	1965	Winner — Mixed Doubles
Australian	1964	Winner — Singles
Australian	1964	Finalist — Doubles

Tournament	Year	Result	Tournament	Year	Result
Australian	1964	Winner — Mixed Doubles	Wimbledon	1964	Finalist — Singles
			Wimbledon	1964	Finalist — Mixed Doubles
Australian	1963	Winner — Singles			
Australian	1963	Winner — Doubles	Wimbledon	1963	Winner — Singles
Australian	1963	Winner — Mixed Doubles	Wimbledon	1963	Winner — Mixed Doubles
Australian	1962	Winner — Singles	Wimbledon	1963	Finalist — Doubles
Australian	1962	Winner — Doubles	Wimbledon	1961	Finalist — Doubles
Australian	1961	Winner — Singles	United States	1975	Winner — Doubles
Australian	1961	Winner — Doubles	United States	1973	Winner — Singles
Australian	1960	Winner — Singles	United States	1973	Winner — Doubles
Australian	1960	Finalist — Doubles	United States	1973	Finalist — Mixed Doubles
French	1973	Winner — Singles			
French	1973	Winner — Doubles	United States	1972	Winner — Mixed Doubles
French	1970	Winner — Singles			
French	1969	Winner — Singles	United States	1972	Finalist — Doubles
French	1969	Winner — Mixed Doubles	United States	1970	Winner — Singles
			United States	1970	Winner — Doubles
French	1969	Finalist — Doubles	United States	1970	Winner — Mixed Doubles
French	1966	Winner — Doubles			
French	1965	Winner — Doubles	United States	1969	Winner — Singles (pro)
French	1965	Winner — Mixed Doubles	United States	1969	Winner — Singles (amateur)
French	1965	Finalist — Singles			
French	1964	Winner — Singles	United States	1969	Winner — Doubles (amateur)
French	1964	Winner — Doubles			
French	1964	Winner — Mixed Doubles	United States	1969	Finalist — Doubles (pro)
French	1963	Winner — Mixed Doubles	United States	1969	Winner — Mixed Doubles
French	1963	Finalist — Doubles	United States	1968	Winner — Singles
French	1962	Winner — Singles	United States	1968	Winner — Doubles (pro)
French	1962	Finalist — Doubles			
Wimbledon	1975	Winner — Mixed Doubles	United States	1968	Winner — Doubles (amateur)
Wimbledon	1971	Finalist — Singles	United States	1965	Winner — Singles
Wimbledon	1971	Finalist — Doubles	United States	1965	Winner — Mixed Doubles
Wimbledon	1971	Finalist — Mixed Doubles	United States	1964	Winner — Mixed Doubles
Wimbledon	1970	Winner — Singles			
Wimbledon	1969	Winner — Doubles	United States	1964	Finalist — Doubles
Wimbledon	1968	Winner — Mixed Doubles	United States	1963	Winner — Doubles
			United States	1963	Winner — Mixed Doubles
Wimbledon	1966	Winner — Mixed Doubles	United States	1962	Winner — Singles
Wimbledon	1966	Finalist — Doubles	United States	1962	Winner — Mixed Doubles
Wimbledon	1965	Winner — Singles			
Wimbledon	1965	Winner — Mixed Doubles	United States	1961	Winner — Mixed Doubles
Wimbledon	1964	Winner — Doubles			

Honors

- In 2005, ranked number 6 on *Tennis Magazine*'s list of the "40 Greatest Players of the Open Tennis Era"
- In 2000, ranked number 16 in *Sports Illustrated for Women*'s "100 Greatest Female Athletes of the 20th Century"
- Selected for the International Women's Sports Hall of Fame in 1986
- Inducted into the International Tennis Hall of Fame in 1979
- Winner of the ABC Sportsman of the Year Award in 1963 and 1970

About Margaret Smith

Margaret Smith started playing tennis at the age of 9 on a public clay court across the street from her parents' modest two-bedroom house. By the time she was 15, she could beat every boy in Albury. She attracted attention in Melbourne with the Australian Lawn Tennis Association. She eventually came under the watchful eye of Wimbledon champion Frank Sedgman. In the early days of her training she worked tirelessly in the gym on strength development and on the courts on her concentration and techniques. The tall country girl was a self-made champion. Although born a left-hander, she was transformed to a right-handed player, which was not unusual for that era.

A prolific winner of major championship tournaments, she won over 60 titles in singles, doubles, and mixed doubles between 1960 and 1975. In 1970, she became the second female to win the Grand Slam and the first in the open era. Maureen Connolly accomplished the feat for the first time in 1953. Smith earlier had won the Grand Slam in mixed doubles with Ken

Fletcher in 1963. She won an amazing 11 Australian singles titles and added 3 Wimbledon, 5 French, and 7 U.S. singles crowns to her record. In arguably her finest Grand Slam moment, she defeated Billie Jean King in the 1970 Wimbledon final, 14–12, 11–9, while in considerable pain from an ankle injury. Her career record against King was 21–13. Her other prime rivalry was against Maria Bueno, whom she defeated 16 of the 22 times they played.

Margaret's style of play was characterized by a heavy serve and volley, but she could also out–steady opponents with her dependable ground strokes. Her cross court forehand soon became a weapon to be avoided by her opponents, some of whom would avoid hitting with pace so as to neutralize her powerful forehand. Occasionally, Smith developed a case of the nerves, such as in her 1971 Wimbledon finals defeat by Evonne Goolagong and during her bizarre match with Bobby Riggs in 1973, which she lost in a lopsided contest. Of her match with Riggs, she recalls, "I played the match in a daze and it remains mercifully foggy to me in retrospect." In 1970, she overcame a case of the "Center Court Jitters" during her 6–2, 2–6, 6–1 victory over diminutive Rosie Casals in the U.S. Open finals.

Smith had an outstanding Fed Cup record. She led her team to victories in 1964, 1965, 1968, and 1971, remaining undefeated in her singles Cup matches for the Australians.

She retired briefly in 1966 to open a boutique with a friend, and the following year married a yachtsman named Barry Court. Smith returned to the tennis court at the urging of her husband and helped to usher in the open era of tennis. She continued to win major titles after the birth of her first three children and competed until the age of 34. During her career,

Margaret Smith following her powerful serve to the net while competing at Wimbledon (courtesy sporting-heroes.net).

which overlapped the amateur and open eras, she earned $550,000 in prize money. The shy, soft-spoken Aussie is a deeply religious woman and was ordained a minister in 1991. Today, she tours Australia and other countries with her mobile ministry. As a lasting tribute to her, the Australian Tennis Association named one of the main venues at Melbourne Park, site of the Australian Open, Margaret Court Stadium.

Notable Quotes About Margaret Smith

"Whenever you talk of great women tennis players you have to start with Margaret. She should go down as the finest woman player of all times." Marty Riessen, mixed doubles partner

"Most of us let up against an opponent at times. Not Margaret. It's not in her make-up. She is determined to win every point, no matter who she is playing." John Newcombe, Australian tennis champion

Writings By and About Margaret Smith

Court, Margaret Smith. *Our Winning Position: Living in Victory Everyday*. Sydney: Strand Pub., 2002.

Court, Margaret Smith, and Don Lawrence. *The Margaret Court Story*. London: Stanley Paul and Co., 1965.

Court, Margaret Smith, and George McGann. *Court On Court: A Life in Tennis*. New York: Dodd, Mead, and Co., 1975.

Oldfield, Barbara. *A Winning Faith: The Margaret Court Story*. Tonbridge, England: Sovereign World, 1993.

BILLIE JEAN KING

Billie Jean Moffitt King

b. November 22, 1943, Long Beach, California
Turned pro 1968; Right-handed; "Mother Freedom"

Career Rankings

USTA Top 10 Singles

Year	Ranking
1980	5
1979	4
1978	2
1977	2
1974	2
1973	1
1972	1
1971	1
1970	1
1967	1
1966	1
1965	1
1964	2
1963	2
1962	3
1961	3
1960	4

WTA Top 10 Singles

Year	Ranking
1983	13
1982	14
1980	6
1979	5
1978	5
1977	2
1975	4
1974	1
1973	2
1972	1
1971	3

Year	Ranking
1970	2
1969	3
1968	1

World Top 10 Singles

Year	Ranking
1980	6
1979	5
1978	5
1977	2
1975	2
1974	1
1973	2
1972	1
1971	1
1970	2
1969	3
1968	1
1967	1
1966	1
1965	4
1964	7
1963	4

Fed Cup

Career Record

Overall: 52–4
Singles: 26–3
Doubles: 26–1

World Group Final Record

Year	Record
1979	Singles: DNP, Doubles: 1–0
1978	Singles: DNP, Doubles: 1–0
1977	Singles: 1–0, Doubles: DNP
1976	Singles: 1–0, Doubles: 1–0
1967	Singles: 1–0, Doubles: Match Suspended
1966	Singles: 1–0, Doubles: 1–0
1965	Singles: 0–1, Doubles: 1–0
1964	Singles: 0–1, Doubles: 1–0
1963	Singles: 1–0, Doubles: 1–0

Wightman Cup Record

Year	Record
1978	Singles: DNP, Doubles: 1–0
1977	Singles: 2–0, Doubles: 1–0
1970	Singles: 2–0, Doubles: 1–0
1967	Singles: 2–0, Doubles: 1–0
1966	Singles: 2–0, Doubles: 1–0
1965	Singles: 1–1, Doubles: 1–0
1964	Singles: 2–0, Doubles: 0–1
1963	Singles: 2–0, Doubles: 1–0
1962	Singles: DNP, Doubles: 0–1
1961	Singles: 1–1, Doubles: 1–0

Grand Slam Highlights

Tournament	Year	Result
Australian	1969	Finalist — Singles
Australian	1969	Finalist — Doubles
Australian	1968	Winner — Singles
Australian	1968	Winner — Mixed Doubles
Australian	1965	Finalist — Doubles
French	1972	Winner — Singles
French	1972	Winner — Doubles
French	1970	Finalist — Doubles
French	1970	Winner — Mixed Doubles
French	1968	Finalist — Doubles
French	1968	Finalist — Mixed Doubles
French	1967	Winner — Mixed Doubles
Wimbledon	1983	Finalist — Mixed Doubles
Wimbledon	1979	Winner — Doubles
Wimbledon	1978	Finalist — Mixed Doubles
Wimbledon	1976	Finalist — Doubles
Wimbledon	1975	Winner — Singles
Wimbledon	1974	Winner — Mixed Doubles
Wimbledon	1973	Winner — Singles
Wimbledon	1973	Winner — Doubles
Wimbledon	1973	Winner — Mixed Doubles
Wimbledon	1972	Winner — Singles
Wimbledon	1972	Winner — Doubles
Wimbledon	1971	Winner — Doubles
Wimbledon	1971	Winner — Mixed Doubles
Wimbledon	1970	Finalist — Singles
Wimbledon	1970	Winner — Doubles
Wimbledon	1969	Finalist — Singles
Wimbledon	1968	Winner — Singles
Wimbledon	1968	Winner — Doubles
Wimbledon	1967	Winner — Singles
Wimbledon	1967	Winner — Doubles
Wimbledon	1967	Winner — Mixed Doubles
Wimbledon	1966	Winner — Singles
Wimbledon	1966	Finalist — Mixed Doubles
Wimbledon	1965	Winner — Doubles
Wimbledon	1964	Finalist — Doubles
Wimbledon	1963	Finalist — Singles
Wimbledon	1962	Winner — Doubles
Wimbledon	1961	Winner — Doubles
United States	1980	Winner — Doubles
United States	1979	Finalist — Doubles
United States	1978	Winner — Doubles
United States	1978	Finalist — Mixed Doubles
United States	1977	Finalist — Mixed Doubles
United States	1976	Winner — Mixed Doubles
United States	1975	Finalist — Doubles
United States	1975	Finalist — Mixed Doubles
United States	1974	Winner — Singles
United States	1974	Winner — Doubles
United States	1973	Finalist — Doubles

Billie Jean King volleying at the net during a match at Wimbledon in 1982 (Carol L. Newsom; courtesy David Newsom).

Tournament	Year	Result	Tournament	Year	Result
United States	1973	Winner — Mixed Doubles	United States	1968	Finalist — Singles
			United States	1968	Finalist — Doubles
United States	1972	Winner — Singles	United States	1967	Winner — Singles
United States	1971	Winner — Singles	United States	1967	Winner — Doubles
United States	1971	Winner — Mixed Doubles	United States	1967	Winner — Mixed Doubles

Tournament	Year	Result
United States	1966	Finalist — Doubles
United States	1965	Finalist — Singles
United States	1965	Finalist — Doubles
United States	1964	Winner — Doubles
United States	1962	Finalist — Doubles

Honors

- In 2005, ranked number 9 on *Tennis Magazine*'s list of the "40 Greatest Players of the Open Tennis Era"
- Inducted into U.S. Open Court of Champions in 2003
- In 2000, ranked number 3 in *Sports Illustrated for Women*'s "100 Greatest Female Athletes of the 20th Century"
- Received the Arthur Ashe Award for Courage in 1999
- Named the Family Circle Magazine Cup's "Player Who Makes a Difference" in 1997
- Selected as captain of U.S. Olympic Women's Tennis Team in 1996 and 2000
- Selected as captain of U.S. Fed Cup Team in 1995–96 and 1998–2001
- Recipient of the Sarah Palfrey Danzig Award in 1995
- Selected for the ITA Women's Collegiate Tennis Hall of Fame in 1995
- Named one of the "100 Most Important Americans of the 20th Century" by *Life* magazine in 1990
- Inducted into the International Tennis Hall of Fame in 1987
- Selected for the International Women's Sports Hall of Fame in 1980
- Founder of the Women's Tennis Association in 1973
- Named the Associated Press Female Athlete of the Year in 1967 and 1973

About Billie Jean King

Billie Jean King had her first tennis lesson at the age of 11. Five years later she was ranked 19th in the USA. Alice Marble, the former world champion, started coaching her at this time. In 1961, Billie Jean won her first Wimbledon title — the women's doubles with partner Karen Hantze. She won her first Grand Slam singles title at Wimbledon in 1966. She won the Wimbledon singles title five more times, added 4 U.S. Open singles titles, and one each at the French and Australian opens. Her doubles accomplishments were even more impressive, she won a total of 27 doubles and mixed doubles Grand Slam tournaments before retiring from professional tennis in 1983.

King played in Fed Cup competition for nine years representing the USA. In each of those years, the Americans reached the final round and won 7 times. Billie Jean's performance was extraordinary, as she won 52 of 56 matches in singles and doubles. In Wightman Cup play she was no less impressive. By winning 22 of 26 singles and doubles matches, she led team USA to nine titles in ten years.

King was an aggressive and extremely competitive player whose game centered around her serve and volley. She was one of the best ever at attacking the net. Although her technically superior ground strokes, volley, and half-volley were perfect for hard court surfaces, her reliable baseline game resulted in success on clay courts as well.

Billie Jean King's most important tennis triumph might have happened on September 30, 1973. On that day she defeated a 55-year-old Wimbledon champ named Bobby Riggs in the Houston Astrodome 6–4, 6–3, 6–3. Earlier in the year, Riggs easily beat Margaret Court in a similar challenge match. The King-Riggs match drew a record crowd of 30,472, and a television audience in the millions. By beating Riggs in straight sets, Billie Jean's victory served as a rallying point for gender equity in sports.

King continually fought ferociously for the women's game during her playing days, and still does today. In 1971, she organized the Virginia Slims tour. In 1973, she founded the Women's Tennis Association, and served as president for several years. She founded the Women's Sports Foundation in 1974, an organization devoted to increasing female participation in sports. Today, she serves as commissioner of the popular and progressive-thinking World Team Tennis league, and administers the Billie Jean King Foundation, which works to "inspire humankind in the pursuit of excellence, ensure equal opportunity and enhance the quality of life for all individuals, regardless of gender, race, religion, appearance, or sexual orientation." In 2006, the USTA's National Tennis Center, site of the U.S. Open, was named after Billie Jean King.

Notable Quote About Billie Jean King

"She needs to win. She loves to be driving herself in an atmosphere of intensity. As soon as one win is under her belt, she is looking forward to the next." Virginia Wade, tennis champion

Writings By and About Billie Jean King

Adams, Mark. "Playbook: Billie Jean King." *Sports Illustrated Women.* September 2001, 136.

Baker, Jim. *Billie Jean King.* New York: Grossett and Dunlop, 1974.

Burchard, Marshall, and Sue H. Burchard. *Sports Hero, Billie Jean King.* New York: Putnam's, 1975.

Church, Carol Bauer. *Billie Jean King: Queen of the Courts.* Minneapolis, Minn.: Greenhaven Press, 1976.

Deford, Frank. "Mrs. Billie Jean King. She Is Something Special, Not Only in Tennis but in the World Beyond the Sidelines." *Sports Illustrated* 19 May 1975: 71–74*ff.*

Fleming, Anne T. "The Battles of Billie Jean King." *Women's Sports and Fitness* Sept.-Oct. 1998: 130–138.

Freeman, Meredith. "The Day Billie Jean King Beat Bobby Riggs." *Ms.* November 1983: 101–02.

Gemme, Leila Boyle, and Bruce Curtis. *King on the Court: Billie Jean King.* Milwaukee, Wis.: Raintree Editions, 1976.

Hahn, James, Lynn Hahn, and Howard Schroeder. *King! The Sports Career of Billie Jean King.* Mankato, Minn.: Crestwood House, 1981.

King, Billie Jean. "I Just Had to Win (1973 Match Against Bobby Riggs)." *Tennis* August 1998: 26–30.

_____. *Pressure Is a Privilege: Lesson I've Learned from Life and the Battle of the Sexes.* New York: LifeTime Media, 2008.

King, Billie Jean, and Cynthia Starr. *We Have Come a Long Way: The Story of Women's Tennis.* New York: McGraw-Hill, 1988.

King, Billie Jean, and Frank Deford. *Billie Jean.* New York: Viking Press, 1982.

King, Billie Jean, and Joe Hyams. *Billie Jean King's Secrets of Winning Tennis.* New York: Holt, Rinehart, and Winston, 1974.

King, Billie Jean, and Kim Chapin. *Billie Jean.* New York: Harper and Row, 1974.

Kort, Michele. "Ms. Conversation: Interview." *Ms.* February 1998: 58–62.

Lannin, Joanne. *Billie Jean King: Tennis Trailblazer.* Minneapolis, Minn.: Lerner Publications, 1999.

Lorge, Barry. "The Once and Future King." *World Tennis* April 1977: 23–31.

Martin, James. "The World According to Billie Jean King." *Tennis* June 2002: 18.

May, Julian. *Billie Jean King: Tennis Champion.* Mankato, Minn.: Crestwood House, 1974.

Morse, Ann. *Tennis Champion, Billie Jean King.* Mankato, Minn.: Creative Education Society, 1976.

Olsen, James T., and John Nelson. *Billie Jean King: The Lady of the Court.* Mankato, Minn.: Creative Education Society, 1974.

Roberts, Selena. *Billie Jean King, Bobby Riggs, and the Tennis Match That Leveled the Game.* New York: Crown Publishers, 2005.

VIRGINIA WADE

Sarah Virginia Wade

b. July 10, 1945, Bournemouth, England
Turned pro 1968; Right-handed; "Ginny," "Wild Woman"

Career Rankings

WTA Top 10 Singles

Year	Ranking
1979	8
1978	4
1977	4
1976	3
1975	5
1974	4
1973	6
1972	6
1971	8
1970	5
1969	9
1968	2

World Top 10 Singles

Year	Ranking
1979	8
1978	4
1977	4
1976	3
1975	5
1974	4
1973	6
1972	5
1971	7
1970	5
1969	9
1968	2
1967	8

Fed Cup

Career Record

Overall: 66–33
Singles: 36–20
Doubles: 30–13

World Group Finals Record

Year	Record
1981	Singles: 0–1, Doubles: 0–1
1972	Singles: 1–0, Doubles: 0–1
1971	Singles: 0–1, Doubles: 0–1
1967	Singles: 0–1, Doubles: DNP

Wightman Cup

Year	Record
1985	Singles: DNP, Doubles: 0–1
1984	Singles: DNP, Doubles: 0–1
1983	Singles: 0–1, Doubles: 1–0
1982	Singles: 0–1, Doubles: 0–1
1981	Singles: 0–2, Doubles: 0–1
1980	Singles: 0–2, Doubles: 0–1
1979	Singles: 0–2, Doubles: 0–1
1978	Singles: 1–1, Doubles: 1–0
1977	Singles: 0–2, Doubles: 0–1
1976	Singles: 1–1, Doubles: 0–1
1975	Singles: 1–1, Doubles: 1–0
1974	Singles: 2–0, Doubles: 0–1
1973	Singles: 1–1, Doubles: 1–0
1972	Singles: 1–1, Doubles: 0–1
1971	Singles: 1–1, Doubles: 1–0
1970	Singles: 1–1, Doubles: 0–1
1969	Singles: 1–1, Doubles: 0–1
1968	Singles: 2–0, Doubles: 1–0

Year	Record
1967	Singles: 0–2, Doubles: 0–1
1966	Singles: 0–2, Doubles: 1–0
1965	Singles: 0–1, Doubles: 0–1

Grand Slam Highlights

Tournament	Year	Result
Australian	1973	Winner — Doubles
Australian	1972	Winner — Singles
French	1979	Finalist — Doubles
French	1973	Winner — Doubles
Wimbledon	1977	Winner — Singles
Wimbledon	1970	Finalist — Doubles
United States	1976	Finalist — Doubles
United States	1975	Winner — Doubles
United States	1973	Winner — Doubles
United States	1972	Finalist — Doubles
United States	1970	Finalist — Doubles
United States	1969	Finalist — Singles (amateur)
United States	1969	Winner — Doubles (amateur)
United States	1969	Finalist — Doubles (pro)
United States	1968	Winner — Singles (pro)
United States	1968	Finalist — Doubles (amateur)

Honors

- In 2005, ranked number 38 on *Tennis Magazine*'s list of the "40 Greatest Players of the Open Tennis Era"
- Inducted into the International Tennis Hall of Fame in 1989
- Recipient of the 2002 Fed Cup Award of Excellence
- First Woman ever elected to Wimbledon Committee in 1982
- Voted WTA Tour Player of the Year in 1977
- Recipient of the BBC Sports Personality of the Year Award in 1977

About Virginia Wade

Virginia Wade loved to play in the garden, climb trees, and walk on her hands while growing up in Cape Town, South Africa. She also learned how to play tennis there and went on to become the most successful Englishwoman ever to play the game. Her long and fruitful career reached its climax in 1977 when she captured the Wimbledon singles title on her 17th try. Her victory on Centre Court was especially meaningful since it was the year of the Wimbledon Centenary, and Queen Elizabeth II presented the women's prize. Earlier in her career, Wade accomplished significant firsts in the sport by winning the inaugural British Hard Court Open in 1968 and by upsetting Billie Jean King to win the initial U.S. Open that same year. Virginia had considered opting out of the Forest Hills tournament after losing in an early round just months before at Wimbledon. "I decided to play, with the emphasis not on winning, but on suffering emotionally as little as possible on court," she later said. She won the Australian singles title in 1972.

As a professional, Wade won 55 singles titles while utilizing her all-court skills. Her versatility also served her well in doubles, as she won three of the four Grand Slam doubles titles (except Wimbledon). Her heavy slice backhand complemented her strong volleying ability to create a powerful game, especially on grass. Many considered her serve to be the best in the game. Wade showed her versatility by winning the Italian Open in Rome on red clay in 1971.

Her reputation for having a temper on court followed her throughout her playing years, resulting in an up and down career. Reporters constantly used words like "tempestuous," "explosive," "unpredictable," and "arrogant" to describe her court demeanor. Some experts blamed her inconsistency on her inability to get her emotions under control for important matches, while others blamed it on her pursuit of technical perfection. There was a scarcity of good coaches at the time, but Wade received momentary guidance from the likes of Pancho Segura, Doris Hart, Maureen Connolly, and Jerry Teeguarden during her career.

Her drive and determination resulted in remarkable accomplishments on and off the court, including a science degree from Sussex University in mathematics and physics, 66 career wins in Fed Cup competition spanning 18 years, and 21 years of Wightman Cup play for her beloved Great Britain. In 1966, she sat for her finals at Sussex University while playing for Britain in the Wightman Cup at Wimbledon.

Midway through her career Virginia Wade had an epiphany. Early in her career before a match she would go through an apocryphal routine about bad calls, poor bounces, and inaccurate line calls. She admitted she was looking for an excuse not to win. Later in her career, however, she took a different approach. She mentally committed herself to winning and the work necessary to achieve victory. She was not intimidated by the thought of losing. She put herself in her own control and no longer felt dependent on factors outside of her control. Although London remains her favorite city, today Wade lives in New York, where she can be "a little more incognito and informal."

Virginia Wade concentrating on hitting a forehand during play in 1983 (Carol L. Newsom; courtesy David Newsom).

Notable Quote About Virginia Wade

"Not until the last point is played can one know whether she will prevail or collapse." Galway Kinnell, sports journalist

Writings By and About Virginia Wade

Collins, Bud. *Total Tennis: The Ultimate Tennis Encyclopedia.* Toronto: Sport Media Publishing, Inc., 2003, pp. 754–755.
Wade, Virginia, and Jean Rafferty. *Ladies of the Court: A Century of Women at Wimbledon.* New York: Atheneum, 1984.
Wade, Virginia, with Mary Lou Mellace. *Courting Triumph.* New York: Mayflower Books, 1978.

EVONNE GOOLAGONG

Evonne Fay Goolagong Cawley

b. July 31, 1951, Griffith, New South Wales, Australia
Right-handed; "Sunshine Super Girl"

Career Rankings

WTA Top 10 Singles

Year	Ranking
1980	5
1979	4
1978	3
1976	2
1975	5
1974	2

World Top 10 Singles

Year	Ranking
1980	5
1979	4
1978	3
1976	2
1975	3
1974	2
1973	3
1972	6
1971	2

Fed Cup

Career Record

Overall: 35–5
Singles: 22–3
Doubles: 13–2

World Group Finals Record

Year	Record
1976	Singles: 0–1, Doubles: DNP
1975	Singles: 0–1, Doubles: DNP
1974	Singles: 1–0, Doubles: 1–0
1973	Singles: 1–0, Doubles: 1–0
1971	Singles: 1–0, Doubles: DNP

Grand Slam Highlights

Tournament	Year	Result
Australian	1977	Winner — Singles (Dec.)
Australian	1977	Co-Winner — Doubles (Dec.) (title was shared)
Australian	1976	Winner — Singles
Australian	1976	Winner — Doubles
Australian	1975	Winner — Singles
Australian	1975	Winner — Doubles
Australian	1974	Winner — Singles
Australian	1974	Winner — Doubles
Australian	1973	Finalist — Singles
Australian	1972	Finalist — Singles
Australian	1971	Finalist — Singles
Australian	1971	Winner — Doubles
French	1972	Finalist — Singles
French	1972	Winner — Mixed Doubles
French	1971	Winner — Singles
Wimbledon	1980	Winner — Singles
Wimbledon	1976	Finalist — Singles
Wimbledon	1975	Finalist — Singles
Wimbledon	1974	Winner — Doubles
Wimbledon	1972	Finalist — Singles

Evonne Goolagong stretching for a backhand while playing on the Virginia Slims Tour (Carol L. Newsom; courtesy David Newsom).

Tournament	Year	Result
Wimbledon	1972	Finalist — Mixed Doubles
Wimbledon	1971	Winner — Singles
Wimbledon	1971	Finalist — Doubles
United States	1976	Finalist — Singles
United States	1975	Finalist — Singles
United States	1974	Finalist — Singles
United States	1973	Finalist — Singles

Honors

- In 2005, ranked number 23 on *Tennis Magazine*'s list of the "40 Greatest Players of the Open Tennis Era"
- In 2000, ranked number 72 in *Sports Illustrated for Women*'s "100 Greatest Female Athletes of the 20th Century"
- Selected for the International Women's Sports Hall of Fame in 1989
- Inducted into the International Tennis Hall of Fame in 1988
- Recipient of the WTA Tour Karen Krantzcke Sportsmanship Award in 1980
- Appointed Member of the Order of the British Empire in 1972 for services to tennis
- Named Associated Press Female Athlete of the Year in 1971

About Evonne Goolagong

Evonne Goolagong was born in a dusty, dreary Aborigine town several hundred miles southwest of Sydney. She was the third of eight children. Her father, a sheep-shearer, bought a secondhand Chevy when Evonne was a year old. Most noteworthy about the purchase, as it turned out, was the presence of several grimy tennis balls in the back seat. Although her parents never took much interest in tennis, at times Mum would give one of these balls to her cranky baby, Evonne. The future Wimbledon champion always walked around the neighborhood with a tennis ball in hand. Evonne started playing tennis at the age of six at the War Memorial Tennis Club in her hometown. She was given special dispensation because of her age to join the local tennis club a year later. She was quickly noticed by Vic Edwards, a proprietor of a tennis school in Sydney. She moved to Sydney in 1965 to focus on her tennis career and while there lived with the Edwards family. Edwards became her coach and personal manager.

Goolagong's rise to the top was swift. In 1971, she won the French and Wimbledon singles titles. She defeated her childhood hero, Margaret Court, 6–4, 6–1, in a stunning upset. Nine years later, in 1980, Evonne won her second Wimbledon singles title and her last Grand Slam tournament. In between those years she was frustrated three times in the finals, losing to Billie Jean King in 1972 and 1975 and Chris Evert in 1976. The thrilling Goolagong-Evert rivalry, which pitted the volleyer against the baseliner, lasted only a few years but excited crowds around the world. Although Evert held a 5–4 edge over Goolagong in major tournaments, Evonne took their initial championship encounter at the 1974 Australian Open. The Aussie went on to win three more consecutive Australian singles titles. Her performances at the U.S. Open, however, had different results. She owns the dubious distinction of being the only woman to lose the finals four successive years. Goolagong was a member of the Australian Fed Cup team for seven years and helped her team win the Cups in 1971, 1973, and 1974. As a professional, she won

the season-ending Virginia Slims championship in 1974 and 1976, both over Chris Evert. She became the fifth woman to surpass $1 million in prize winnings.

Her style of play is best described as brisk and buoyant with a sense of enjoyment and an enthusiastic serenity. She uniquely combined lightning fast reflexes with a carefree temperament. Her smile, good-natured shrug, and tiny shriek when she made a mistake separated her from the rest of the field. She never took the game too seriously so that it would impede her feeling of pleasure on the court. Her movements were swift but graceful. She was able to quickly assess the strengths and weaknesses of her opponents and respond with her own superior tactics and flexible array of strokes. Many times while in a close match her seeming lack of concentration resulted in her renowned "walkabouts."

In 1975, Evonne Goolagong married Roger Cawley. The marriage brought a break with Vic Edwards, her long time coach. The couple had their first child, a daughter, in 1977. After giving birth to a son in 1981, Goolagong made a brief comeback attempt. After the 1983 season, Goolagong retired. She returned to live in Queensland after the death of her mother in 1991. Previously, she lived in Hilton Head Island, South Carolina, and Naples, Florida. Upon her return to Australia she began to research her Aboriginal family roots and wrote her autobiography. She was a member of the Board of the Australian Sports Commission from 1995 to 1997. Since 1977, she has held the position of sports ambassador to Aboriginal and Torres Strait Island Communities.

Notable Quotes About Evonne Goolagong

"Tennis is Evonne's being, and it becomes a very special celebration of beauty and verve when she plays it." Bud Collins, sports journalist

"She's happy. No brooding, no introspection. Her head is just there. No problems. She's just Evonne, that's all. Who can be like that? Nobody else I've run into in this life." Rosie Casals, tennis champion

"You can tell she's playing for the sheer fun of it. Now that the big money is here, none of them would play for free. But Evonne would." Sarah Palfrey Cooke Danzig, tennis champion

Writings By and About Evonne Goolagong

Cawley, Evonne, and Phil Jarratt. *Home! The Evonne Goolagong Story*. East Roseville, NSW: Simon and Schuster Australia, 1993.

Goolagong, Evonne, and Bud Collins. *Evonne! On the Move*. New York: Dutton, 1975.

Wind, Herbert Warren. *Evonne Goolagong*. St. Paul, Minn.: EMC, 1975.

CHRIS EVERT

Christine Marie Evert

b. December 21, 1954, Fort Lauderdale, Florida
Turned pro 1972; Right-handed with two-handed backhand;
"The Ice Maiden"; "Little Miss Cool"; "Chrissie"; "Chris America"

Career Rankings

USTA Top 10 Singles

Year	Ranking
1989	3
1988	2
1987	2
1986	2
1985	2
1984	2
1983	2
1982	2
1981	1
1980	2
1979	2
1978	1
1977	1
1976	1
1975	1
1974	1
1973	2
1972	3
1971	3

WTA Top 10 Singles

Year	Ranking
1988	3
1987	3
1986	2
1985	2
1984	2
1983	2
1982	2

Year	Ranking
1981	1
1980	1
1979	2
1978	1
1977	1
1976	1
1975	1
1974	3
1973	3
1972	3
1971	10

World Top 10 Singles

Year	Ranking
1989	10
1988	3
1987	3
1986	2
1985	2
1984	2
1983	2
1982	2
1981	1
1980	1
1979	2
1978	2
1977	1
1976	1
1975	1
1974	3
1973	4
1972	4
1971	10

Fed Cup

Career Record

Overall: 57–4
Singles: 40–2
Doubles: 17–2

World Group Finals Record

Year	Record
1989	Singles: 1–0, Doubles: DNP
1987	Singles: 0–1, Doubles: 0–1
1986	Singles: 1–0, Doubles: DNP
1982	Singles: 1–0, Doubles: 1–0
1981	Singles: 1–0, Doubles: DNP
1980	Singles: 1–0, Doubles: DNP
1979	Singles: 1–0, Doubles: DNP
1978	Singles: 1–0, Doubles: 1–0
1977	Singles: 1–0, Doubles: 0–1

Wightman Cup Record

Year	Record
1985	Singles: 2–0, Doubles: 1–0
1984	Singles: 2–0, Doubles: 1–0
1982	Singles: 2–0, Doubles: DNP
1981	Singles: 2–0, Doubles: 1–0
1980	Singles: 2–0, Doubles: 1–0
1979	Singles: 2–0, Doubles: 1–0
1978	Singles: 2–0, Doubles: 0–1
1977	Singles: 2–0, Doubles: 1–0
1976	Singles: 2–0, Doubles: 1–0
1975	Singles: 2–0, Doubles: 1–0
1973	Singles: 2–0, Doubles: 0–1
1972	Singles: 2–0, Doubles: 1–0
1971	Singles: 2–0, Doubles: 0–1

Grand Slam Highlights

Tournament	Year	Result
Australian	1988	Finalist — Singles
Australian	1988	Finalist — Doubles
Australian	1985	Finalist — Singles
Australian	1984	Winner — Singles
Australian	1982	Winner — Singles
Australian	1981	Finalist — Singles
Australian	1974	Finalist — Singles
French	1986	Winner — Singles
French	1985	Winner — Singles
French	1984	Finalist — Singles
French	1983	Winner — Singles
French	1980	Winner — Singles
French	1979	Winner — Singles
French	1975	Winner — Singles
French	1975	Winner — Doubles
French	1974	Winner — Singles
French	1974	Winner — Doubles
French	1973	Finalist — Singles
Wimbledon	1985	Finalist — Singles
Wimbledon	1984	Finalist — Singles
Wimbledon	1982	Finalist — Singles
Wimbledon	1981	Winner — Singles
Wimbledon	1980	Finalist — Singles
Wimbledon	1979	Finalist — Singles
Wimbledon	1978	Finalist — Singles
Wimbledon	1976	Winner — Singles
Wimbledon	1976	Winner — Doubles
Wimbledon	1974	Winner — Singles
Wimbledon	1973	Finalist — Singles
United States	1984	Finalist — Singles
United States	1983	Finalist — Singles
United States	1982	Winner — Singles
United States	1980	Winner — Singles
United States	1979	Finalist — Singles
United States	1978	Winner — Singles
United States	1977	Winner — Singles
United States	1976	Winner — Singles
United States	1975	Winner — Singles
United States	1974	Finalist — Mixed Doubles

Honors

- In 2005, ranked number 4 on *Tennis Magazine*'s list of the "40 Greatest Players of the Open Tennis Era"
- One of the first inductees into the U.S. Open Court of Champions in 2003
- In 2000, ranked number 6 in *Sports Illustrated for Women*'s "100 Greatest Female Athletes of the 20th Century"
- Inducted into the International Tennis Hall of Fame in 1995

Chris Evert following through as she hits her classic two-handed backhand at the U.S. Open (Carol L. Newsom; courtesy David Newsom).

- Received the Family Circle Player Who Makes a Difference Award in 1995
- Presented the Flo Hyman Award by President George H.W. Bush in 1990
- Founded Chris Evert Charities in 1989
- Named Greatest Woman Athlete of the Last 25 Years by Women's Sports Foundation in 1985
- Received the WTA Tour Player Service Award in 1981, 1986, and 1987
- Women's Sports Foundation Sportswoman of the Year in 1981
- Selected for the International Women's Sports Hall of Fame in 1981
- Received the *Sports Illustrated* Sportsman of the Year Award in 1976
- WTA Players Association president in 1975–1976 and 1983–1991
- Named Associated Press Female Athlete of the Year in 1974, 1975, 1977, and 1980

About Chris Evert

Chris Evert grew up hitting tennis balls on the clay courts at Holiday Park Tennis Center, a public tennis facility in Fort Lauderdale, Florida, where her father was a teaching pro. Jimmy Evert's passion for tennis spread throughout the family. Chris, her mother, both brothers, and her 2 sisters all embraced the game at some level. At age 6, Chris was not strong enough to hit a one-handed backhand so instead used two hands. Nearly 30 years later, still blasting balls with her two-handed backhand, Evert left behind a path of destruction unprecedented in the sport. Her two-handed backhand became a trademark and inspired generations of future players. From 1971 through 1989, Evert maintained a world top 10 ranking and for many of those years was ranked number 1 or 2. She

amassed one of the most impressive individual career records of all time — a 1309–146 won–loss record, 154 singles and 8 doubles WTA Tour titles, 18 singles and 3 doubles Grand Slam titles, a remarkable 57–4 overall record in Fed Cup competition, 26 consecutive singles victories in Wightman Cup matches, and a 125-match win streak on clay from 1973 to 1979.

In 1970, a 15-year-old teenager burst upon the tennis scene by beating Margaret Smith Court. At the time, Court was the holder of all four Grand Slam singles titles. A year later, the pony-tailed Evert advanced to the semi-finals of the U.S. Open. Although she lost to the eventual winner, Billie Jean King, Evert won the acclaim and hearts of tennis fans world wide. King immediately recognized and acknowledged the talents of her young opponent by commenting to her fellow competitors on the tour, "This is a 16-year-old kid who's beating the best people in the world. It's beautiful." Evert's first Grand Slam victories came in 1974 when she won the singles and doubles titles at Roland Garros. She added another Grand Slam title a few weeks later by winning the singles title at Wimbledon. During her illustrious career she won 7 times in Paris, 6 U.S. Opens, 3 Wimbledons, and 2 Australian Opens. Evert was best in the USA, where she compiled an Open record of 101–13.

Evert was most comfortable hugging the baseline and slamming her reliable ground strokes deep and cross court. Although her precise ground strokes were best suited for clay courts, she showed early in her career an ability to win on all surfaces. Her serve was adequate, but she relied heavily on her outstanding return of serve to pull her through many tight matches. She possessed great concentration and anticipation. She played with an impassive efficiency which some observers characterized as a boring style of play. Her cool stoicism, steadiness, and craftiness were practically impenetrable. In 1979, her record setting win streak on clay was stopped in Rome when she lost to Tracy Austin in a thriller 6–4, 2–6, 7–6 (4). Evert's on-court nemesis was Martina Navratilova. Evert lost 40 of 76 singles matches against the Czech, including 6 Grand Slam finals. Chris's last major victory came in the 1986 French Open. Although she missed several tournaments in late 1986 because of a knee injury, she became the first woman tennis player to earn one million dollars in prize money.

Chris Evert and Jimmy Connors were engaged in 1974, but the romance quickly faded and a wedding planned for November was called off. In April 1979, she married English tennis pro John Lloyd. In 1987, the couple divorced with no children. She married Olympic skier Andy Mill in 1988. The couple has three sons. In 2006, Evert filed for divorce and by the end of the year the divorce was finalized. In 2008, Evert and Australian golfer Greg Norman were married at a ceremony in the Bahamas. It was reported that wedding guests were offered an opportunity to play a round of golf with Norman and tennis with Evert.

Chris Evert Charities, founded in 1989, has raised millions of dollars to fight drug abuse and to assist neglected and abused children. Each year she hosts a popular fund raiser in Florida which includes pro-celebrity matches and a black-tie gala. Evert is also actively involved with Robert Seguso and his wife, Carling Bassett-Seguso, in operating a tennis academy. Christine Marie Evert has left an indelible mark on the women's game with her unsurpassed contributions both on and off the tennis court.

Notable Quotes About Chris Evert

"She never left the baseline. She knocked everybody out at long range like the USS *Missouri*. She played tennis the way an orchestra played Beethoven, deftly, lovingly but with intense concentration on the notes. Other players might be rock 'n' roll or bombast. Chris Evert was a Moonlight Sonata." Jim Murray, sports journalist

"She enters a cocoon the moment she goes on court. It's as though she flicks on a switch and automatically she is in a frame of reference where all that matters is her apparatus working at precision efficiency." Virginia Wade, tennis champion

Writings By and About Chris Evert

Burchard, Sue H. *Chris Evert*. New York: Harcourt, 1976.

Hahn, James, and Lynn Hahn. *Chris! The Sports Career of Chris Evert Lloyd*. Mankato, Minn.: Crestwood House, 1981.

Haney, Lynn. *Chris Evert: The Young Champion*. New York: Putnam's, 1976.

Howard, Johnette. *The Rivals: Chris Evert vs. Martina Navratilova, Their Epic Duels and Extraordinary Friendship*. New York: Broadway Books, 2005.

Lloyd, Chris Evert, with Neil Amdur. *Chrissie: My Own Story*. New York: Simon and Schuster, 1982.

Lloyd, Chris Evert, and John Lloyd with Carol Thatcher. *Lloyd on Lloyd*. New York: Beaufort Books, 1986.

May, Julian. *Chris Evert: Princess of Tennis*. Mankato, Minn.: Crestwood House, 1975.

Phillips, Betty Lou. *Chris Evert: First Lady of Tennis*. New York: Putnam's, 1977.

Sabin, Francene. *Set Point: The Story of Chris Evert*. New York: Putnam's, 1977.

Schmitz, Dorothy Childers. *Chris Evert: Women's Tennis Champion*. Mankato, Minn.: Crestwood House, 1977.

MARTINA NAVRATILOVA

b. October 18, 1956, Prague, Czechoslovakia
Turned pro 1975; Left-handed; "Marvelous Martina"

Career Rankings

USTA Top 10 Singles

Year	Ranking
1994	2
1993	1
1992	1
1991	1
1990	1
1989	1
1988	1
1987	1
1986	1
1985	1
1984	1
1983	1
1982	1
1981	3
1980	3
1979	1

WTA Top 10 Singles

Year	Ranking
1994	8
1993	3
1992	5
1990	3
1989	2
1988	2
1987	2
1986	1
1985	1
1984	1
1983	1
1982	1
1981	3
1980	3

Year	Ranking
1979	1
1978	1
1977	3
1976	4
1975	3

World Top 10 Singles

Year	Ranking
1994	8
1993	3
1992	5
1991	5
1990	3
1989	2
1988	2
1987	2
1986	1
1985	1
1984	1
1983	1
1982	1
1981	3
1980	3
1979	1
1978	1
1977	3
1976	4
1975	4

Fed Cup

Career Record

Overall: 40–1
Singles: 20–0
Doubles: 20–1

World Group Finals Record

Year	Record
2003	Singles: 1–0, Doubles: DNP
1989	Singles: 1–0, Doubles: DNP
1986	Singles: 1–0, Doubles: 1–0
1982	Singles: 1–0, Doubles: 1–0
1975	Singles: 1–0, Doubles: 1–0

Wightman Cup Record

Year	Record
1983	Singles: 2–0, Doubles: 1–0

Grand Slam Highlights

Tournament	Year	Result
Australian	2004	Finalist — Mixed Doubles
Australian	2003	Winner — Mixed Doubles
Australian	1989	Winner — Doubles
Australian	1988	Winner — Doubles
Australian	1988	Finalist — Mixed Doubles
Australian	1987	Finalist — Singles
Australian	1987	Winner — Doubles
Australian	1985	Winner — Singles
Australian	1985	Winner — Doubles
Australian	1984	Winner — Doubles
Australian	1983	Winner — Singles
Australian	1983	Winner — Doubles
Australian	1982	Finalist — Singles
Australian	1982	Winner — Doubles
Australian	1981	Winner — Singles
Australian	1981	Finalist — Doubles
Australian	1980	Winner — Doubles
Australian	1975	Finalist — Singles
French	2005	Finalist — Mixed Doubles
French	1988	Winner — Doubles
French	1987	Finalist — Singles
French	1987	Winner — Doubles
French	1986	Finalist — Singles
French	1986	Winner — Doubles
French	1985	Finalist — Singles
French	1985	Winner — Doubles
French	1985	Winner — Mixed Doubles
French	1984	Winner — Singles
French	1984	Winner — Doubles
French	1982	Winner — Singles
French	1982	Winner — Doubles
French	1975	Finalist — Singles
French	1975	Winner — Doubles
French	1974	Winner — Mixed Doubles
Wimbledon	2003	Winner — Mixed Doubles
Wimbledon	1995	Winner — Mixed Doubles
Wimbledon	1994	Finalist — Singles
Wimbledon	1993	Winner — Mixed Doubles
Wimbledon	1990	Winner — Singles
Wimbledon	1989	Finalist — Singles
Wimbledon	1988	Finalist — Singles
Wimbledon	1987	Winner — Singles
Wimbledon	1986	Winner — Singles
Wimbledon	1986	Winner — Doubles
Wimbledon	1986	Finalist — Mixed Doubles
Wimbledon	1985	Winner — Singles
Wimbledon	1985	Finalist — Doubles
Wimbledon	1985	Winner — Mixed Doubles
Wimbledon	1984	Winner — Singles
Wimbledon	1984	Winner — Doubles
Wimbledon	1983	Winner — Singles
Wimbledon	1983	Winner — Doubles
Wimbledon	1982	Winner — Singles
Wimbledon	1982	Winner — Doubles
Wimbledon	1981	Winner — Doubles
Wimbledon	1979	Winner — Singles
Wimbledon	1979	Winner — Doubles
Wimbledon	1978	Winner — Singles
Wimbledon	1977	Finalist — Doubles
Wimbledon	1976	Winner — Doubles
United States	2006	Winner — Mixed Doubles
United States	2003	Finalist — Doubles
United States	1993	Finalist — Mixed Doubles
United States	1991	Finalist — Singles
United States	1990	Winner — Doubles
United States	1989	Finalist — Singles
United States	1989	Winner — Doubles
United States	1987	Winner — Singles
United States	1987	Winner — Doubles
United States	1987	Winner — Mixed Doubles

Martina Navratilova attacking her opponent at the net in Eastbourne, England, in 1984 (Carol L. Newsom; courtesy David Newsom).

Tournament	Year	Result	Tournament	Year	Result
United States	1986	Winner — Singles	United States	1985	Finalist — Doubles
United States	1986	Winner — Doubles	United States	1985	Winner — Mixed
United States	1986	Finalist — Mixed			Doubles
		Doubles	United States	1984	Winner — Singles
United States	1985	Finalist — Singles	United States	1984	Winner — Doubles

Tournament	Year	Result
United States	1983	Winner — Singles
United States	1983	Winner — Doubles
United States	1981	Finalist — Singles
United States	1980	Winner — Doubles
United States	1979	Finalist — Doubles
United States	1978	Winner — Doubles
United States	1977	Winner — Doubles

Honors

- Ranked number 14 on *Sports Illustrated*'s "Top 40 Athletes of All Time"
- In 2005, ranked number 2 on *Tennis Magazine*'s list of the "40 Greatest Players of the Open Tennis Era"
- Recipient of the Laureus World Comeback of the Year Award in 2004
- Received the BBC Lifetime Achievement Award in 2003
- In 2000, ranked number 5 in *Sports Illustrated for Women*'s "100 Greatest Female Athletes of the 20th Century"
- Selected for the International Tennis Hall of Fame in 2000
- Voted World Team Tennis Female Most Valuable Player in 1991, 1992, and 1993
- Named Female Athlete of the Decade (1980s) by *The National Sports Review*, UPI, and AP
- Received Women's Sports Foundation Flo Hyman Award in 1987
- Selected for the International Women's Sports Hall of Fame in 1984
- Named Associated Press Female Athlete of the Year in 1983 and 1986
- Women's Sports Foundation Sportswoman of the Year in 1982, 1983, and 1984
- Named WTA Tour Player of the Year in 1978–1979 and from 1982–1986

About Martina Navratilova

Martina Navratilova learned to play tennis from her stepfather, whom her mother married when Martina was 6 years old. Her first tennis racket found its way into her hands when she was just 4 years old, a hand-me-down from her grandmother. Both her grandmother and mother were athletic. Her mother was an accomplished gymnast, tennis player, and ski instructor. While watching her parents play tennis, Martina would hit an old tennis ball against a practice wall. Martina benefited greatly by the early tutelage of her stepfather/tennis coach and the renewed interest in sports in the late 1960s by the Communist government. She began receiving lessons from George Parma, who taught her the mechanics of the game and encouraged her aggressive play at net, when Martina was just 9 years old.

Navratilova arrived in the United States for the first time in 1973. She won her first title as a professional at a tournament in Orlando, Florida, in 1974. Toward the end of the year, her career took off in earnest when she defeated Margaret Court in Australia and a few weeks later beat Chris Evert in a match in Washington, D.C. She resisted the Czech regime's attempt to restrict her travels and defected in 1975. She became a naturalized citizen in 1981. She's lived in several parts of the United States, including California, Texas, Florida, Virginia, and New York. Particularly fond of the USA, she flourishes in the freedom to be herself and exhibits her independent spirit wherever she goes.

Navratilova became the world's most prominent woman tennis player in the 1980s while successfully unseating her most competitive rival, Chris Evert. Of her astounding career record, her triumphs at Wimbledon are the most impressive. Martina's game always revolved around the serve and volley, making her favorite court surface that of grass. She captured the singles title in 1978, 1979, and 1982–1987. She played in 12 singles finals at Wimbledon, winning 9 of those matches. Her style of play was also effective on other surfaces; she captured at least 2 Grand Slam titles at each of the other major venues during her illustrious career. Although eventually winning all four Grand Slam singles titles, the net-hugging southpaw found the U.S. Championships the most elusive. Finally, in 1983 she captured the coveted career Grand Slam in singles with a win over Chris Evert in a come-from-behind 3 set victory in New York. She went on to win 34 of her last 35 matches in five U.S. Opens from 1983 to 1987. In total, she won 18 Grand Slam singles titles, 31 doubles titles, and 10 mixed doubles crowns. She raised the women's game to new heights with her power and aggressiveness.

Martina revolutionized the way women prepared for matches by identifying a daily program for weight training, running, and eating. Her innovative approach to the game, which had a permanent influence on women's tennis, was documented in a collaborative effort with Mary Carillo in a breakthrough book titled *Tennis My Way*. In the early 1980s Navratilova built a support network around her. Under the guidance of basketball star Nancy Lieberman, she started lifting weights. She worked with Renee Richards on court tactics and strategy. Mike Estep coached her on the technical aspects of the game. Her hard work and meticulous preparation paid off for Navratilova and she became a tennis phenom in the 1980s. In 1982, she lost just 3 times in 93 singles matches. In 1983, she did even better losing only once in 87 matches. She continued her unprecedented dominance in the sport by winning 74 consecutive singles matches in 1984. During her career she won 167 singles titles and 177 doubles titles. In 2006, she won the U.S. Open mixed doubles title with Bob Bryan just a few weeks before her 50th birthday, extending her record as the oldest player to win a major tournament.

In her autobiography, *Martina*, Navratilova admits to having her first gay relationship at the age of 18. In 1981, after becoming a U.S. citizen, she publicly disclosed her sexual orientation. She had a long-term relationship with Judy Nelson from 1983 to 1991. During her first retirement from tennis in 1995–2000 she skied, piloted planes, played ice hockey, and co–authored several novels. Today, she is involved with various organizations which benefit animal rights, help underprivileged children, and promote gay rights in professional sports. She lives with her partner in Sarasota, Florida.

Notable Quotes About Martina Navratilova

"She's the greatest singles, doubles, and mixed doubles player who's ever lived." Billie Jean King, tennis champion

"Martina revolutionized the game by her superb athleticism and aggressiveness, not to mention, her outspokenness and her candor. She brought athleticism to a whole new level." Chris Evert, tennis champion

Writings By and About Martina Navratilova

Blue, Adrianne. *Martina: The Lives and Times of Martina Navratilova*. Secaucus, N.J.: Carol Pub. Group, 1995.
Elstein, Rick. *Tennis Kinetics with Martina*

Navratilova. New York: Simon and Schuster, 1985.

Faulkner, Sandra, with Judy Nelson. *Love Match: Nelson vs. Navratilova.* New York: Carol Pub. Group, 1993.

Howard, Johnette. *The Rivals: Chris Evert vs. Martina Navratilova, Their Epic Duels and Extraordinary Friendship.* New York: Broadway Books, 2005.

Navratilova, Martina. *Shape Your Self: My 6-Step Diet and Fitness Plan to Achieve the Best Shape of Your Life.* Emmaus, Pa.: Rodale, 2006.

Navratilova, Martina, with George Vecsey. *Martina.* New York: Knopf, 1985.

Navratilova, Martina, with Mary Carillo. *Tennis My Way.* New York: Charles Scribner's Sons, 1983.

HANA MANDLIKOVA

b. February 19, 1962, Prague, Czechoslovakia
Turned pro 1978; Right-handed

Career Rankings

WTA Top 10 Singles

Year	Ranking
1987	5
1986	4
1985	3
1984	3
1982	7
1981	5
1980	4

World Top 10 Singles

Year	Ranking
1987	5
1986	4
1985	3
1984	3
1982	7
1981	5
1980	4

Fed Cup

Career Record

Overall: 49–12
Singles: 34–6
Doubles: 15–6

World Group Finals Record

Year	Record
1986	Singles: 0–1, Doubles: 0–1
1985	Singles: 1–0, Doubles: DNP

Year	Record
1984	Singles: 1–0, Doubles: 1–0
1983	Singles: 1–0, Doubles: DNP

Hopman Cup

Career Record

Overall: 6–6
Singles: 2–4
Doubles: 4–2

Finals Round Record

Year	Record
1989	Singles: 0–1, Doubles: 0–1

Grand Slam Highlights

Tournament	Year	Result
Australian	1987	Winner — Singles
Australian	1980	Winner — Singles
French	1984	Finalist — Doubles
French	1981	Winner — Singles
Wimbledon	1986	Finalist — Singles
Wimbledon	1986	Finalist — Doubles
Wimbledon	1981	Finalist — Singles
United States	1989	Winner — Doubles
United States	1986	Finalist — Doubles
United States	1985	Winner — Singles
United States	1982	Finalist — Singles
United States	1980	Finalist — Singles

Hana Mandlikova slicing her backhand during competition on the Virginia Slims Tour in 1984 (Carol L. Newsom; courtesy David Newsom).

Honors

- In 2005, ranked number 33 on *Tennis Magazine*'s list of the "40 Greatest Players of the Open Tennis Era"

- Inducted into the International Tennis Hall of Fame in 1994

- Voted 1980 WTA Tour Most Improved Player

About Hana Mandlikova

Hana Mandlikova was deliberately raised by her father to become a "sports child." Along with her brother, who played professional hockey, she was introduced to sports at a very young age. Her father is Vilem Mandlik, an Olympic 100-meter finalist. He built a scaled-down wooden tennis racket for Hana and showed her how to hit imaginary tennis balls while standing in front of a mirror. When Mandlikova was 9, her father enrolled her in the Sparta Sports Club in Prague. Growing up she idolized the Czech Hall of Fame player Jan Kodes. Later, at age 12, she was a ball girl for Martina Navratilova at the club. "It was not really a dream, but always I was thinking about when I would beat Martina," she once admitted to a sportswriter.

Mandlikova was a magnificent athlete who relentlessly attacked the net. She combined grace and agility on the court. She possessed extraordinary versatility, mixing strong serves with heavy topspin backhands and flat forehands on her way to winning 4 majors, including 2 Australian, a French, and the U.S. Open in 1985, when she beat Martina Navratilova 7–6 (3), 1–6, 7–6 (2) in a thrilling finals match. Two years later, the two powerhouses hooked up again in the finals in Melbourne, where once again Hana prevailed in a close match 7–5, 7–6 (2).

Early in her career, Hana Mandlikova developed a reputation for "choking." At crucial moments during a match she would lose concentration and eventually lose the match. In 1980, in a pre–Wimbledon tournament in Eastbourne, she squandered a big lead and lost to Tracy Austin. At Wimbledon that same year, she blew another lead against Evonne Goolagong in a fourth-round contest. Sensing something was missing from her tennis arsenal, Hana hired a veteran player, Betty Stove, to serve as her coach, trainer, and manager. Dividends paid off almost immediately from this action. Only months later, she defeated both Navratilova and Andrea Jaegar to win a tournament in the United States. At the U.S. Open that year she stormed into the finals only to succumb to the incomparable Chris Evert. Mandlikova finished the season in a flurry by winning several tournaments, including the Australian Open, her first Grand Slam title. After a slow start in 1981, Hana ended Chris Evert's 64 match win streak on clay by beating her in the semi-finals at Roland Garros and went on to take her 2nd Grand Slam singles title.

Hana went into a slump in 1982 precipitated by nagging injuries. The slump lasted nearly two years. She admits that she became a victim of her own success. She felt the pressure of being labeled the heir apparent to Evert and Navratilova. By 1984, she was once again back on track, helped by her coach, Betty Stove, who designed a rigorous physical training program for the Czech. With an abbreviated playing schedule, Hana made her way back up to number 3 in the world in 1985. She capped off her comeback year by winning the U.S. Open with consecutive wins against Evert and Navratilova. In Fed Cup play, Hana had an exceptional record, leading her country to 3 consecutive championships from 1983 to 1985.

Noted for her dark hair held in place by a trademark red bandana tied Indian-style around her forehead, the tall right-hander maintained a serious demeanor on court. Off court, however, she was known for her sense of humor. In 1986, Mandlikova married Jan Sedlak, a childhood friend. Today, she divides her time between Prague and Boca West, Florida.

Notable Quote About Hana Mandlikova

"One of the most natural athletes in women's tennis." John Newcombe, tennis champion

Writings By and About Hana Mandlikova

Collins, Bud. *Total Tennis: The Ultimate Tennis Encyclopedia*. Toronto: Sport Media Pub. Inc., 2003, pp. 699–700.

Mandlikova, Hana. "I Gave 100 Percent." *Tennis* (Australia) November 1992: 50–53.

Mandlikova, Hana, and Betty Stove. *Total Tennis: A Guide to the Fundamentals of the Game*. Australia: Simon and Schuster, 1990.

Mandlikova, Hana, and Malcolm Folley. *Hana: An Autobiography*. London: Arthur Baker, 1989.

Mandlikova, Hana, and Vladimir Skutina. *Hana*. Praha, Czechoslovakia: Olympia, 1991.

TRACY AUSTIN

b. December 12, 1962, Palos Verdes, California
Turned pro 1978; Right-handed with two-handed backhand

Career Rankings

USTA Top 10 Singles

Year	Ranking
1983	5
1982	4
1981	2
1980	1
1979	3
1978	3
1977	4

WTA Top 10 Singles

Year	Ranking
1983	9
1982	4
1981	2
1980	2
1979	3
1978	6

World Top 10 Singles

Year	Ranking
1983	9
1982	4
1981	2
1980	2
1979	3
1978	6

Fed Cup

Career Record

Overall: 13–1
Singles: 13–1
Doubles: DNP

World Group Finals Record

Year	Record
1980	Singles: 1–0, Doubles: DNP
1979	Singles: 1–0, Doubles: DNP
1978	Singles: 0–1, Doubles: DNP

Wightman Cup Record

Year	Record
1981	Singles: 2–0, Doubles: DNP
1979	Singles: 2–0, Doubles: 1–0
1978	Singles: 0–2, Doubles: 1–0

Grand Slam Highlights

Tournament	Year	Result
Wimbledon	1981	Finalist — Mixed Doubles
Wimbledon	1980	Winner — Mixed Doubles
United States	1981	Winner — Singles
United States	1979	Winner — Singles

Honors

- In 2005, ranked number 32 on *Tennis Magazine*'s list of the "40 Greatest Players of the Open Tennis Era"

Tracy Austin, teenage sensation, preparing to hit a forehand lob (Carol L. Newsom; courtesy David Newsom).

- Inducted into the International Tennis Hall of Fame in 1992
- Women's Sports Foundation Sportswoman of the Year in 1980
- WTA Player of the Year in 1980
- Named Associated Press Female Athlete of the Year in 1979 and 1981
- WTA Most Impressive Newcomer in 1977

About Tracy Austin

Easily recognizable on the tennis court by her pigtails and pinafores, Tracy Austin's competitive playing career ended as abruptly as it began in 1977. By 1983, her astonishing career was virtually over due to a number of injuries. In the intervening years she turned the tennis world upside down winning 32 singles titles, including two Grand Slam singles tournaments and a doubles crown. She also represented the USA as a member of the Fed Cup and Wightman Cup teams between the years 1978 and 1981.

Her style of play was characterized by tenacity, mental toughness, patience, and torrid passing shots from behind the baseline. Her competitive nature probably resulted from her tennis playing parents and siblings. Her three brothers all held rankings in California, and her sister played professional tennis for several years. Tracy had a spectacular junior tennis record. She won a record 27 national titles, including the USLTA girls' 12 singles in 1974, girls' 14 singles in 1975 and 1976, girls' 16 singles in 1978, and the girls' 18 singles in 1977 and 1978.

At the age of 14 Austin competed in her first Wimbledon singles tournament; at 17 she attained the world's number 1 ranking, and by 21 she had won 2 U.S.

Open titles. In 1979, she was the youngest tennis player to win a U.S. Open title when she beat Chris Evert in straight sets. She was also the youngest professional player to earn one million dollars in prize money. The highlight of her career came in 1981 when she defeated Martina Navratilova to win her second U.S. Open singles title while fighting a bout of sciatica. During the years 1982–1989 Austin played sporadically while fighting several injuries. In August 1989, she was in a terrible automobile accident that severely damaged her right knee. Determined to get back on to the tennis court, she went through a regimen of intense physical therapy for months. In 1994, she was back on the courts playing in professional tournaments, but never regained her competitive edge. Today, she is active in the world of tennis as a sports commentator, a motivational speaker, and a sponsor of pro-celebrity charity tennis tournaments. She is married to Scott Holt and is the mother of three sons.

Notable Quote About Tracy Austin

"Tracy's mental strength was scary. She had no weaknesses, she was obsessive about winning." Chris Evert, tennis champion

Writings By and About Tracy Austin

Austin, Tracy, and Christine Brennan. *Beyond Center Court: My Story.* New York: W. Morrow, 1992.
Austin, Tracy, and Steve Eubanks. *I Know Absolutely Nothing About Tennis.* Nashville, Tenn.: Rutledge Hill Press, 1997.
Burchard, Sue. *Sports Star: Tracy Austin.* New York: Harcourt, 1982.

Friend, Tom. "A Tennis Life Begins Again at 30." *New York Times* 24 February 1993: B9.

Jenkins, Sally. "Tracy Austin." *Sports Illustrated* 8 March 1993: 40–41.

Lorge, Barry. "Why Tracy Austin Decided to Make a Comeback." *Tennis* November 1988: 25–26.

Miklowitz, Gloria D. *Tracy Austin*. New York: Grossett and Dunlop, 1978.

Robison, Nancy. *Tracy Austin: Teenage Superstar*. New York: Harvey House, 1978.

Scher, Jon. "Served: Tracy Austin, with an Invitation to Become, at 29, the Youngest Member of the Tennis Hall of Fame." *Sports Illustrated* 3 February 1992: 66.

JANA NOVOTNA

b. October 2, 1968, Brno, Czech Republic
Turned pro 1986; Right-handed

Career Rankings

WTA Top 10 Singles

Year	Ranking
1998	3
1997	2
1996	3
1994	4
1993	6
1992	10
1991	7

World Top 10 Singles

Year	Ranking
1998	3
1997	2
1996	3
1994	4
1993	6
1992	10
1991	7

Fed Cup

Career Record

Overall: 33–12
Singles: 22–7
Doubles: 11–5

World Group Finals Record

Year	Record
1988	Singles: DNP, Doubles: 0–1

Hopman Cup

Career Record

Overall: 6–8
Singles: 3–4
Doubles: 3–4

Finals Round Record

Year	Record
1994	Singles: 1–0, Doubles: 0–1

Olympic Tennis Medals

Year	Medal
1996	Singles: Bronze, Doubles: Silver
1988	Doubles: Silver

Grand Slam Highlights

Tournament	Year	Result
Australian	1995	Winner — Doubles
Australian	1991	Finalist — Singles
Australian	1990	Winner — Doubles
Australian	1989	Winner — Mixed Doubles
Australian	1988	Winner — Mixed Doubles
French	1998	Winner — Doubles
French	1991	Winner — Doubles
French	1990	Winner — Doubles
Wimbledon	1998	Winner — Singles
Wimbledon	1998	Winner — Doubles
Wimbledon	1997	Finalist — Singles
Wimbledon	1995	Winner — Doubles
Wimbledon	1994	Finalist — Doubles

Tournament	Year	Result
Wimbledon	1993	Finalist — Singles
Wimbledon	1993	Finalist — Doubles
Wimbledon	1992	Finalist — Doubles
Wimbledon	1991	Finalist — Doubles
Wimbledon	1990	Winner — Doubles
Wimbledon	1989	Winner — Doubles
Wimbledon	1989	Winner — Mixed Doubles
United States	1998	Winner — Doubles
United States	1997	Winner — Doubles
United States	1996	Finalist — Doubles
United States	1994	Winner — Doubles
United States	1994	Finalist — Mixed Doubles
United States	1988	Winner — Mixed Doubles

Honors

- Inducted into the International Tennis Hall of Fame in 2005
- Winner of the International Tennis Federation Doubles Team of the Year in 1997 (with Lindsay Davenport)
- Winner of WTA Tour Doubles Team of the Year in 1989 and 1990 (with Helena Sukova), in 1991 (with Gigi Fernandez), in 1996 (with Arantxa Sanchez-Vicario), and in 1998 (with Martina Hingis)

About Jana Novotna

Despite winning an impressive seventeen Grand Slam titles, Jana Novotna is remembered more as a runner-up rather than a singles champion. Her one and only major singles title was won on the sacred grounds of Centre Court at Wimbledon in 1998 when she beat Nathalie Tauziat in straight sets. Five years earlier, she lost a heart-breaking finals match to Steffi Graf and instead of holding the famed Wimbledon trophy over her head, she cried on the shoulder of the Duchess of Kent.

Playing with another player on the same side of the net with her, however, was a different story for Jana. The doubles specialist won 12 Grand Slam women's doubles titles and 4 Grand Slam mixed doubles crowns. She was the season ending top ranked doubles player 11 times. Although she was soft-spoken off the court, Novotna relied on dependable and well-placed volleys to do the talking for her while on the court. She consistently followed her serve to the net and immediately put her opponents on the defensive.

While known primarily as a doubles player in the early years of her career, she had modest success in singles competition. Experts believe her successful singles play is attributed to Hana Mandlikova, who became her coach in the early 1990s. In 1991, at the Australian Open, she reached her first Grand Slam singles final, but lost to Monica Seles in a 3 set match. Two years later, in London, after making a remarkable comeback against Steffi Graf in the finals, she seemed on her way to winning the coveted trophy until she started to lose her nerve and began missing easy shots. In 1998, she finally redeemed herself by beating Venus Williams and Martina Hingis on her way to winning both the singles and doubles titles at Wimbledon. Earlier in her career she was a member of the Czech team that won the Fed Cup in 1988. At the Olympic Games, Novotna was a women's doubles silver medalist in 1988 and 1996, and a singles bronze medalist in 1996.

Despite her reputation as a runner-up, Jana seems at peace with her tennis career. During retirement ceremonies in New York at the U.S. Open in 1999, she said goodbye to the game with these words, "I can look back and just be very thankful for the long and very healthy career that I had." In 2006, Jana continued to show her doubles prowess when she won the women's

Jana Novotna after her victory over Nathalie Tauziat in the finals at the 1998 Wimbledon Championships (courtesy Sportingheroes.net).

membered as one of the great women volleyers of all time.

Notable Quote About Jana Novotna

"She's one of the few players who comes into the net and can also stay in the back. She doesn't give you any shots. You just kind of always have to wait and be very patient against her." Martina Hingis, tennis champion

Writings About Jana Novotna

Robertson, Linda. "Blonde Ambition." *Tennis* July 1999: 68*ff.*
Rosenbaum, Dan. "Czech Her Out." *World Tennis* March 1990: 50.
Shmerler, Cindy. "The World According to Jana Novotna." *Tennis* February 1999: 16.

35 and over doubles tournament at Wimbledon. Especially known for her heavy slice backhand shot which she used when attacking the net, Jana Novotna will be re-

STEFFI GRAF

b. June 14, 1969, Bruhl, Germany
Turned pro 1982; Right-handed; "Fraulein Forehand"

Career Rankings

WTA Top 10 Singles

Year	Ranking
1996	1
1995	1
1994	1
1993	1
1992	2
1991	2
1990	1
1989	1
1988	1
1987	1
1986	3
1985	6

World Top 10 Singles

Year	Ranking
1996	1
1995	1 (tied with Monica Seles)
1994	1
1993	1
1992	2
1991	2
1990	1
1989	1
1988	1
1987	1
1986	3
1985	6

Fed Cup

Career Record

Overall: 28–4
Singles: 20–2
Doubles: 8–2

World Group Finals Record

Year	Record
1992	Singles: 1–0, Doubles: DNP
1987	Singles: 1–0, Doubles: 1–0

Hopman Cup

Career Record

Overall: 8–6
Singles: 6–1
Doubles: 2–5

Finals Round Record

Year	Record
1993	Singles: 1–0, Doubles: 0–1

Olympic Tennis Medals

Year	Medal
1992	Singles: Silver
1988	Singles: Gold, Doubles: Bronze

Grand Slam Highlights

Tournament	Year	Result
Australian	1994	Winner — Singles
Australian	1993	Finalist — Singles
Australian	1990	Winner — Singles
Australian	1989	Winner — Singles
Australian	1988	Winner — Singles
French	1999	Winner — Singles
French	1996	Winner — Singles
French	1995	Winner — Singles
French	1993	Winner — Singles
French	1992	Finalist — Singles
French	1990	Finalist — Singles
French	1989	Finalist — Singles
French	1989	Finalist — Doubles
French	1988	Winner — Singles
French	1987	Winner — Singles
French	1987	Finalist — Doubles
French	1986	Finalist — Doubles
Wimbledon	1999	Finalist — Singles
Wimbledon	1996	Winner — Singles
Wimbledon	1995	Winner — Singles
Wimbledon	1993	Winner — Singles
Wimbledon	1992	Winner — Singles
Wimbledon	1991	Winner — Singles
Wimbledon	1989	Winner — Singles
Wimbledon	1988	Winner — Singles
Wimbledon	1988	Winner — Doubles
Wimbledon	1987	Finalist — Singles
United States	1996	Winner — Singles
United States	1995	Winner — Singles
United States	1994	Finalist — Singles
United States	1993	Winner — Singles
United States	1990	Finalist — Singles
United States	1989	Winner — Singles
United States	1988	Winner — Singles
United States	1987	Finalist — Singles

Honors

- In 2005, ranked number 3 in *Tennis Magazine*'s "40 Greatest Players of the Open Tennis Era"
- Inducted into the International Tennis Hall of Fame in 2004
- In 2000, ranked number 14 in *Sports Il-lustrated for Women*'s "100 Greatest Female Athletes of the 20th Century"
- WTA Most Exciting Player in 1996, 1998, and 1999
- Steffi Graf Youth Tennis Center was founded and dedicated October 1991 in Leipzig, Germany
- Associated Press Female Athlete of the Year in 1989
- Women's Sports Foundation Sportswoman of the Year in 1989
- WTA Most Improved Player in 1986
- WTA Player of the Year 1987–1990 and 1993–1996

About Steffi Graf

Steffi Graf is the older of two children born to Peter and Heidi Graf. Both her parents played tennis, and Steffi received her first racket at the age of 4. She grew up on the tennis court after her father opened a tennis school in Bruhl. At the young age of 5, she played in her first tournament. She played constantly as a junior, winning the European Championships in the 12s and 18s. Peter Graf remained her coach and business manager until 1995, when he was sentenced to 45 months in prison for tax evasion in connection with handling financial matters for Steffi during her early career. Her father always kept a tight rein on Steffi both on and off the court. Graf typically practiced several hours a day. She had no close friends on the tour, especially during the early years. Many believe that the extremely restricted lifestyle imposed by her father resulted in her steady tennis improvement, and ultimately, her meteoric rise to the top of the tennis world.

In 1988, Graf became the only player, male or female, to win the Golden Slam — all 4 Grand Slam singles titles and the

Olympic gold medal in the same year. She is also the only male or female player to win at least 4 times in singles play at each Grand Slam venue. Her Grand Slam singles record is incomparable in the open tennis era. She played in 36 majors from 1987 to 1996. In those tournaments she reached the final round 29 times while winning the championship crown 21 times. At one stretch during that period she played in 13 consecutive Grand Slam singles finals, winning 9 of them.

In 1990, personal problems threatened Graf's reign atop the world of women's tennis more than any of her on-court opponents. Her father was connected to a fraudulent paternity suit which distracted Steffi at Wimbledon. She uncharacteristically lost in a semi-final match to Zina Garrison. She had already lost to Monica Seles in the finals at the French Open just weeks before. At the culminating Slam event of the year, she lost to Gabriela Sabatini in straight sets in the finals at Flushing Meadows. Her downturn continued into 1991. Plagued by injuries and personal struggles, she watched Monica Seles win at Melbourne, Paris, and New York. Although managing to capture another singles title in London, Graf lost her number 1 world ranking in March to Seles. In 1992, Graf repeated her win at Wimbledon, led Germany to the Fed Cup championship, and won a silver medal at the Olympics in Barcelona. For most tennis players, these accomplishments would have been considered highly rewarding, but for Steffi and her fans, they fell short of the potential she showed at the beginning of 1990 when she beat Mary Joe Fernandez in the finals at the Australian Open. That victory was her eighth win in her last nine Grand Slam events.

Following the tragic events surrounding the inexplicable stabbing of Monica

Seles in Hamburg, Graf once again dominated women's tennis. After her victory over Arantxa Sanchez-Vicario at the Australian Open in 1994, she held all four major titles simultaneously. Unfortunately, Graf's personal problems resurfaced in 1995 when she was accused of tax evasion. The German government eventually dropped its case against her in 1997. Despite the distraction, she won three of four Grand Slam tournaments in 1995 and successfully defended her titles in 1996 in Paris, London, and New York. Such a feat is a testimonial to the determination and tenacity of the German superstar.

Towards the end of her career Graf played through nagging knee and back injuries. After regaining and maintaining the world's number 1 ranking from 1993 to 1996, her injuries caused her to miss the 1997 season. She failed to win a Grand Slam title for the first time in ten years. In 1999, she won her 22nd and last major tournament by coming from behind to beat Martina Hingis in the finals at the French Open. The win would be her last in Grand Slam competition. Graf retired with an overall won–loss record of 902–115. She won 107 WTA Tour singles titles, 11 doubles titles, 22 Grand Slam singles titles, 1 Grand Slam doubles title, and 3 Olympic medals.

The main weapon in Graf's tennis arsenal was her powerful and consistent forehand. She used this blistering stroke to set up easy winners later in a point, or many times, she used it to hit instant winners. Graf developed a classic slice backhand that was the best in the game. When she hit deep into her opponent's court she would approach the net and be in a position to hit a easy winning volley. If she returned her deftly sliced backhand short over the net, her opponents were forced to hit a high and oftentimes weak return, setting

Graf announced her retirement on August 13, 1999, shortly after retiring from a second round match due to a hamstring strain in her left leg. She was ranked number 3 in the world when she retired. Two years later she married former men's tennis star Andre Agassi. The superstar tennis couple lives in Las Vegas, Nevada, with their son and daughter.

Notable Quote About Steffi Graf

"I think Steffi is the ideal, what any athlete in tennis would want to reach." Monica Seles, tennis champion

Writings About Steffi Graf

Steffi Graf celebrating her 6th French Open singles title in 1999 after beating Martina Hingis in three sets (Carol L. Newsom; courtesy David Newsom).

up another easy winning shot. After taking her game to the highest level by developing a reliable volley and powerful serve, her all-court game was virtually unstoppable.

Brooks, Philip. *Steffi Graf: Tennis Champ*. New York: Children's Press, 1996.

Heady, Sue. *Steffi: Public Power, Private Pain*. London: Virgin, 1995.

Hilgers, Laura. *Steffi Graf*. New York: Little, Brown, 1990.

Knapp, Ron. *Sports Great Steffi Graf*. Springfield, N.J.: Enslow Pub., 1995.

Monroe, Judy. *Steffi Graf*. Mankato, Minn.: Crestwood House, 1988.

ARANTXA SANCHEZ-VICARIO

b. December 18, 1971, Barcelona, Spain
Turned pro 1985; Right-handed with two-handed backhand;
"The Barcelona Bumblebee"

Career Rankings

WTA Top 10 Singles

Year	Ranking
2000	9
1998	4
1997	9
1996	2 (tied with Monica Seles)
1995	4
1994	2
1993	2
1992	4
1991	5
1990	7
1989	5

World Top 10 Singles

Year	Ranking
2000	9
1998	4
1997	9
1996	2 (tied with Monica Seles)
1995	3
1994	2
1993	2
1992	4
1991	5
1990	7
1989	5

Fed Cup Record

Career Record

Overall: 72–28
Singles: 50–22
Doubles: 22–6

World Group Finals Record

Year	Record
2002	Singles: 0–1, Doubles: DNP
2000	Singles: 0–2, Doubles: DNP
1998	Singles: 1–1, Doubles: 1–0
1996	Singles: 0–2, Doubles: DNP
1995	Singles: 1–1, Doubles: DNP
1994	Singles: 1–0, Doubles: 1–0
1993	Singles: 1–0, Doubles: 1–0
1992	Singles: 0–1, Doubles: 1–0
1991	Singles: 1–0, Doubles: 1–0
1989	Singles: 0–1, Doubles: 0–1

Hopman Cup

Career Record

Overall: 24–12
Singles: 13–5
Doubles: 11–7

Finals Round Record

Year	Record
2002	Singles: 0–1, Doubles: 1–0
1993	Singles: 0–1, Doubles: 1–0
1990	Singles: 1–0, Doubles: 0–1

Arantxa Sanchez-Vicario ready to hit a backhand at Wimbledon in 1999 (Carol L. Newsom; courtesy David Newsom).

Olympic Tennis Medals

Year	Medal
1996	Singles: Silver, Doubles: Bronze
1992	Singles: Bronze, Doubles: Silver

Grand Slam Highlights

Tournament	Year	Result
Australian	2002	Finalist — Doubles
Australian	2000	Finalist — Mixed Doubles
Australian	1996	Winner — Doubles
Australian	1995	Finalist — Singles
Australian	1995	Winner — Doubles
Australian	1994	Finalist — Singles
Australian	1993	Winner — Mixed Doubles
Australian	1992	Winner — Doubles
Australian	1992	Finalist — Mixed Doubles
French	1998	Winner — Singles
French	1996	Finalist — Singles
French	1995	Finalist — Singles
French	1995	Finalist — Doubles
French	1994	Winner — Singles
French	1992	Finalist — Doubles
French	1992	Winner — Mixed Doubles
French	1991	Finalist — Singles
French	1990	Winner — Mixed Doubles
French	1989	Finalist — Mixed Doubles
French	1989	Winner — Singles
Wimbledon	1996	Finalist — Singles
Wimbledon	1995	Finalist — Singles
Wimbledon	1995	Winner — Doubles
Wimbledon	1994	Finalist — Doubles
United States	2000	Winner — Mixed Doubles
United States	1999	Finalist — Doubles
United States	1996	Finalist — Doubles
United States	1994	Winner — Singles
United States	1994	Winner — Doubles
United States	1993	Winner — Doubles
United States	1992	Finalist — Singles
United States	1991	Finalist — Mixed Doubles

Honors

- Recipient of the Principe De Asturiasi, Spain's highest award, for her lifetime achievement in tennis
- Inducted into the International Tennis Hall of Fame in 2007
- In 2005, ranked number 27 on *Tennis Magazine*'s "40 Greatest Players of the Open Tennis Era"
- Received the 2001 inaugural Award of Excellence from the ITF and the International Tennis Hall of Fame for dedication to Fed Cup play for participating 15 years while helping Spain win the Cup five times (with Conchita Martinez)
- Received the 2000 Family Circle Cup Player Who Makes a Difference Award
- Named *Tennis Magazine*'s Comeback Player in 1998
- Named the WTA Tour Doubles Team of the Year (with Jana Novotna) in 1996
- Recipient of the first-ever WTA Tour ACES Award in 1995
- Received the Infiniti Commitment to Excellence Award in 1992
- Named Spain's Best Athlete in 1991, 1994, and 1998 by the newspaper *El Mundo Deportivo*
- Recipient of the WTA Tour Most Improved Player Award in 1988 and 1989
- Recipient of the WTA Tour Most Impressive Newcomer Award in 1987

About Arantxa Sanchez-Vicario

Arantxa Sanchez-Vicario was practically born with a tennis racket in her hand. She had no choice but to pick up a racket lying around the house that belonged to one of her tennis playing brothers, Emilio or Javier. Her mother, Marisa, was totally committed to supporting Arantxa's tennis career and often traveled with her not as an overbearing "tennis mother," but just as a caring mother watching over one of her children. The Sanchez family grew up on the red clay courts at the Real Club de Tenis in Barcelona, the oldest and most prestigious tennis club in Spain. Arantxa emphasized the importance of her family as being responsible for her success on the tennis court during her emotional induction speech in 2007 at the International Tennis Hall of Fame.

Although her 4 Grand Slam singles titles don't compare with the records of some of her contemporaries, Sanchez-Vicario brought to the game a unique commitment, dedication, and charm. She represented the soul of women's tennis for three decades. The over-achieving Spaniard capitalized on her work ethic and perseverance. While lacking the powerful weapons of many of her opponents, Arantxa conquered them with her court craftiness and ingenuity. She was a ferocious competitor. Known for her fighting spirit, she would scamper around the court refusing to concede a point. Time after time she turned seemingly certain defeat into victory with her piercing passing shots and topspin lobs. Her never-say-die attitude propelled her to wins against stronger opponents. In the dramatic finals of the French Open in 1989 against heavily favored Steffi Graf, Sanchez-Vicario showed her unmatched spirit. She outlasted the German superstar by winning 7–5 in the third set. Chris Evert once commented that no one in tennis had a bigger heart than Arantxa. At the time, her victory made her the youngest French champion in history.

In 1994, Sanchez-Vicario became the first-ever Spanish woman to win the U.S. Open. She held the world's number 1 ranking in singles and doubles simultaneously during the early part of 1995. She was one of only 4 women players to ever achieve that distinction. Her career peaked in 1996. She did not win a WTA Tour title in 1997. In 1998, she surprised everyone by winning her third French Open singles title by beating Monica Seles in 3 sets. It would be her last Slam title. During her stellar career, she combined 6 doubles and 4 mixed doubles Grand Slam titles with her 4 singles titles to bring her total to a very respectable 14. Sanchez-Vicario announced her retirement on November 12, 2001, in Barcelona. Before she retired, however, she won 29 singles WTA Tour titles, 67 doubles Tour championships, 4 Olympic medals, 2 Hopman Cup titles, and was a member of Spain's championship Fed Cup team 5 times.

She was married in August 2000 to sports journalist Joan Vehils, but the marriage lasted only 10 months. She returned to the WTA Tour in 2004 and played in selected doubles events. No longer playing competitive tennis, Sanchez-Vicario is still involved in the game. She keeps busy working with the Real Federacion Espanola de Tenis and the International Tennis Federation. She travels worldwide presenting workshops and clinics for elite female tennis players. The charismatic Spaniard continues to be one of the sport's great ambassadors.

Notable Quote About Arantxa Sanchez-Vicario

"Arantxa is absolutely wonderful. She is feisty and fiery and laughs back at the public when she misses an easy shot. But beneath all the fun and the giggles, she's a lion." Ted Tinling, tennis player and fashion designer

Writings By and About Arantxa Sanchez-Vicario

Lidz, Franz. "Tennis with Plenty of Bounce, Arantxa Sanchez-Vicario's Winning Style." *Sports Illustrated* 14 May 1990: 12–13.

Preston, Mark. "Arantxa Sanchez: Still the Same, Only Better." *Tennis* January 1990: 32–36.

Sanchez-Vicario, Arantxa. *Tennis*. New York: DK Pub., 2000.

Sanchez-Vicario, Arantxa. *The Young Tennis Player: A Young Enthusiast's Guide to Tennis*. New York: DK Pub., 1996.

MONICA SELES

b. December 2, 1973, Novi Sad, Yugoslavia
Turned pro 1989, Left-handed with two-handed forehand and backhand

Career Rankings

WTA Top 10 Singles

Year	Ranking
2002	7
2001	10
2000	4
1999	6
1998	6
1997	5
1996	2 (tied with Arantxa Sanchez-Vicario)
1995	1
1993	8
1992	1
1991	1
1990	2
1989	6

World Top 10 Singles

Year	Ranking
2002	7
2001	10
2000	4
1999	6
1998	6
1997	5
1996	2 (tied with Arantxa Sanchez-Vicario)
1995	1 (tied with Steffi Graf)
1993	8
1992	1
1991	1
1990	2
1989	6

Fed Cup

Career Record

Overall: 17–2
Singles: 15–2
Doubles: 2–0

World Group Finals Record

Year	Record
2000	Singles: 1–0, Doubles: DNP
1996	Singles: 2–0, Doubles: DNP

Hopman Cup

Career Record

Overall: 20–4
Singles: 10–2
Doubles: 10–2

Finals Round Record

Year	Record
2002	Singles: 1–0, Doubles: 0–1
2001	Singles: 0–1, Doubles: 1–0
1991	Singles: 1–0, Doubles: 1–0

Olympic Tennis Medals

Year	Medal
2000	Singles: Bronze

Grand Slam Highlights

Tournament	Year	Result
Australian	1996	Winner — Singles
Australian	1993	Winner — Singles
Australian	1992	Winner — Singles
Australian	1991	Winner — Singles
French	1998	Finalist — Singles
French	1992	Winner — Singles
French	1991	Winner — Singles
French	1990	Winner — Singles
Wimbledon	1992	Finalist — Singles
United States	1996	Finalist — Singles
United States	1995	Finalist — Singles
United States	1992	Winner — Singles
United States	1991	Winner — Singles

Honors

- In 2005, ranked number 13 on *Tennis Magazine*'s list of the "40 Greatest Players of the Open Tennis Era"
- WTA Sanex Hero of the Year Award in 2002
- Women's Sports Foundation Flo Hyman Memorial Award in 2000
- Commitment to Community Award by Florida's *Times-Union* in 1999
- Named Family Circle Cup Player Who Makes a Difference in 1999
- Named Female Pro Athlete of the Year by the Florida Sports Hall of Fame in 1998
- WTA Tour Comeback Player of the Year Award in 1995 and 1998
- Named one of *People Magazine*'s "Most Intriguing People of 1995"
- *Tennis Magazine* Comeback Player of the Year in 1995
- Recipient of the 1993 ESPY Best Female Athlete Award
- WTA Tour Player of the Year in 1991 and 1992
- Associated Press Female Athlete of the Year in 1991 and 1992
- Ted Tinling Diamond Award for Dedication to the Game in 1990
- WTA Tour Most Improved Player in 1990
- *Tennis Magazine* Female Rookie of the Year in 1989

About Monica Seles

Monica Seles' favorite cartoon as a child was Tom and Jerry. She first learned how to play tennis wearing a T-shirt with a cat drawn on it by her father, who was a cartoonist. She chased after tennis balls containing images of a mouse. Her father's strategy worked. By the time she was eight years old, she was the highest ranked junior tennis player in Yugoslavia. In 1986, the Seles family moved to the United States when Monica enrolled in the Nick Bollettieri Tennis Academy.

She reached the semi-finals in her professional debut. In April 1989, when playing in only her second professional tournament in Houston, she defeated top-seeded Chris Evert in 3 sets. She won her first Grand Slam title in 1990 at the French Open by beating Steffi Graf in straight sets, becoming the youngest-ever French champion.

Famous for her grunts and squeals, Monica possessed a unique style of play. She hit both her forehand and backhand while holding the racket with two hands. Combined with her strong return of serve, Monica's baseline game was punishing to opponents. Seles completely dominated the women's game in 1991 and 1992. During those two years she won 6 of 8 Grand Slam titles, helped Yugoslavia win the Hopman Cup, and held the number one ranking in the world.

The hardest defeat Monica took on

Monica Seles playing her baseline game while hitting her two-handed forehand at the U.S. Open (courtesy Mark M. Mayers).

the court was not at the hands of one of her female competitors, but rather from a 38-year-old unemployed German named Guenter Parche. On April 30, 1993, while playing against Magdalena Maleeva in a tournament in Hamburg, Parche attacked and stabbed Seles courtside during a changeover. He later told police that he did it to help Steffi Graf regain her number one ranking in the world. Initially, it was thought that the attack would sideline Seles for a few weeks, but it wasn't until July 29, 1995, that she returned to the court by playing an exhibition match against Martina Navratilova in Atlantic City, New Jersey.

She won her first come-back tournament in August 1995 by beating Amanda Coetzer in the Canadian Open. A few weeks later she lost to Steffi Graf in the finals of the U.S. Open. In January 1996, Seles won her 4th Australian Open. Unfortunately, this was her last Grand Slam title, although she played in the finals of the U.S. Open in 1996 and the French Open in 1998. Most observers agree that she never regained the powerful game and psychological toughness she had before the stabbing incident. In 2007, when asked by a reporter if she would like to be on the court again, she answered, "Maybe one of these days."

Notable Quote About Monica Seles

"The lefty, with two-fisted strokes off both sides, overflows with confidence and a sense of limitless possibilities. Her ground game is devastatingly potent...." Steve Fink, sports journalist

Writings By and About Monica Seles

Burby, Liza N. *Monica Seles: Champion Tennis Player*. New York: Rosen Publishing Group, 1997.

Layden, Joseph. *Return of a Champion: The Monica Seles Story*. New York: St. Martin's Press, 1996.

Seles, Monica, and Nancy Ann Richardson. *Monica: From Fear to Victory*. New York: HarperCollins, 1996.

Stewart, Mark. *Monica Seles: The Comeback Kid*. New York: Children's Press, 1997.

LINDSAY DAVENPORT

b. June 8, 1976, Laguna Beach, California
Turned pro 1993; Right-handed with two-handed backhand
"The Dav," "The Big L"

Career Rankings

USTA Top 10 Singles

Year	Ranking
2005	1
2004	1
2003	2
2002	5
2001	1
2000	1
1999	1
1998	1
1997	1
1996	2
1995	2
1994	1
1993	5

WTA Top 10 Singles

Year	Ranking
2005	1
2004	1
2003	5
2001	1
2000	2
1999	2
1998	1
1997	3
1996	9
1994	6

World Top 10 Singles

Year	Ranking
2005	1
2004	1

Year	Ranking
2003	5
2001	1
2000	2
1999	2
1998	1
1997	3
1996	9
1994	6

Fed Cup

Career Record

Overall: 31–2
Singles: 25–2
Doubles: 6–0

World Group Finals Record

Year	Record
2000	Singles: 2–0, Doubles: DNP
1999	Singles: 2–0, Doubles: DNP
1996	Singles: 2–0, Doubles: DNP
1995	Singles: DNP, Doubles: 1–0
1994	Singles: 0–1, Doubles: DNP

Olympic Tennis Medals

Year	Medal
1996	Singles: Gold

Lindsay Davenport striking her explosive backhand during match play at the U.S. Open (courtesy Mark M. Mayers).

Hopman Cup

Career Record

Overall: 12–4
Singles: 6–2
Doubles: 6–2

Final Round Record

Year   Record
2004   Singles: 1–0, Doubles: 1–0

Grand Slam Highlights

Tournament	Year	Result
Australian	2005	Finalist — Singles
Australian	2005	Finalist — Doubles
Australian	2001	Finalist — Doubles
Australian	2000	Winner — Singles
Australian	1999	Finalist — Doubles
Australian	1998	Finalist — Doubles
Australian	1997	Finalist — Doubles
Australian	1996	Finalist — Doubles
French	1998	Finalist — Doubles
French	1996	Winner — Doubles
French	1994	Finalist — Doubles
Wimbledon	2005	Finalist — Singles
Wimbledon	2000	Finalist — Singles
Wimbledon	1999	Winner — Singles
Wimbledon	1999	Winner — Doubles
Wimbledon	1998	Finalist — Doubles
United States	2000	Finalist — Singles
United States	1998	Winner — Singles
United States	1998	Finalist — Doubles
United States	1997	Winner — Doubles

Honors

- In 2005, ranked number 29 on *Tennis Magazine*'s list of the "40 Greatest Players of the Open Tennis Era"
- Winner of the Karen Krantzchke Sportsmanship Award in 2004
- Voted Tour Player of the Month for February 2003 by the International Tennis Writers Association

- Nominee for the Laureus World Sports Award for Sportswoman of the Year in 2000
- Voted by journalists as the winner of 2000 Prix Orange at Roland Garros as Friendliest and Most Approachable Player on Tour
- Recipient of the 1998 *Tennis Magazine* Player of the Year Award
- Recipient of the 1998 and 1999 WTA Tour Player of the Year Award
- Recipient of the 1998 and 1999 Tour Diamond ACES Award
- World Team Tennis Most Valuable Player in 1997
- Named by *Tennis Magazine* and World Team Tennis as the 1993 Rookie of the Year
- 1991 *Tennis Magazine* Female Junior Player of the Year

About Lindsay Davenport

Lindsay Davenport rejuvenated American women's tennis following a dormant period after the Chris Evert era. When Davenport won the U.S. Open in 1998, she became the first American woman to win the tournament since Evert won the singles title in 1982. Her 6 Grand Slam titles (3 singles and 3 doubles), an Olympic gold medal in singles, 3 Fed Cup championships, and 2 year-end world number 1 rankings achieved from 1996 to 2001 secured her place in tennis history. Born the daughter of Wink Davenport, a U.S. volleyball Olympian, Lindsay started playing tennis at age 5 when her mother put her in an afternoon clinic at the local tennis club to keep her occupied. Her mom's decision was a good one, as her daughter went on to earn more than $21,000,000 playing professional tennis.

While struggling with her lack of confidence and unusually large body-frame for a tennis player, Davenport got off to a slow start after turning pro in 1993. Often during matches her opponents moved her around the court from side to side and up and back as part of their winning strategy. In 1995, Lindsay turned her game around. She hired Robert Van't Hof, a former NCAA tennis champion at the University of Southern California, as her tennis coach. As a result, she slimmed down, revised her fitness program, and strengthened her mental game. This mid-career adjustment started to pay off almost immediately.

In 1996, Lindsay won her first major tournament by capturing the doubles title with Mary Joe Fernandez at Roland Garros. She followed that doubles title with another in 1997 at Flushing Meadows. Finally, after years of hearing that she could not win a major singles title, Lindsay captured the crown at the U.S. Open in 1998. The following year Davenport made a strong statement in London by winning both the singles and doubles championships. She defeated Steffi Graf in a tight three-set match after dropping the first set tie-breaker. Her last major singles title was captured in Melbourne in 2000. Her victory Down Under marked the 5th consecutive year she won a Grand Slam title.

Davenport's game centered around her ground strokes. She hit them as cleanly and powerfully as any woman in the sport. Her serve and return of serve were also major weapons in her tennis arsenal. The lanky Southern Californian made up for her sometimes sluggish court speed by keeping her opponents on the defensive. She was always embraced by the media and perceived by them as cooperative, polite, and well-balanced. Although flashier players of the day stole the limelight, Lindsay remained a fan favorite throughout her career.

Near the end of 2001, Lindsay underwent knee surgery which knocked her out of competition for most of the 2002 season. She did not win a tournament that year and dropped out of the top 10 rankings. In 2003, she married investment banker and former University of Southern California tennis player Jon Leach. The marriage apparently inspired her to play tennis because by the latter part of 2004, she was back on top of the tennis world and remained there throughout most of 2005. By the end of the year, however, she announced that she would play an abbreviated schedule in 2006. The most noteworthy event which took place in 2006 was her announcement in December that she was pregnant. After taking a year off to have her baby, Lindsay was back on the courts playing competitive tennis within a few months following the birth of her first child. She won WTA Tour singles titles in Bali and Quebec City toward the end of the year by beating Daniela Hantuchova and Julia Vakulenko respectively in the finals. The victory in the Quebec City Challenge was the 53rd title of her career.

Notable Quote About Lindsay Davenport

"Lindsay is totally unpretentious and laid back but when she wants to achieve something her work ethic is unbelievable." Robert Van't Hof, Davenport's coach

Writings By and About Lindsay Davenport

Davenport, Lindsay. "My Rookie Year." *Tennis* Mar. 1994: 50–52ff.

Greer, Jim. "The Nice Girl Who Finished First." *Tennis* September 1999: 52ff.

Howard, Johnette. "A Women's Liberation: Thought You Knew Lindsay Davenport, Didn't You? Nice, Quiet, Boring. Wake Up! There's a New Champ in Town. She Cusses. She Criticizes. And She's Just as Cocky as You'd Expect a No. 1 Player to Be." *Tennis* July–August 2000: 34–38*ff.*

McCann, John T. *Lindsay Davenport.* Philadelphia: Chelsea House, 2002.

Miles, Ellen. *Superstars of Women's Tennis.* New York: Aladdin Paperbacks, 2000.

Pare, Michael A., and Julie Carnagie. *Sports Stars, Series 5.* Detroit: UXL, 1999.

Rutledge, Rachel. *Women of Sports: The Best of the Best in Tennis.* Brookfield, Conn.: Millbrook Press, 1998.

VENUS WILLIAMS

b. June 17, 1980, Lynwood, California
Turned pro 1994; Right-handed with two-handed backhand;
"Cinderella of the Ghetto"

Career Rankings

USTA Top 10 Singles

Year	Ranking
2005	2
2004	3
2003	5
2002	2
2001	3
2000	2
1999	2
1998	2
1997	5

WTA Top 10 Singles

Year	Ranking
2005	10
2004	9
2002	2
2001	3
2000	3
1999	3
1998	5

World Top 10 Singles

Year	Ranking
2007	7
2005	10
2004	9
2002	2
2001	3
2000	3
1999	3
1998	5

Fed Cup

Career Record

Overall: 17–4
Singles: 14–2
Doubles: 3–2

World Group Finals Record

Year	Record
1999	Singles: 1–1, Doubles: 1–0

Olympic Tennis Medals

Year	Medal
2008	Doubles: Gold
2000	Singles: Gold, Doubles: Gold

Grand Slam Highlights

Tournament	Year	Result
Australian	2003	Finalist — Singles
Australian	2003	Winner — Doubles
Australian	2001	Winner — Doubles
Australian	1998	Winner — Mixed Doubles
French	2002	Finalist — Singles
French	1999	Winner — Doubles
French	1998	Winner — Mixed Doubles
Wimbledon	2008	Winner — Singles
Wimbledon	2008	Winner — Doubles
Wimbledon	2007	Winner — Singles
Wimbledon	2005	Winner — Singles
Wimbledon	2003	Finalist — Singles

Venus Williams prepares to hit a topspin forehand at the Wimbledon Championships in 2002 (Carol L. Newsom; courtesy David Newsom).

Tournament	Year	Result
Wimbledon	2002	Finalist — Singles
Wimbledon	2002	Winner — Doubles
Wimbledon	2001	Winner — Singles
Wimbledon	2000	Winner — Singles
Wimbledon	2000	Winner — Doubles
United States	2002	Finalist — Singles
United States	2001	Winner — Singles
United States	2000	Winner — Singles
United States	1999	Winner — Doubles
United States	1997	Finalist — Singles

Honors

- In 2005, ranked number 25 on *Tennis Magazine*'s list of the "40 Greatest Players of the Open Tennis Era"
- Appeared on July 5, 2004, *Forbes Magazine* "Celebrity 100" list at number 77
- Won 2002 ESPY Best Female Athlete and Best Female Tennis Player
- Ranked number 25 on *Ladies Home Journal* 30 Most Powerful Women in America List in 2001
- Nominee for the Laureus World Sports Award for Sportswoman of the Year in 2001 and 2002
- In 2000, one of five female tennis players named to the *Forbes Magazine* "Power 100 in Fame and Fortune" list at number 62
- 2000 WTA Tour Player of the Year
- Recipient of the Women's Sports Foundation's Athlete of the Year Award in 2000
- 1998 *Tennis Magazine* Most Improved Female Pro

- Recipient of the 1997 WTA Tour Most Impressive Newcomer Award

About Venus Williams

Venus Ebone Starr Williams learned how to play tennis on the glass-strewn, crime-infested public courts of Compton, California. Her father, Richard Williams, worked tirelessly with Venus and her sister until they emerged from the ghetto ready to make their indelible mark on the game of women's tennis like no one could have imagined, except for their father. Venus, the quiet, introspective sister, blazed the family tennis trail. Her sister, Serena, followed closely behind and eventually overtook Venus on the path to stardom.

In 1991, Richard moved the Williams family to Florida, where Venus was enrolled in the Rick Macci Tennis Academy. Although she compiled a 63–0 record as a junior and held a number one ranking in the USTA 12 and under division, Richard pulled her off the junior circuit. Controversy surrounded her turning pro in 1994 at the age of 14 because of her lack of tournament experience as a junior. She participated in only one professional tournament in 1994. That didn't stop Reebok from offering her a $12 million endorsement contract. Many so-called tennis experts were skeptical of the gangly teenager's ability to compete successfully in the "big leagues." Venus put that theory to rest in 1997 when she made it to the finals at the U.S. Open. Although she lost in straight sets to Martina Hingis, she gave notice to the sports world of her arrival. The following year she won her first two Grand Slam titles. The first came Down Under when she teamed with Justin Gimelstob in the mixed doubles. Her second major title came later in the year in Paris when again with Gimel-

stob she won the mixed doubles. Williams added two more major trophies to her collection the following year by winning the women's doubles in Paris and New York. That same year she helped the United States win the Fed Cup and finished the season ranked number 3 in the world.

Recovering from tendonitis, which kept her out most of the season leading up to the tournament, Williams amazed the tennis world in 2000 by winning her first Grand Slam singles title at Wimbledon. She defeated Lindsay Davenport in a hard-fought straight set match. The Williams sisters also won the doubles title for the first time. Venus proved her singles victory at Wimbledon was no fluke by beating Davenport again for the singles championship in New York. The win was her 7th Grand Slam title. Her titles were almost equally distributed among singles (2), doubles (3), and mixed doubles (2).

Her reign continued in 2001. She captured three Grand Slam titles, including the singles in London and New York, and the doubles in Melbourne. She decimated her opponents at the U.S. Open. After making it into the finals without losing a set, she beat Serena Williams in straight sets 6–2, 6–4. No one seemed to be in Venus' path — a path that threatened to rewrite the record books. No one except for her sister, who was raised on the same high energy tennis diet served up by her father during their developmental years. Over the next two years, Venus lost to Serena in the finals of 5 Grand Slam singles tournaments. Some critics accused Venus of throwing a match to Serena, but it's unlikely given Venus' competitive spirit on the court and her drive to always play her best.

Injuries and the murder of Yetunde Price, her half-sister, added to Venus' sudden fall from glory. Utilizing her lean, muscular frame to hit powerful ground strokes, the fastest serve in the sport, and penetrating volleys, Williams struggled to add three more titles to her elite collection of tennis hardware from 2002 to 2005. Although her deep-rooted confidence started to wane and her forehand became inconsistent, she managed to orchestrate a magnificent comeback against Lindsay Davenport in the finals at Wimbledon in 2005. Venus continued her tennis magic by winning the 2007 Wimbledon Championships as the lowest seeded player ever to take home the Venus Rosewater Dish. Her victory had added meaning since it marked the 50th anniversary of Althea Gibson's singles win in London in 1957. In 2008, Venus successfully defended her singles title and added another Grand Slam trophy to her collection by teaming with her sister, Serena, to capture the women's doubles title. Her total Grand Slam titles stood at 16 after her two victories at Wimbledon in 2008 — 7 singles, 7 doubles, and 2 mixed doubles.

Recently, the former teenage player who once sported colorful bouncing beads in her braids has become a spokesperson for the Women's Tennis Association. Williams is following in the footsteps of legends Arthur Ashe and Billie Jean King. She is working with the WTA and UNESCO on gender equity issues, particularly in African countries. Venus, who was once a lonely figure in the locker-room, is becoming a focal point for women around the world. Her artistic and creative energies are spent working with clients within the context of her own business enterprise, V Starr Interiors. Along with her team of talented designers, Venus is helping her customers successfully implement interior plans to achieve a more comfortable lifestyle. At the 2007 U.S. Open, Venus launched her new line of clothing, which she named "EleVen."

Notable Quote About Venus Williams

"The thunder claps whenever Venus strikes her forehand." Richard Williams, father of Venus Williams

Writings By and About Venus Williams

Armentrout, David. *Venus and Serena Williams.* Vero Beach, Fla.: Rourke Pub., 2004.
Aronson, Virginia. *Venus and Serena Williams.* Philadelphia: Chelsea House, 2001.
Aronson, Virginia, and Elaine K. Andrews. *Venus Williams.* Philadelphia: Chelsea House, 1999.
Asirvatham, Sandy. *Venus Williams.* Philadelphia: Chelsea House, 2002.
Bankston, John. *Venus Williams.* Bear, Del.: Mitchell Lane Pub., 2003.
Boekhoff, P.M, and Stuart A. Kallen. *Venus Williams.* San Diego: Kidhaven Press, 2003.
Buckley, James. *Venus and Serena Williams.* Milwaukee, Wis.: World Almanac, 2003.
Christopher, Matt. *On the Court with Venus and Serena.* Boston: Little, Brown, 2003.
Donaldson, Madeline. *Venus and Serena Williams.* Minneapolis, Minn.: LernerSports, 2003.
Dorrie, Roxanne. *Venus and Serena Williams: The Smashing Sisters.* Bloomington, Minn.: Red Brick Learning, 2004.
Edmondson, Jacqueline. *Venus and Serena Williams: A Biography.* Westport, Conn.: Greenwood Press, 2005.
Feldman, Heather. *Venus Williams: Tennis Champion.* New York: Powerkids Press, 2001.
Fillon, Mike. *Young Superstars of Tennis: The Venus and Serena Williams Story.* Greensboro, N.C.: Avisson Press, 1999.
Flynn, Gabriel. *Venus and Serena Williams.* Chanhassen, Minn.: Child's World, 2000.
Franzen, Lenore. *Venus Williams.* Mankato, Minn.: Creative Education, 2003.
Gutman, Bill. *Venus and Serena: The Grand Slam Williams Sisters.* New York: Scholastic, 2001.
Hill, Mary. *Serena and Venus Williams.* New York: Children's Press, 2003.

Miklowitz, Gloria D. *Venus and Serena Williams.* Carlsbad, Calif.: Dominie Press, 2002.

Morgan, Terri. *Venus and Serena Williams: Grand Slam Sisters.* Minneapolis, Minn.: Lerner Sports, 2001.

Pyle, Lydia. *Venus and Serena Williams.* Edina, Minn.: Abdo Pub., 2004.

Rineberg, Dave. *Venus and Serena: My Seven Years as Hitting Coach for the Williams Sisters.* Hollywood, Fla.: Frederick Fell Pub., Inc., 2001.

Sander, Michael. *Tennis: Victory for Venus Williams.* New York: Bearport Pub., 2006.

Schaefer, A. R. *Serena and Venus Williams.* Mankato, Minn.: Capstone High-Interest Books, 2002.

Schimel, Lawrence. *Venus and Serena Williams.* Kansas City, Mo.: Andrews McMeel Pub., 2000.

Sherman, Joseph. *Venus Williams.* Chicago: Heinemann Library, 2001.

Sparling, Ken. *Venus and Serena Williams.* Chicago: Warwick Pub., 2000.

Stewart, Mark. *Venus and Serena Williams: Sisters in Arms.* Brookfield, Conn.: Millbrook Press, 2000.

Stout, Glenn. *On the Court with ... Venus and Serena Williams.* Boston: Little, Brown, 2002.

Teitelbaum, Michael. *Grand Slam Stars: Martina Hingis and Venus Williams.* New York: HarperActive, 1998.

Watson, Galadriel Findlay. *Venus and Serena Williams.* New York: Weigl Pub., 2006.

Wertheim, L. Jon. *Venus Envy: A Sensational Season Inside the Women's Tennis Tour.* New York: HarperCollins, 2001.

Wertheim, L. Jon. *Venus Envy: Power Games, Teenage Vixens, and Million-Dollar Egos on the Women's Tennis Tour.* 2002.

Williams, Venus, and Serena Williams. *How to Be the Best: Tennis.* London: Dorling Kindersley, 2004.

Williams, Venus, Serena Williams, and Hilary Beard. *Venus and Serena: Serving from the Hip; Ten Rules for Living, Loving, and Winning.* Boston: H. Mifflin, 2005.

Williams, Venus, Serena Williams, and Russell Sadur. *How to Play Tennis: Learn How to Play Tennis with the Williams Sisters.* New York: DK Pub., 2004.

Wilson, Mike. *The Williams Sisters: Venus and Serena.* London: Hodder and Stoughton, 2002.

MARTINA HINGIS

b. September 30, 1980, Kosice, Slovakia
Turned pro 1994; Right-handed with two-handed backhand; "Swiss Miss"

Career Rankings

WTA Top 10 Singles

Year	Ranking
2002	10
2001	4
2000	1
1999	1
1998	2
1997	1
1996	4

World Top 10 Singles

Year	Ranking
2006	7
2002	10
2001	4
2000	1
1999	1
1998	2
1997	1
1996	4

Fed Cup

Career Record

Overall: 26–4
Singles: 18–2
Doubles: 8–2

World Group Finals Record

Year	Record
1998	Singles: 2–0, Doubles: 0–1

Hopman Cup

Career Record

Overall: 20–6
Singles: 13–0
Doubles: 7–6

Finals Round Record

Year	Record
2001	Singles: 1–0, Doubles: 0–1
1996	Singles: 1–0, Doubles: 0–1

Grand Slam Highlights

Tournament	Year	Result
Australian	2006	Winner — Mixed Doubles
Australian	2002	Finalist — Singles
Australian	2002	Winner — Doubles
Australian	2001	Finalist — Singles
Australian	2000	Finalist — Singles
Australian	1999	Winner — Singles
Australian	1999	Winner — Doubles
Australian	1998	Winner — Singles
Australian	1998	Winner — Doubles
Australian	1997	Winner — Singles
Australian	1997	Winner — Doubles
French	2000	Winner — Doubles
French	1999	Finalist — Singles
French	1998	Winner — Doubles
French	1997	Finalist — Singles
Wimbledon	1998	Winner — Doubles
Wimbledon	1997	Winner — Singles
Wimbledon	1996	Winner — Doubles
United States	1999	Finalist — Singles
United States	1998	Finalist — Singles

United States	1998	Winner — Doubles
United States	1997	Winner — Singles

Honors

- Recipient of the Laureus World Sports World Comeback of the Year Award in 2006
- Recipient of the 2006 WTA Tour Comeback Player of the Year Award
- In 2005, ranked number 22 on *Tennis Magazine*'s list of the "40 Greatest Players of the Open Tennis Era"
- Elected to WTA Tour Players' Council in 2002
- Named the 2001 Family Circle/ Hormel Foods Player Who Makes a Difference
- Recipient of the 2000 WTA Tour Diamond ACES Award
- One of Only Five Female Tennis Players Named to the 2000 *Forbes Magazine* "Power 100 in Fame and Fortune" list at number 51
- Named 1999 WTA Tour Doubles Team of the Year (with Anna Kournikova) and in 1998 (with Jana Novotna)
- First female athlete to be on the cover of *GQ* in June 1998
- Selected as the Player of the Year by the WTA Tour in 1997
- Named the Associated Press Female Athlete of the Year in 1997
- Named the 1996 WTA Tour Most Improved Player
- Recipient of the 1995 WTA Tour Most Impressive Newcomer Award

Martina Hingis using her two-handed backhand to crush a return at the 2000 French Open (Carol L. Newsom; courtesy David Newsom).

- Named the 1995 *Tennis Magazine* Female Rookie of the Year

About Martina Hingis

Martina Hingis, the daughter of tennis playing parents, was named after Martina Navratilova. Although Hingis' parents divorced when she was a young girl, her mother, Melanie, coached and managed her to tennis superstardom. The two moved to Switzerland when Martina was

8 years old. By this time, she had already been playing tennis for several years. She entered her first tournament at age four. When she was 12 she became the youngest player to win a Grand Slam junior title. In 1994, Martina was ranked the World Number 1 Junior. After turning professional just two weeks after her 14th birthday, she quickly rose to the top of the tennis world and by 1997 was the undisputed world's number 1 female tennis player. She was the youngest ever number 1 and she held it for the next 80 weeks. She started the year by winning a minor tournament in Sydney in preparation for the Australian Open. Her victory was a preview of what was to come, as she went on to become the youngest 20th century Grand Slam champion by capturing the singles title in Melbourne at the age of 16 years and 3 months. As a follow-up to that historic event, Hingis became the youngest singles champion at Wimbledon since Lottie Dod was crowned champ in 1887. She capped off her fabulous year by beating Venus Williams in the singles finals at the U.S. Open. Her only major loss that year was to Iva Majoli in Paris.

In 1998, Hingis swept all four Grand Slam doubles titles. She became only the third woman to hold simultaneously the number 1 ranking in both singles and doubles. Although Hingis lost her world number 1 ranking when she dropped a match to Lindsay Davenport in the finals at the U.S. Open, she finished the year on a positive note by beating Davenport in the finals of the lucrative WTA Tour Championships. Hingis' dominance continued in 1999, but she started showing signs of vulnerability. She won her third successive Australian Open, but not without controversy. Her outspoken comments regarding Amelie Mauresmo's sexual preferences temporarily became the focus of attention.

She continued her success on the court, however, by adding the doubles title, solidifying her presence Down Under.

However, Paris was another story. Only three points from a singles victory against Steffi Graf in the finals, Martina let the match slip away, losing in three sets. To make matters worse, she alienated the crowd by arguing several line calls, took an uncharacteristic bathroom break during the third set, and hit insulting underhanded serves to Graf on two match points. Later in the year, she shockingly lost to Jelena Dokic in a first round match at Wimbledon, and lost to Serena Williams in the finals in New York. Her seven singles titles in 1999, despite her uneven performances in the majors, resulted in her reclaiming the number 1 year-end ranking. She retained her number 1 ranking in 2000 by winning 9 tournaments, including the WTA Tour Championships, but she did not win a Grand Slam singles title.

Representing Switzerland in 2001, Martina Hingis and Roger Federer won the Hopman Cup. Martina was undefeated during the event. She couldn't keep her early season momentum going, however, yielding to Jennifer Capriati in the finals in Melbourne. It was Martina's fifth consecutive appearance in the finals. Soon after her loss, Martina severed her long lasting player-coach relationship with her mother, only to re-establish the daughter-mother connection just before the beginning of the French Open. Her frustration manifested itself in other ways later in the year when she made remarks pertaining to alleged preferential treatment afforded the Williams sisters. Hingis underwent ankle surgery in late 2001, and a year later, another ankle operation significantly hampered her effectiveness on the court. In 2003, Hingis retired from tennis at the age of 22.

In 2005, Hingis' tennis career was

reincarnated. She starred for the New York Sportimes while leading her World Team Tennis team to the league championship for the first time in franchise history. Along the way, she had some decisive victories against top 100 players, including her namesake, Martina Navratilova. Hingis returned to the WTA Tour by the end of the year. In Melbourne in 2006, she added another Grand Slam title to her collection of trophies by winning the mixed doubles with Mahesh Bhupathi of India. The win brought her Grand Slam total to a very respectable 15 (5 singles, 9 doubles, and 1 mixed doubles).

She continued her successful comeback in Rome when she won the Italian Open, her first WTA title in over 4 years. After losing in the quarterfinals or earlier in Grand Slam singles events in 2006, she won another comeback tournament when she was victorious at the Sunfeast Open in Kolkata, India. She ended the year at a respectable 7th in the WTA rankings. Martina Hingis, recently engaged to Czech tennis player Radek Stepanek, continued to play in 2007 in Grand Slam events and WTA competition. Late in the year, she called a press conference to announce that she had been accused of testing positive for cocaine at Wimbledon, and announced her retirement from professional tennis.

Hingis built her game around her tremendous poise on the court. The thoughtful right-hander used ball placement and spin to outmaneuver her opponents. By minimizing her unforced errors, remaining consistent from the baseline, and developing a reliable volley and serve,

she accumulated more than 500 singles match victories and close to 300 doubles wins in WTA tournaments. Her major accomplishments included 5 Grand Slam singles titles, 9 Grand Slam women's doubles titles, and 2 Sony Ericsson Championships. She also posted an impressive Fed Cup record by winning 26 of 30 matches.

Notable Quote About Martina Hingis

"She had an animal instinct for the game, an exceptionally strong mentality.... Talents like this happen once or twice in a lifetime.... She's just a born winner." Nick Bolletieri, tennis coach

Writings About Martina Hingis

Ditchfield, Christin. *Martina Hingis*. Philadelphia: Chelsea House, 2001.
Jenkins, Sally. "Mind Over Matter: Martina Hingis Knows That if It Comes Down to a Power Struggle on the Court She Can't Win. So the Undersized Champion Has Cut Out the Distractions and Adopted a New Game Plan, Realizing That the Only Way to Grow as a Player Is to Grow Up." *Tennis* June 2001: 28–32ff.
Miles, Ellen. *Superstars of Women's Tennis*. New York: Alladdin Paperbacks, 2000.
Rutledge, Rachel. *Women of Sports: The Best of the Best in Tennis*. Brookfield, Conn.: Millbrook Press, 1998.
Spencer, Bev. *Martina Hingis*. Toronto: Warwick Pub., 1999.
Teitelbaum, Michael. *Grand Slam Stars: Martina Hingis and Venus Williams*. New York: HarperActive, 1998.

Serena Williams

b. September 26, 1981, Saginaw, Michigan
Turned pro 1995; Right-handed with two-handed backhand;"Meeka"

Career Rankings

USTA Top 10 Singles

Year	Ranking
2005	3
2004	2
2003	1
2002	1
2001	4
2000	4
1999	3
1998	4

WTA Top 10 Singles

Year	Ranking
2004	7
2003	3
2002	1
2001	6
2000	6
1999	4

World Top 10 Singles

Year	Ranking
2007	5
2004	7
2003	3
2002	1
2001	6
2000	6
1999	4

Fed Cup

Career Record

Overall: 7–0
Singles: 4–0
Doubles: 3–0

World Group Finals Record

Year	Record
1999	Singles: DNP, Doubles: 1–0

Hopman Cup

Career Record

Overall: 8–0
Singles: 4–0
Doubles: 4–0

Finals Round Record

Year	Record
2003	Singles: 1–0, Doubles: 1–0

Olympic Tennis Medals

Year	Medal
2008	Doubles: Gold
2000	Doubles: Gold

Grand Slam Highlights

Tournament	Year	Result
Australian	2007	Winner — Singles
Australian	2005	Winner — Singles

Tournament	Year	Result
Australian	2003	Winner — Singles
Australian	2003	Winner — Doubles
Australian	2001	Winner — Doubles
French	2002	Winner — Singles
French	1999	Winner — Doubles
French	1998	Finalist — Mixed Doubles
Wimbledon	2008	Finalist — Singles
Wimbledon	2008	Winner — Doubles
Wimbledon	2004	Finalist — Singles
Wimbledon	2003	Winner — Singles
Wimbledon	2002	Winner — Singles
Wimbledon	2002	Winner — Doubles
Wimbledon	2000	Winner — Doubles
Wimbledon	1998	Winner — Mixed Doubles
United States	2008	Winner — Singles
United States	2002	Winner — Singles
United States	2001	Finalist — Singles
United States	1999	Winner — Singles
United States	1999	Winner — Doubles
United States	1998	Winner — Mixed Doubles

Honors

- In 2005, ranked number 17 in *Tennis Magazine*'s list of the "40 Greatest Players of the Open Tennis Era"
- Nominee for the Laureus World Sports Award for Sportswoman of the Year in 2004
- Named WTA Tour Comeback Player of the Year for 2004
- Appeared on July 5, 2004, *Forbes Magazine* "Celebrity 100" list at number 63
- Named 2004 Family Circle/Prudential Financial "Player Who Makes a Difference"
- Won 2003 ESPY Best Female Athlete Award
- Received 2003 Celebrity Role Model Award from Avon Foundation for her charitable work in breast cancer awareness

- Winner of the Laureus World Sports Award for Sportswoman of the Year in 2003
- Named by *People Magazine* as one of the Top 25 Most Intriguing People in 2002
- Named by *Ebony Magazine* as one of the 57 Most Intriguing African-Americans in 2002
- Named one of BBC's 2002 Sports Personalities of the Year
- Named Associated Press Female Athlete of the Year in 2002
- Named 2002 WTA Tour Player of the Year
- In 2000, one of five female tennis players named to the *Forbes Magazine* "Power 100 in Fame and Fortune" at number 68
- 2000 WTA Tour Doubles Team of the Year (with Venus Williams)
- Recipient of the Women's Sports Foundation Athlete of the Year Award in 2000
- Named *Tennis Magazine*'s Player of the Year in 1999
- Named WTA Tour Most Improved Player in 1999
- Named one of *People Magazine*'s 25 Most Intriguing People of 1999
- Named 1998 *Tennis Magazine*/Rolex Rookie of the Year
- Recipient of the 1998 WTA Tour Most Impressive Newcomer Award

About Serena Williams

When Serena Jamika Williams was a young child her parents would make her order first at a restaurant so she wouldn't simply duplicate Venus' meal order. Trouble was, when Serena ordered first but heard what Venus wanted, Serena would change her mind. She wanted to be just like her older sister and at times actually pretended to be Venus. Serena eventually outgrew the "admiration" stage and made it official when she defeated her older sister in straight sets in 3 Grand Slam finals in 2002. On the international level, by winning 3 of 4 major titles that year, the powerful right-hander made her mark on the game of women's tennis.

Williams started playing tennis when she was five and a half years old. By age 10, she had entered 49 tournaments, winning 46 of them. After the Williams family moved to Florida in 1991, Serena (and Venus) received full scholarships to Rick Macci's renowned tennis academy in Delray Beach. While at the academy Serena did not play in junior competition because her father was fearful of possible injury or burn out. After four years, Richard Williams pulled the sisters out of the academy to work with them at his private estate in West Palm Beach.

Serena turned pro in 1995 at age 14. In her first professional appearance in Quebec she lost in less than one hour. By 1997, she started to climb up in the rankings and had some impressive wins, including two against Monica Seles and Mary Pierce. Her first Grand Slam titles came a year later when she won the mixed doubles at Wimbledon and the U.S. Open, both with Max Mirnyi. At the U.S. Open in 1999, Williams won her first Grand Slam singles title by beating Martina Hingis in a hard fought, straight set victory. By doing so, she became the first African-American woman to win a Grand Slam singles tournament since Althea Gibson in 1958. After winning a doubles gold medal at the Sydney Olympics with her sister Venus in 2000, the following year saw Serena play in her first Grand Slam singles final since 1999. She lost to Venus in the finals at the

U.S. Open 6–2, 6–4. It would be the last time Serena would lose to Venus in a Grand Slam final until 2008.

After her breakthrough year in 2002, Serena Williams continued her dominance over her sister when she beat Venus in the finals of the Australian Open in 2003. It was her fourth straight Grand Slam singles title and completed the "Serena Slam." The accomplishment was particularly noteworthy because Serena defeated her sister in each of the finals. Williams added another major singles title when she won Wimbledon by once again overcoming the futile efforts of her older sister.

In that same year the 22-year-old tennis superstar began to develop interests off the tennis court. After dabbling in professional acting years earlier, Serena appeared in a dramatic role on cable TV and filmed a part for the movie *Beauty Shop* starring Queen Latifah. Some of her non-tennis commitments resulted in her withdrawal from a few WTA Tour stops and her critics predicted the distractions would lead to her tennis demise. Always under close watch by the media, Serena was linked romantically around this same time to professional athletes including Keyshawn Johnson and Corey Maggette. More recently she began a public and controversial relationship with Hollywood director Brett Ratner. In September 2003, Williams' older sister, Yetunde Price, was killed by gunshots from a passing car in Compton, California. The murder had a profound effect on both Serena and her sister Venus.

At the beginning of 2004, Williams was still rehabilitating her left knee, on which she had had surgery the previous year. Finally, after eight months away from the WTA Tour, she began her comeback in Miami by crushing Elena Dementieva in the finals. After Williams lost in the quarterfinals in Paris and in the finals at Wimbledon to Maria Sharapova, another left knee injury forced her to withdraw from the Summer Olympics. She finished the year ranked number 8 in the world. Her relatively disappointing performance in 2004 was in part linked to her continued outside interests in acting and fashion. In 2005, however, Serena captured her seventh major singles title in Melbourne. The victory turned out to be the high point of her season, as a stress fracture in her ankle and a lack of conditioning resulted in a sub-par year.

Williams' downward spiral continued into 2006 when her early exit from the Australian Open provoked media reports that she had lost her enthusiasm for the sport. After withdrawing from a WTA Tour event in South Carolina, Serena dropped out of the Top-100 in the world for the first time in almost a decade. She described her six-month break from competition as much "mental" as it was to rehabilitate her

Serena Williams' fist pumping after hitting a winner at Wimbledon in 2000 (Carol L. Newsom; courtesy David Newsom).

recurring knee injury. Williams picked up her game later in the year by defeating Daniela Hantuchova, the player who was responsible for her early exit in Melbourne at the beginning of the year. Playing in the U.S. Open as a wildcard entry, she lost to Amelie Mauresmo in the fourth round. At the end of 2006, she was ranked 95th in the world.

In one of the most amazing performances in the sport's history, the unseeded Serena Williams won the 2007 Australian Open by annihilating her Russian opponent, Maria Sharapova, in the finals 6–1,

6–2. It was one of the most lopsided matches in Grand Slam finals history. Serena seemed to have played herself into the tournament; she got stronger, faster, and more confident as she progressed through the rounds. By the time she met Sharapova in the finals, she was once again entertaining the crowd with her fist-pumping ebullience. Many points which Serena won were either on service winners or set up with her angled slice serves. Williams dedicated the win to her deceased sister, Yetunde Price. In 2008, Serena and her sister, Venus, won the women's doubles title at Wimbledon. She continued her outstanding play in 2008 culminating in her reaching the number one world ranking after her triumph over Jelena Jankovic in the finals of the U.S. Open. The win was the ninth Grand Slam singles title for Serena. Earlier in the year, she lost to her sister, Venus, in the singles final at Wimbledon.

Throughout her playing career, Serena Williams has been known for her colorful and controversial tennis outfits, including leather-looking cat suits, micromini denim skirts, black studded tank tops, and black knee-high boots. Recently, she released her own line of clothing designed for Nike. Never one to let the grass grow under her feet, unless it's on Centre Court at Wimbledon, Serena continues to work on several projects outside of tennis. She's actively involved in charity work with several organizations, including Ronald McDonald House, the HollyRod Foundation, and the Make-A-Wish Foundation. She continues to remain active in Hollywood. Recently, she appeared in her own reality show with her sister and guest starred in episodes of *ER* and *Law and Order: Special Victims Unit*.

Notable Quote About Serena Williams

"To grow up in someone's shadow can be a cold, dark place. Many people said that Serena grew up in Venus' shadow and she definitely did. But being in someone's shadow can make a person stronger or wiser and in the end even better, if they have the will to break out of that shadow and become their own person." Dave Rineberg, the Williams' hitting coach from 1992 to 1999

Writings By and About Serena Williams

Armentrout, David. *Venus and Serena Williams*. Vero Beach, Fla.: Rourke Pub., 2004.

Aronson, Virginia. *Venus and Serena Williams*. Philadelphia: Chelsea House, 2001.

Buckley, James. *Venus and Serena Williams*. Milwaukee, Wis.: World Almanac, 2003.

Christopher, Matt. *On the Court with Venus and Serena*. Boston: Little, Brown, 2003.

Donaldson, Madeline. *Venus and Serena Williams*. Minneapolis, Minn.: LernerSports, 2003.

Dorrie, Roxanne. *Venus and Serena Williams: The Smashing Sisters*. Bloomington, Minn.: Red Brick Learning, 2004.

Edmondson, Jacqueline. *Venus and Serena Williams: A Biography*. Westport, Conn.: Greenwood Press, 2005.

Fillon, Mike. *Young Superstars of Tennis: The Venus and Serena Williams Story*. Greensboro, N.C.: Avisson Press, 1999.

Flynn, Gabriel. *Venus and Serena Williams*. Chanhassen, Minn.: Child's World, 2000.

Gutman, Bill. *Venus and Serena: The Grand Slam Williams Sisters*. New York: Scholastic, 2001.

Hill, Mary. *Serena and Venus Williams*. New York: Children's Press, 2003.

Miklowitz, Gloria D. *Venus and Serena Williams*. Carlsbad, Calif.: Dominie Press, 2002.

Morgan, Terri. *Venus and Serena Williams: Grand Slam Sisters*. Minneapolis, Minn.: Lerner Sports, 2001.

Pyle, Lydia. *Venus and Serena Williams*. Edina, Minn.: Abdo Pub., 2004.

Rineberg, Dave. *Venus and Serena: My Seven Years as Hitting Coach for the Williams Sisters*. Hollywood, Fla.: Frederick Fell Pub., Inc., 2001.

Schaefer, A. R. *Serena and Venus Williams*. Mankato, Minn.: Capstone High-Interest Books, 2002.

Schimel, Lawrence. *Venus and Serena Williams*. Kansas City, Mo.: Andrews McMeel Pub., 2000.

Sparling, Ken. *Venus and Serena Williams*. Chicago: Warwick Pub., 2000.

Stewart, Mark. *Venus and Serena Williams: Sisters in Arms*. Brookfield, Conn.: Millbrook Press, 2000.

Stout, Glenn. *On the Court with ... Venus and Serena Williams.* Boston: Little, Brown, 2002.

Watson, Galadriel Findlay. *Venus and Serena Williams.* New York: Weigl Pub., 2006.

Williams, Venus, and Serena Williams. *How to Be the Best: Tennis.* London: Dorling Kindersley, 2004.

Williams, Venus, Serena Williams, and Hilary Beard. *Venus and Serena: Serving from the Hip; Ten Rules for Living, Loving, and Winning.* Boston: H. Mifflin, 2005.

Williams, Venus, Serena Williams, and Russell Sadur. *How to Play Tennis: Learn How to Play Tennis with the Williams Sisters.* New York: DK Pub., 2004.

Wilson, Mike. *The Williams Sisters: Venus and Serena.* London: Hodder and Stoughton, 2002.

JUSTINE HENIN

b. June 1, 1982, Liege, Belgium
Turned pro 1999; Right-handed; "Juju"

Career Rankings

WTA Top 10 Singles

Year	Ranking
2007	1
2006	1
2005	6
2004	8
2003	1
2002	5
2001	7

World Top 10 Singles

Year	Ranking
2007	1
2006	1
2004	8
2003	1
2002	5
2001	7

Fed Cup

Career Record

Overall: 15–3
Singles: 15–1
Doubles: 0–2

World Group Finals Record

Year	Record
2006	Singles: 2–0, Doubles: 0–1
2001	Singles: 1–0, Doubles: DNP

Olympic Tennis Medals

Year	Medal
2004	Singles: Gold

Grand Slam Highlights

Tournament	Year	Result
Australian	2006	Finalist — Singles
Australian	2004	Winner — Singles
French	2007	Winner — Singles
French	2006	Winner — Singles
French	2005	Winner — Singles
French	2003	Winner — Singles
Wimbledon	2006	Finalist — Singles
Wimbledon	2001	Finalist — Singles
United States	2007	Winner — Singles
United States	2006	Finalist — Singles
United States	2003	Winner — Singles

Honors

- In 2005, ranked number 25 in *Tennis Magazine*'s list of the "40 Greatest Players Over the Last 40 Years"
- Received the 2005 Family Circle/State Farm "Player Who Makes a Difference" Award
- Nominee for the Laureus World Sports Award for Sportswoman of the Year in 2004
- Appeared on July 5, 2004, *Forbes Magazine* "Celebrity 100" list at number 81

- Nominated for 2004 ESPY Award for Best Female Athlete and Best Female Tennis Player
- In 2004, presented with the Great Cross of the Order of the Crown by Belgian King Albert II at the Royal Palace in Brussels
- Named 2003 Female Player of the Year by the International Tennis Writers Association
- Voted 2003 Sanex Hero of the Year by an Internet poll of more than 30,000 tennis fans worldwide
- Presented with the Commitment to Community Award by the *Florida Times-Union/Waters Edge* magazine in 2003 in recognition of her generous contributions to the Make-A-Wish Foundation
- In 2002 received the Trophy for National Sporting Excellence from the Belgian government
- In 1997, received the "Trophy 40-15" as Belgium's most popular tennis personality

About Justine Henin

Noted for her picture perfect one-handed backhand and her mental toughness, Justine Henin played tennis for the first time at age 2 at a local club near her home. By age 5 she was playing tennis exclusively during her summer vacations. A year later she joined Tennis Club Ciney, where she received professional training for the first time. She began to compete in tournaments shortly thereafter. Since age 14, Henin has been continuously coached by Carlos Rodriguez. She won five International Tennis Federation tournaments before turning pro, including the 1997 junior girls' singles title at the French Open. The young Henin had fond memories at

Roland Garros. Her mother routinely took her to watch the greatest women in the world play in Paris. One year after watching Steffi Graf and Monica Seles play in the finals, rumor had it that Justine was so moved by the experience that she told her mother, "One day I will play here and I will win." Henin was true to her word. As of 2007, she has won 4 titles at Roland Garros, 7 Grand Slam singles titles in all, and a gold medal in singles at the 2004 Summer Olympics.

Henin started her professional career in 1999 as a wild card entry in the Belgian Open in Antwerp. She became only the fifth player in WTA Tour history to win in her pro debut. By 2001, she had established herself as a major competitor. Although she lost to Venus Williams in the singles finals at Wimbledon, she was ranked seventh in the world by the end of the year. She climbed to fifth in the rankings in 2002 by reaching four WTA Tour finals, winning two of them. Her victory at the German Open was her first Tier I tournament title. In the process, she beat Jennifer Capriati and Serena Williams.

The all-court player had a breakthrough year in 2003. Relying on her powerful ground strokes, which included her legendary cross-court driving backhand, her devastating slice backhand, and her reliable net game, Henin won her first Grand Slam tournament in style at the French Open. She defeated top-seeded Serena Williams in the semi-finals in straight sets, coming back from a 2–4 deficit in the third set. In the finals, she played nearly flawless tennis while dominating Kim Clijsters 6–0, 6–4. Henin quickly added a second singles Grand Slam title in New York defeating her compatriot Kim Clijsters once again in a straight set finals. Her major victories catapulted her to the top of the world in women's tennis. In memory of her mother,

Justine Henin is a study in concentration as she prepares to hit a forehand volley (Carol L. Newsom; courtesy David Newsom).

who died of intestinal cancer when Justine was only 12 years old, Henin created her own charity, Justine's Winner Circle, in 2003 to provide joy and hope to children with cancer.

Henin had an up and down year in 2004. It began in Australia when she won a warm-up tourney in Sydney, and went on to defeat Clijsters in the finals to win the Australian Open for her 3rd Slam singles title. In late spring, however, Justine developed an immune system infection which adversely affected her. It sapped her of most of her energy. Competitive tennis was the farthest thing from her mind; she barely had enough strength to get out of bed and walk. In a surprising move, she decided to defend her French Open crown

but was defeated in the second round by a low ranking player. At the Summer Olympics in August, she won the women's singles gold medal in Athens. She reached the gold medal round by staging a major comeback in a semi-final match after trailing 1–5 in the third set. She defeated Amelie Mauresmo in the finals. Her rollercoaster year continued at the U.S. Open when she lost in the fourth round. The defeat caused her to lose her number 1 ranking. After winning the French Open in 2005, she had sub-par performances in London and New York. A hamstring injury sustained earlier in the year limited her play throughout the year.

At the Australian Open in 2006, Henin suddenly retired during her finals match against Mauresmo early in the second set. Criticized heavily by the media, she came storming back in Paris to win her third singles title in four years. Relying on her crisp volleying and her court quickness, she won the title without losing a set and became the first French Open champion to defend her title successfully since Steffi Graf. Although she was beaten in the finals at Wimbledon and the U.S. Open, she guaranteed her year end World number 1 ranking by winning the WTA Tour Championships.

Her four-year marriage to Pierre-Yves Hardenne, which ended in late 2006, was the cause of her distraction from tennis at the beginning of 2007. In January, Henin withdrew from the Australian Open for personal reasons. Later in the year, however, she won her 4th French Open singles title. More importantly, she reconciled her estranged relationship with her father and siblings. She capped off her outstanding year by winning her 7th Grand Slam singles title in New York. On her way to victory she did not lose a set, and she became the first woman to win a major title after beating both Williams sisters in the same tournament. Her late season victory solidified her position as the number 1 female player in the world.

In May 2008, the Belgian star shocked the tennis world when she announced her sudden retirement as a professional tennis player. At age 25, she became the first female player to retire while holding the world's number 1 ranking. She planned to spend time with her family, charities, and working with young players enrolled in her tennis academy.

Notable Quotes About Justine Henin

"One of the more extraordinary aspects of the women's game since the turn of the millennium has been the success of Belgium's Justine Henin." *The Guardian* (London)

"Pound for pound the best woman athlete I have ever seen." Billie Jean King, tennis champion

Writings About Justine Henin

Ryan, Mark. *Tie-Break! Justine Henin-Hardenne, Tragedy and Triumph.* London: Robson, 2004.

Ryan, Mark. *Justine Henin: From Tragedy to Triumph.* New York: St. Martin's Press, 2008.

II

RECORDS

THE GRAND SLAMS

The Australian Championships

The Australian Open began in 1905, but the women's tournament did not begin until 1922. The championships moved around among several major cities in Australia and New Zealand until 1972, when the tournament was permanently moved to the Kooyong Lawn Tennis Club in Melbourne. In 1988, the National Tennis Centre at Melbourne Park, formerly known as Flinders Park, was opened and with it came the change from playing on grass courts to a hard surface court called Rebound Ace. During the calendar year 1977 the tournament was played twice when the event was moved from January to December. In 1986 the event was moved back to January of the next year, so no competition took place in that calendar year.

During the early years, the geographical remoteness of Australia discouraged many of the world's top players from participating in the tournament. In 1906, when the tournament was played in New Zealand, only 10 players entered the competition. Travel by ship took more than a month from the Mediterranean Sea. The first tennis players to travel by plane were members of the United States Davis Cup team in 1946. The trend of the world's top players staying away from the Australian Championships continued through the early 1980s. In 1983, Ivan Lendl, John McEnroe, and Mats Wilander went Down Under to play in the Davis Cup. They decided to enter the Australian Championships, which were played just before the Davis Cup. That year marked a turning point and established the Melbourne tournament as one of the Grand Slam events of the tennis season.

The two major venues in Melbourne are called Rod Laver Arena and Vodafone Arena. They are distinctive because each features a retractable roof which can be closed in case of rain or excessive heat. A third venue, known as Margaret Court Arena, was re-named in 2003 as a tribute to Australia's most successful female tennis player. In 2008, the hard court surface used since 1988 was replaced by an acrylic surface called Plexicushion. The new surface has a thinner top layer, retains less heat, and reduces player injuries.

Women's Singles

Year	Final Round Results	Scores
1922	Mall Molesworth d. Esna Boyd	6–3, 10–8
1923	Mall Molesworth d. Esna Boyd	6–1, 7–5
1924	Sylvia Lance d. Esna Boyd	6–3, 3–6, 6–4
1925	Daphne Akhurst d. Esna Boyd	1–6, 8–6, 6–4
1926	Daphne Akhurst d. Esna Boyd	6–1, 6–3
1927	Esna Boyd d. Sylvia Lance Harper	5–7, 6–1, 6–2
1928	Daphne Akhurst d. Esna Boyd	7–5, 6–2
1929	Daphne Akhurst d. Louie Bickerton	6–1, 5–7, 6–2
1930	Daphne Akhurst d. Sylvia Lance Harper	10–8, 2–6, 7–5
1931	Coral McInnes Buttsworth d. Marjorie Cox Crawford	1–6, 6–3, 6–4
1932	Coral McInnes Buttsworth d. Kathrine Le Messurier	9–7, 6–4
1933	Joan Hartigan d. Coral McInnes Buttsworth	6–4, 6–3
1934	Joan Hartigan d. Mall Molesworth	6–1, 6–4
1935	Dorothy Round d. Nancy Lyle	1–6, 6–1, 6–3
1936	Joan Hartigan d. Nancye Wynne	6–4, 6–4
1937	Nancye Wynne d. Emily Hood Westacott	6–3, 5–7, 6–4
1938	Dorothy Bundy d. Dorothy Stevenson	6–3, 6–2
1939	Emily Hood Westacott d. Nell Hall Hopman	6–1, 6–2
1940	Nancye Wynne d. Thelma Coyne	5–7, 6–4, 6–0
1941–1945	Not held because of World War II	
1946	Nancye Wynne Bolton d. Joyce Fitch	6–4, 6–4
1947	Nancye Wynne Bolton d. Nell Hall Hopman	6–3, 6–2
1948	Nancye Wynne Bolton d. Marie Toomey	6–3, 6–1
1949	Doris Hart d. Nancye Wynne Bolton	6–3, 6–4
1950	Louise Brough d. Doris Hart	6–4, 3–6, 6–4
1951	Nancye Wynne Bolton d. Thelma Coyne Long	6–1, 7–5
1952	Thelma Coyne Long d. Helen Angwin	6–2, 6–3
1953	Maureen Connolly d. Julia Sampson	6–3, 6–2
1954	Thelma Coyne Long d. Jenny Staley	6–3, 6–4
1955	Beryl Penrose d. Thelma Coyne Long	6–4, 6–3
1956	Mary Carter d. Thelma Coyne Long	3–6, 6–2, 9–7
1957	Shirley Fry d. Althea Gibson	6–3, 6–4
1958	Angela Mortimer d. Lorraine Coghlan	6–3, 6–4
1959	Mary Carter Reitano d. Renee Schuurman	6–2, 6–3
1960	Margaret Smith d. Jan Lehane	7–5, 6–2
1961	Margaret Smith d. Jan Lehane	6–1, 6–4
1962	Margaret Smith d. Jan Lehane	6–0, 6–2
1963	Margaret Smith d. Jan Lehane	6–2, 6–2
1964	Margaret Smith d. Lesley Turner	6–3, 6–2
1965	Margaret Smith d. Maria Bueno	5–7, 6–4, 5–2 retired
1966	Margaret Smith d. Nancy Richey	default
1967	Nancy Richey d. Lesley Turner	6–1, 6–4
1968	Billie Jean King d. Margaret Smith	6–1, 6–2
1969	Margaret Smith Court d. Billie Jean King	6–4, 6–1
1970	Margaret Smith Court d. Kerry Melville	6–1, 6–3
1971	Margaret Smith Court d. Evonne Goolagong	2–6, 7–6, 7–5
1972	Virginia Wade d. Evonne Goolagong	6–4, 6–4
1973	Margaret Smith Court d. Evonne Goolagong	6–4, 7–5

Year	Final Round Results	Scores
1974	Evonne Goolagong d. Chris Evert	7–5, 4–6, 6–0
1975	Evonne Goolagong d. Martina Navratilova	6–3, 6–2
1976	Evonne Goolagong d. Renata Tomanova	6–2, 6–2
1977 (Jan.)	Kerry Melville Reid d. Dianne Fromholtz Balestrat	7–5, 6–2
1977 (Dec.)	Evonne Goolagong Cawley d. Helen Gourlay Cawley	6–3, 6–0
1978	Chris O'Neil d. Betsy Nagelsen	6–3, 7–6
1979	Barbara Jordan d. Sharon Walsh	6–3, 6–3
1980	Hana Mandlikova d. Wendy Turnbull	6–0, 7–5
1981	Martina Navratilova d. Chris Evert	6–7 (4), 6–4, 7–5
1982	Chris Evert d. Martina Navratilova	6–3, 2–6, 6–3
1983	Martina Navratilova d. Kathy Jordan	6–2, 7–6 (5)
1984	Chris Evert d. Helena Sukova	6–7 (4), 6–1, 6–3
1985	Martina Navratilova d. Chris Evert	6–2, 4–6, 6–2
1986	Not held. Moved to January 1987.	
1987	Hana Mandlikova d. Martina Navratilova	7–5, 7–6 (2)
1988	Steffi Graf d. Chris Evert	6–1, 7–6 (3)
1989	Steffi Graf d. Helena Sukova	6–4, 6–4
1990	Steffi Graf d. Mary Joe Fernandez	6–3, 6–4
1991	Monica Seles d. Jana Novotna	5–7, 6–3, 6–1
1992	Monica Seles d. Mary Joe Fernandez	6–2, 6–3
1993	Monica Seles d. Steffi Graf	4–6, 6–3, 6–2
1994	Steffi Graf d. Arantxa Sanchez-Vicario	6–0, 6–2
1995	Mary Pierce d. Arantxa Sanchez-Vicario	6–3, 6–2
1996	Monica Seles d. Anke Huber	6–4, 6–1
1997	Martina Hingis d. Mary Pierce	6–2, 6–2
1998	Martina Hingis d. Conchita Martinez	6–3, 6–3
1999	Martina Hingis d. Amelie Mauresmo	6–2, 6–3
2000	Lindsay Davenport d. Martina Hingis	6–1, 7–5
2001	Jennifer Capriati d. Martina Hingis	6–4, 6–3
2002	Jennifer Capriati d. Martina Hingis	4–6, 7–6 (7), 6–2
2003	Serena Williams d. Venus Williams	7–6 (4), 3–6, 6–4
2004	Justine Henin d. Kim Clijsters	6–3, 4–6, 6–3
2005	Serena Williams d. Lindsay Davenport	2–6, 6–3, 6–0
2006	Amelie Mauresmo d. Justine Henin	6–1, 2–0 retired
2007	Serena Williams d. Maria Sharapova	6–1, 6–2
2008	Maria Sharapova d. Ana Ivanovic	7–5, 6–3

Women's Doubles

Year	Final Round Results	Scores
1922	Esna Boyd, Marjorie Mountain d. Floris St. George, Lorna Utz	1–6, 6–4, 7–5
1923	Esna Boyd, Sylvia Lance d. Mall Molesworth, H. Turner	6–1, 6–4
1924	Daphne Akhurst, Sylvia Lance d. Kathrine LeMesurier, Meryl O'Hara Wood	7–5, 6–2
1925	Sylvia Lance Harper, Daphne Akhurst d. Esna Boyd, Kathrine LeMesurie	6–4, 6–3
1926	Meryl O'Hara Wood, Esna Boyd d. Daphne Akhurst, Marjorie Cox	6–3, 6–8, 8–6

Year	Final Round Results	Scores
1927	Meryl O'Hara Wood, Louie Bickerton	
	d. Esna Boyd, Sylvia Lance Harper	6–3, 6–3
1928	Daphne Akhurst, Esna Boyd	
	d. Kathrine LeMesurier, Dorothy Weston	6–3, 6–1
1929	Daphne Akhurst, Louie Bickerton	
	d. Sylvia Lance Harper, Meryl O'Hara Wood	6–2, 3–6, 6–2
1930	Mall Molesworth, Emily Hood	
	d. Marjorie Cox, Sylvia Harper	6–3, 0–6, 7–5
1931	Daphne Akhurst Cozens, Louie Bickerton	
	d. N. Lloyd, Lorna Utz	6–0, 6–4
1932	Coral Buttsworth, Marjorie Cox	
	d. Kathrine LeMesurier, Dorothy Weston	6–2, 6–2
1933	Mall Molesworth, Emily Hood Westacott	
	d. Joan Hartigan, Marjorie Gladman Van Ryn	6–3, 6–2
1934	Mall Molesworth, Emily Hood Westacott	
	d. Joan Hartigan, Ula Valkenburg	6–8, 6–4, 6–4
1935	Evelyn Dearman, Nancy Lyle	
	d. Louie Bickerton, Nell Hall Hopman	6–3, 6–4
1936	Thelma Coyne, Nancye Wynne	
	d. May Blick, K. Woodward	6–2, 6–4
1937	Thelma Coyne, Nancye Wynne	
	d. Nell Hall Hopman, Emily Hood Westacott	6–2, 6–2
1938	Thelma Coyne, Nancye Wynne	
	d. Dorothy Bundy, Dorothy Workman	9–7, 6–4
1939	Thelma Coyne, Nancye Wynne	
	d. May Hardcastle, Emily Hood Westacott	7–5, 6–4
1940	Thelma Coyne, Nancye Wynne	
	d. Joan Hartigan, Emily Niemeyer	7–5, 6–2
1941–1945	Not held because of World War II	
1946	Joyce Fitch, Mary Bevis	
	d. Nancye Wynne Bolton, Thelma Coyne Long	9–7, 6–4
1947	Thelma Coyne Long, Nancye Wynne Bolton	
	d. Mary Bevis, Joyce Fitch	6–3, 6–3
1948	Thelma Coyne Long, Nancye Wynne Bolton	
	d. Mary Bevis, P. Jones	6–3, 6–3
1949	Thelma Coyne Long, Nancye Wynne Bolton	
	d. Doris Hart, Marie Toomey	6–0, 6–1
1950	Louise Brough, Doris Hart	
	d. Nancye Wynne Bolton, Thelma Coyne Long	6–2, 2–6, 6–3
1951	Thelma Coyne Long, Nancye Wynne Bolton	
	d. Joyce Fitch, Mary Hawton	6–2, 6–1
1952	Thelma Coyne Long, Nancye Wynne Bolton	
	d. R. Baker, Mary Hawton	6–1, 6–1
1953	Maureen Connolly, Julia Sampson	
	d. Mary Hawton, Beryl Penrose	6–4, 6–2
1954	Mary Hawton, Beryl Penrose	
	d. Hazel Redick-Smith, Julia Wipplinger	6–3, 8–6
1955	Mary Hawton, Beryl Penrose	
	d. Nell Hall Hopman, Gwen Thiele	7–5, 6–1

Year	Final Round Results	Scores
1956	Mary Hawton, Thelma Coyne Long	
	d. Mary Carter, Beryl Penrose	6–2, 5–7, 9–7
1957	Althea Gibson, Shirley Fry	
	d. Mary Hawton, Fay Muller	6–2, 6–1
1958	Mary Hawton, Thelma Coyne Long	
	d. Lorraine Coghlan, Angela Mortimer	7–5, 6–8, 6–2
1959	Renee Schuurman, Sandra Reynolds	
	d. Lorraine Coghlan, Mary Carter Reitano	7–5, 6–4
1960	Maria Bueno, Christine Truman	
	d. Lorraine Coghlan Robinson, Margaret Smith	6–2, 5–7, 6–2
1961	Mary Carter Reitano, Margaret Smith	
	d. Mary Hawton, Jan Lehane	6–4, 3–6, 7–5
1962	Margaret Smith, Robyn Ebbern	
	d. Darlene Hard, Mary Carter Reitano	6–4, 6–4
1963	Margaret Smith, Robyn Ebbern	
	d. Jan Lehane, Lesley Turner	6–1, 6–3
1964	Judy Tegart Dalton, Lesley Turner	
	d. Robyn Ebbern, Margaret Smith	6–4, 6–4
1965	Margaret Smith, Lesley Turner	
	d. Robyn Ebbern, Billie Jean King	1–6, 6–2, 6–3
1966	Carole Caldwell Graebner, Nancy Richey	
	d. Margaret Smith, Lesley Turner	6–4, 7–5
1967	Lesley Turner, Judy Tegart Dalton	
	d. Lorraine Coghlan Robinson, Evelyn Terras	6–0, 6–2
1968	Karen Krantzcke, Kerry Melville	
	d. Judy Tegart Dalton-Lesley Turner	6–4, 3–6, 6–2
1969	Margaret Smith Court, Judy Tegart Dalton	
	d. Rosie Casals, Billie Jean King	6–4, 6–4
1970	Margaret Smith Court, Judy Tegart Dalton	
	d. Karen Krantzcke, Kerry Melville	6–3, 6–1
1971	Margaret Smith Court, Evonne Goolagong	
	d. Jill Emmerson, Lesley Hunt	6–0, 6–0
1972	Kerry Harris, Helen Gourlay	
	d. Patricia Coleman, Karen Krantzcke	6–0, 6–4
1973	Margaret Smith Court, Virginia Wade	
	d. Kerry Harris, Kerry Melville	6–4, 6–4
1974	Evonne Goolagong, Peggy Michel	
	d. Kerry Harris, Kerry Melville	7–5, 6–3
1975	Evonne Goolagong, Peggy Michel	
	d. Margaret Smith Court, Olga Morozova	7–6, 7–6
1976	Evonne Goolagong, Helen Gourlay	
	d. Lesley Turner Bowrey, Renata Tomanova	8–1
	(one pro set determined championship)	
1977 (Jan.)	Dianne Fromholtz Balestrat, Helen Gourlay	
	d. Betsy Nagelsen, Kerry Melville Reid	5–7, 6–1, 7–6
1977 (Dec.)	Evonne Goolagong Cawley, Helen Gourlay vs.	
	Mona Schallau Guerrant, Kerry Melville Reid	
	(title shared; rain out)	

Year	Final Round Results	Scores
1978	Betsy Nagelsen, Renata Tomanova	
	d. Naoko Sato, Pam Whytcross	7–5, 6–2
1979	Judy Chaloner, Dianne Evers	
	d. Leanne Harrison, Marcella Mesker	6–1, 3–6, 6–0
1980	Martina Navratilova, Betsy Nagelsen	
	d. Ann Kiyomura, Candy Reynolds	6–4, 6–4
1981	Kathy Jordan, Anne Smith	
	d. Martina Navratilova, Pam Shriver	6–2, 7–5
1982	Martina Navratilova, Pam Shriver	
	d. Claudia Kohde Kilsch, Eva Pfaff	6–4, 6–2
1983	Martina Navratilova, Pam Shriver	
	d. Anne Hobbs, Wendy Turnbul	6–4, 6–7, 6–2
1984	Martina Navratilova, Pam Shriver	
	d. Claudia Kohde Kilsch, Helena Sukova	6–3, 6–4
1985	Martina Navratilova, Pam Shriver	
	d. Claudia Kohde Kilsch, Helena Sukova	6–3, 6–4
1986	Not held. Moved to January 1987.	
1987	Martina Navratilova, Pam Shriver	
	d. Zina Garrison, Lori McNeil	6–1, 6–0
1988	Martina Navratilova, Pam Shriver	
	d. Chris Evert, Wendy Turnbull	6–0, 6–4
1989	Martina Navratilova, Pam Shriver	
	d. Patty Fendick, Jill Hetherington	3–6, 6–3, 6–2
1990	Jana Novotna, Helena Sukova	
	d. Patty Fendick, Mary Joe Fernandez	7–6 (5), 7–6 (6)
1991	Patty Fendick, Mary Joe Fernandez	
	d. Gigi Fernandez, Jana Novotna	7–6 (4), 6–1
1992	Arantxa Sanchez-Vicario, Helena Sukova	
	d. Mary Joe Fernandez, Zina Garrison-Jackson	6–4, 7–6 (3)
1993	Gigi Fernandez, Natasha Zvereva	
	d. Pam Shriver, Elizabeth Smylie	6–4, 6–3
1994	Gigi Fernandez, Natasha Zvereva	
	d. Patty Fendick, Meredith McGrath	6–3, 4–6, 6–4
1995	Jana Novotna, Arantxa Sanchez-Vicario	
	d. Gigi Fernandez, Natasha Zvereva	6–3, 6–7 (3), 6–4
1996	Chanda Rubin, Arantxa Sanchez-Vicario	
	d. Lindsay Davenport, Mary Joe Fernandez	7–5, 2–6, 6–4
1997	Martina Hingis, Natasha Zvereva	
	d. Lindsay Davenport, Lisa Raymond	6–2, 6–2
1998	Martina Hingis, Mirjana Lucic	
	d. Lindsay Davenport, Natasha Zvereva	6–4, 2–6, 6–3
1999	Martina Hingis, Anna Kournikova	
	d. Lindsay Davenport, Natasha Zvereva	7–5, 6–3
2000	Lisa Raymond, Rennae Stubbs	
	d. Martina Hingis, Mary Pierce	6–4, 5–7, 6–4
2001	Serena Williams, Venus Williams	
	d. Lindsay Davenport, Corina Morariu	6–2, 4–6, 6–4
2002	Martina Hingis, Anna Kournikova	
	d. Daniela Hantuchova, Arantxa Sanchez-Vicario	6–2, 6–7(4), 6–1

Year	Final Round Results	Scores
2003	Serena Williams, Venus Williams	
	d. Virginia Ruano Pascual, Paola Suarez	4–6, 6–4, 6–3
2004	Virginia Ruano Pascual, Paola Suarez	
	d. Svetlana Kuznetsova, Elena Likhovtseva	6–4, 6–3
2005	Svetlana Kuznetsova, Alicia Molik	
	d. Lindsay Davenport, Corina Morariu	6–3, 6–4
2006	Zi Yan, Jie Zheng	
	d. Lisa Raymond, Samantha Stosur	2–6, 7–6 (7), 6–3
2007	Cara Black, Liezel Huber	
	d. Yung-Jan Chan, Chia-Yung Chuang	6–4, 6–7 (4), 6–1
2008	Alona Bondarenko, Kateryna Bondarenko	
	d. Victoria Azarenka, Shahar Peer	2–6, 6–1, 6–4

Mixed Doubles

Year	Final Round Results	Scores
1922	Esna Boyd, John Hawkes d. Lorna Utz, H.S. Utz	6–1, 6–1
1923	Sylvia Lance, Horace Rice	
	d. Mall Molesworth, C.B. St. John	2–6, 6–4, 6–4
1924	Daphne Akhurst, John Willard	
	d. Esna Boyd, Gar Hone	6–3, 6–4
1925	Daphne Akhurst, John Willard	
	d. Sylvia Lance Harper, Bob Schlesinger	6–4, 6–4
1926	Esna Boyd, John Hawkes	
	d. Daphne Akhurst, Jim Willard	6–2, 6–4
1927	Esna Boyd, John Hawkes	
	d. Youtha Anthony, Jim Willard	6–1, 6–3
1928	Daphne Akhurst, Jean Borotra	
	d. Esna Boyd, John Hawkes	default
1929	Daphne Akhurst, Gar Moon	
	d. Marjorie Cox, Jack Crawford	6–0, 7–5
1930	Nell Hall, Harry Hopman	
	d. Marjorie Cox, Jack Crawford	11–9, 3–6, 6–3
1931	Marjorie Cox Crawford, Jack Crawford	
	d. Emily Hood Westacott, A. Willard	7–5, 6–4
1932	Marjorie Cox Crawford, Jack Crawford	
	d. Meryl O'Hara Wood, Jiri Satoh	6–8, 8–6, 6–3
1933	Marjorie Cox Crawford, Jack Crawford	
	d. Marjorie Gladman Van Ryn, Ellsworth Vines	3–6, 7–5, 13–11
1934	Joan Hartigan, Gar Moon	
	d. Emily Hood Westacott, Ray Dunlop	6–3, 6–4
1935	Louie Bickerton, Christian Boussus	
	d. Mrs. Bond, Vernon Kirby	1–6, 6–3, 6–3
1936	Nell Hall Hopman, Harry Hopman	
	d. May Blick, A. A. Kay	6–2, 6–0
1937	Nell Hall Hopman, Harry Hopman	
	d. Dorothy Stevenson, Don Turnbull	3–6, 6–3, 6–2
1938	Margaret Wilson, John Bromwich	
	d. Nancye Wynne, Colin Long	6–3, 6–2

Year	*Final Round Results*	*Scores*
1939	Nell Hall Hopman, Harry Hopman	
	d. Margaret Wilson, John Bromwich	6–8, 6–2, 6–3
1940	Nancye Wynne, Colin Long	
	d. Nell Hall Hopman, Harry Hopman	7–5, 2–6, 6–4
1941–1945	Not held because of World War II	
1946	Nancye Wynne Bolton, Colin Long	
	d. Joyce Fitch, John Bromwich	6–0, 6–4
1947	Nancye Wynne Bolton, Colin Long	
	d. Joyce Fitch, John Bromwich	6–3, 6–3
1948	Nancye Wynne Bolton, Colin Long	
	d. Thelma Coyne Long, Billy Sidwell	7–5, 4–6, 8–6
1949	Doris Hart, Frank Sedgman	
	d. Joyce Fitch, John Bromwich	6–1, 5–7, 12–10
1950	Doris Hart, Frank Sedgman	
	d. Joyce Fitch, Eric Sturgess	8–6, 6–4
1951	Thelma Coyne Long, George Worthington	
	d. Clare Proctor, J. May	6–4, 3–6, 6–2
1952	Thelma Coyne Long, George Worthington	
	d. Mrs. A.R. Thiele, T. Warhurst	9–7, 7–5
1953	Julia Sampson, Rex Hartwig	
	d. Maureen Connolly, Hamilton Richardson	6–4, 6–3
1954	Thelma Coyne Long, Rex Hartwig	
	d. Beryl Penrose, John Bromwich	4–6, 6–1, 6–2
1955	Thelma Coyne Long, George Worthington	
	d. Jenny Staley, Lew Hoad	6–2, 6–1
1956	Beryl Penrose, Neale Fraser	
	d. Mary Bevis Hawton, Roy Emerson	6–2, 6–4
1957	Fay Muller, Mal Anderson d. J. Langley, Billy Knight	7–5, 3–6, 6–1
1958	Mary Bevis Hawton, Bob Howe	
	d. Angela Mortimer, Peter Newman	9–11, 6–1, 6–2
1959	Sandra Reynolds, Bob Mark	
	d. Renee Schuurman, Rod Laver	4–6, 13–11, 6–1
1960	Jan Lehane, Trevor Fancutt	
	d. Mary Carter Reitano, Bob Mark	6–2, 7–5
1961	Jan Lehane, Bob Hewitt	
	d. Mary Carter Reitano, J. Pearce	9–7, 6–2
1962	Lesley Turner, Fred Stolle	
	d. Darlene Hard, Roger Taylor	6–3, 9–7
1963	Margaret Smith, Ken Fletcher	
	d. Lesley Turner, Fred Stolle	7–5, 5–7, 6–4
1964	Margaret Smith, Ken Fletcher	
	d. Jan Lehane, Mike Sangster	6–1, 6–2
1965	Margaret Smith, John Newcombe	(final match was not
	vs. Robyn Ebbern, Owen Davidson	played; teams
		shared title)
1966	Judy Tegart, Tony Roche	
	d. Robyn Ebbern, Bill Bowery	6–1, 6–3
1967	Lesley Turner, Owen Davidson	
	d. Judy Tegart, Tony Roche	9–7, 6–4

Year	Final Round Results	Scores
1968	Billie Jean King, Dick Crealy	
	d. Margaret Smith Court, Allan Stone	6–2, 9–7
1969	Margaret Smith Court, Marty Riessen	(final match was not
	vs. Ann Haydon Jones, Fred Stolle	played; teams
		shared title)
1970–1986	Not held	
1987	Zina Garrison, Sherwood Stewart	
	d. Anne Hobbs, Andrew Castle	3–6, 7–6, 6–3
1988	Jana Novotna, Jim Pugh	
	d. Martina Navratilova, Tim Gullikson	5–7, 6–2, 6–4
1989	Jana Novotna, Jim Pugh	
	d. Zina Garrison, Sherwood Stewart	6–3, 6–4
1990	Natalia Zvereva, Jim Pugh	
	d. Zina Garrison, Rick Leach	4–6, 6–2, 6–3
1991	Jo Durie, Jeremy Bates d. Robin White, Scott Davis	2–6, 6–4, 6–4
1992	Nicole Provis, Mark Woodforde	
	d. Arantxa Sanchez-Vicario, Todd Woodbridge	6–3, 4–6, 11–9
1993	Arantxa Sanchez-Vicario, Todd Woodbridge	
	d. Zina Garrison-Jackson, Rick Leach	7–5, 6–4
1994	Larisa Neiland, Andrei Olhovskiy	
	d. Helena Sukova, Todd Woodbridge	7–5, 6–7, 6–2
1995	Natalia Zvereva, Rick Leach	
	d. Gigi Fernandez, Cyril Suk	7–6 (4), 6–7 (3), 6–4
1996	Larisa Neiland, Mark Woodforde	
	d. Nicole Arendt, Luke Jensen	4–6, 7–5, 6–0
1997	Manon Bollegraf, Rick Leach	
	d. Larisa Neiland, John Laffnie De Jager	6–3, 6–7 (5), 7–5
1998	Venus Williams, Justin Gimelstob	
	d. Helena Sukova, Cyril Suk	6–2, 6–1
1999	Mariaan DeSwardt, David Adams	
	d. Serena Williams, Max Mirnyi	6–4, 4–6, 7–6 (5)
2000	Rennae Stubbs, Jared Palmer	
	d. Arantxa Sanchez-Vicario	7–5, 7–6 (3)
2001	Corina Morariu, Ellis Ferreira	
	d. Barbara Schett, Josh Eagle	6–1, 6–3
2002	Daniela Hantuchova, Kevin Ullyett	
	d. Paola Suarez, Gaston Etis	6–2, 6–3
2003	Martina Navratilova, Leander Paes	
	d. Eleni Daniilidou, Todd Woodbridge	6–4, 7–5
2004	Elena Bovina, Nenad Zimonjic	
	d. Martina Navratilova, Leander Paes	6–1, 7–6 (3)
2005	Samantha Stosur, Scott Draper	
	d. Liezel Huber, Kevin Ullyett	6–2, 2–6, 7–6 (6)
2006	Martina Hingis, Mahesh Bhupathi	
	d. Elena Likhovtseva, Daniel Nestor	6–3, 6–3
2007	Elena Likhovtseva, Daniel Nestor	
	d. Viktoria Azarenka, Max Mirnyi	6–4, 6–4
2008	Tiantian Sun, Nenad Zimonjic	
	d. Sania Mirza, Mahesh Bhupathi	7–6 (4), 6–4

The French Championships

Tournoi de Roland-Garros or Roland Garros Tournament, the competition more commonly referred to as the French Open, is the second Grand Slam tournament on the annual tennis calendar. It is played in late May and early June in the southwest region of Paris, France. The event is named after its stadium, Stade Roland Garros, which in turn is named after the famous French World War I pilot. The tournament has been played at Stade Roland Garros since 1928, when the new stadium was built for Davis Cup competition. Court Suzanne Lenglen, built in 1994, was named after the legendary French female champion in 1997. In 2001, Center Court was named Court Philippe Chatrier in honor of the French tennis player, journalist, and former president of the International Tennis Federation.

Although the French Championships began in 1897 for women's competition, it was not until 1925 that the tournament was open to players other than French residents. Of the four Grand Slam tournaments, it is the only one currently played on a red clay court surface composed of crushed wastes from red brick. The slow playing surface is considered to be the most physically demanding of the Grand Slams. The French Open has prevented players like Lindsay Davenport and Martina Hingis from achieving a career Grand Slam. In 1968, the French Open became the first of the Grand Slams to allow both amateurs and professionals to compete together in the same tournament. Equal prize money for both men and women was awarded for the first time in 2007.

Women's Singles

Year	Final Round Results	Scores
1925	Suzanne Lenglen d. Kitty McKane	6–1, 6–2
1926	Suzanne Lenglen d. Mary K. Browne	6–1, 6–0
1927	Kea Bouman d. Irene Peacock	6–2, 6–4
1928	Helen Wills d. Eileen Bennett	6–1, 6–2
1929	Helen Wills d. Simone Passemard Mathieu	6–3, 6–4
1930	Helen Wills Moody d. Helen Jacobs	6–2, 6–1
1931	Cilly Aussem d. Betty Nuthall	8–6, 6–1
1932	Helen Wills Moody d. Simone Passemard Mathieu	7–5, 6–1
1933	Margaret Scriven d. Simone Passemard Mathieu	6–2, 4–6, 6–4
1934	Margaret Scriven d. Helen Jacobs	7–5, 4–6, 6–1
1935	Hilde Krahwinkel Sperling d. Simone Passemard Mathieu	6–2, 6–1
1936	Hilde Krahwinkel Sperling d. Simone Passemard Mathieu	6–3, 6–4
1937	Hilde Krahwinkel Sperling d. Simone Passemard Mathieu	6–2, 6–4
1938	Simone Passemard Mathieu d. Nelly Adamson Landry	6–0, 6–3
1939	Simone Passemard Mathieu d. Jadwiga Jedrzejowska	6–3, 8–6
1940–1945	Not held because of World War II	
1946	Margaret Osborne d. Pauline Betz	1–6, 8–6, 7–5
1947	Patricia Canning Todd d. Doris Hart	6–3, 3–6, 6–4
1948	Nelly Landry d. Shirley Fry	6–2, 0–6, 6–0

Year	Final Round Results	Scores
1949	Margaret Osborne duPont d. Nelly Adamson	7–5, 6–2
1950	Doris Hart d. Patricia Canning Todd	6–4, 4–6, 6–2
1951	Shirley Fry d. Doris Hart	6–3, 3–6, 6–3
1952	Doris Hart d. Shirley Fry	6–4, 6–4
1953	Maureen Connolly d. Doris Hart	6–2, 6–4
1954	Maureen Connolly d. Ginette Bucaille	6–4, 6–1
1955	Angela Mortimer d. Dorothy Head Knode	2–6, 7–5, 10–8
1956	Althea Gibson d. Angela Mortimer	6–0, 12–10
1957	Shirley Bloomer d. Dorothy Head Knode	6–1, 6–3
1958	Suzi Kormoczy d. Shirley Bloomer	6–4, 1–6, 6–2
1959	Christine Truman d. Suzi Kormoczy	6–4, 7–5
1960	Darlene Hard d. Yola Ramirez	6–3, 6–4
1961	Ann Haydon d. Yola Ramirez	6–2, 6–1
1962	Margaret Smith d. Lesley Turner	6–3, 3–6, 7–5
1963	Lesley Turner d. Ann Haydon Jones	2–6, 6–3, 7–5
1964	Margaret Smith d. Maria Bueno	5–7, 6–1, 6–2
1965	Lesley Turner d. Margaret Smith	6–3, 6–4
1966	Ann Haydon Jones d. Nancy Richey	6–3, 6–1
1967	Francoise Durr d. Lesley Turner	4–6, 6–3, 6–4
1968	Nancy Richey d. Ann Haydon Jones	5–7, 6–4, 6–1
1969	Margaret Smith Court d. Ann Jones	6–1, 4–6, 6–3
1970	Margaret Smith Court d. Helga Niessen	6–2, 6–4
1971	Evonne Goolagong d. Helen Gourlay	6–3, 7–5
1972	Billie Jean King d. Evonne Goolagong	6–3, 6–3
1973	Margaret Smith Court d. Chris Evert	6–7 (5), 7–6 (6), 6–4
1974	Chris Evert d. Olga Morozova	6–1, 6–2
1975	Chris Evert d. Martina Navratilova	2–6, 6–2, 6–1
1976	Sue Barker d. Renata Tomanova	6–2, 0–6, 6–2
1977	Mima Jausovec d. Florenta Mihai	6–2, 6–7 (5), 6–1
1978	Virginia Ruzici d. Mima Jausovec	6–2, 6–2
1979	Chris Evert d. Wendy Turnbull	6–2, 6–0
1980	Chris Evert d. Virginia Ruzici	6–0, 6–3
1981	Hana Mandlikova d. Sylvia Hanika	6–2, 6–4
1982	Martina Navratilova d. Andrea Jaeger	7–6 (6), 6–1
1983	Chris Evert d. Mima Jausovec	6–1, 6–2
1984	Martina Navratilova d. Chris Evert	6–3, 6–1
1985	Chris Evert d. Martina Navratilova	6–3, 6–7 (4), 7–5
1986	Chris Evert d. Martina Navratilova	2–6, 6–3, 6–3
1987	Steffi Graf d. Martina Navratilova	6–4, 4–6, 8–6
1988	Steffi Graf d. Natasha Zvereva	6–0, 6–0
1989	Arantxa Sanchez-Vicario d. Steffi Graf	7–6 (6), 3–6, 7–5
1990	Monica Seles d. Steffi Graf	7–6 (6), 6–4
1991	Monica Seles d. Arantxa Sanchez-Vicario	6–3, 6–4
1992	Monica Seles d. Steffi Graf	6–2, 3–6, 10–8
1993	Steffi Graf d. Mary Joe Fernandez	4–6, 6–2, 6–4
1994	Arantxa Sanchez-Vicario d. Mary Pierce	6–4, 6–4
1995	Steffi Graf d. Arantxa Sanchez-Vicario	7–5, 4–6, 6–0
1996	Steffi Graf d. Arantxa Sanchez-Vicario	6–3, 6–7 (4), 10–8
1997	Iva Majoli d. Martina Hingis	6–4, 6–2

Year	Final Round Results	Scores
1998	Arantxa Sanchez-Vicario d. Monica Seles	7–6 (5), 0–6, 6–2
1999	Steffi Graf d. Martina Hingis	4–6, 7–5, 6–2
2000	Mary Pierce d. Conchita Martinez	6–2, 7–5
2001	Jennifer Capriati d. Kim Clijsters	1–6, 6–4, 12–10
2002	Serena Williams d. Venus Williams	7–5, 6–3
2003	Justine Henin d. Kim Clijsters	6–0, 6–4
2004	Anastasia Myskina d. Elena Dementieva	6–1, 6–2
2005	Justine Henin d. Mary Pierce	6–1, 6–1
2006	Justine Henin d. Svetlana Kuznetsova	6–4, 6–4
2007	Justine Henin d. Ana Ivanovic	6–1, 6–2
2008	Ana Ivanovic d. Dinara Safina	6–4, 6–3

Women's Doubles

Year	Final Round Results	Scores
1925	Suzanne Lenglen, Didi Vlasto	
	d. Evelyn Colyer, Kitty McKane	6–1, 9–11, 6–2
1926	Suzanne Lenglen, Didi Vlasto	
	d. Evelyn Colyer, Kitty McKane Godfree	6–1, 6–1
1927	Irene Peacock, Bobbie Heine	
	d. Peggy Saunders, Phoebe Watson	6–2, 6–1
1928	Phoebe Watson, Eileen Bennett	
	d. Suzanne Deve, Sylvia Lafaurie	6–0, 6–2
1929	Lili de Alvarez, Kea Bouman	
	d. Bobbie Heine, Alida Neave	7–5, 6–3
1930	Helen Wills Moody, Elizabeth Ryan	
	d. Simone Barbier, Simone Passemard Mathieu	6–3, 6–1
1931	Eileen Bennett Whittingstall, Betty Nuthall	
	d. Cilly Aussem, Elizabeth Ryan	9–7, 6–2
1932	Helen Wills Moody, Elizabeth Ryan	
	d. Betty Nuthall, Eileen Bennett Whittingstall	6–1, 6–3
1933	Simone Passemard Mathieu, Elizabeth Ryan	
	d. Sylvie Jung Henrotin, Colette Rosambert	6–1, 6–3
1934	Simone Passemard Mathieu, Elizabeth Ryan	
	d. Helen Jacobs, Sarah Palfrey	3–6, 6–4, 6–2
1935	Margaret Scriven, Kay Stammers	
	d. Ida Adamoff, Hilde Krahwinkel Sperling	6–4, 6–0
1936	Simone Passemard Mathieu, Adeline Yorke	
	d. Susan Noel, Jadwiga Jedrzejowska	2–6, 6–4, 6–4
1937	Simone Passemard Mathieu, Adeline Yorke	
	d. Dorothy Andrus, Sylvia Henrotin	3–6, 6–2, 6–2
1938	Simone Passemard Mathieu, Adeline Yorke	
	d. Arlette Halff, Nelly Adamson Landry	6–3, 6–3
1939	Simone Passemard Mathieu, Jadwiga Jedrzejowska	
	d. Alice Florian, Hella Kovac	7–5, 7–5
1940–1945	Not held because of World War II	
1946	Louise Brough, Margaret Osborne	
	d. Pauline Betz, Doris Hart	6–4, 0–6, 6–1

Year	Final Round Results	Scores
1947	Louise Brough, Margaret Osborne	
	d. Doris Hart, Patricia Canning Todd	7–5, 6–2
1948	Doris Hart, Patricia Canning Todd	
	d. Shirley Fry, Mary Arnold Prentiss	6–4, 6–2
1949	Margaret Osborne duPont, Louise Brough	
	d. Joy Gannon, Betty Hilton	7–5, 6–1
1950	Doris Hart, Shirley Fry	
	d. Louise Brough, Margaret Osborne duPont	1–6, 7–5, 6–2
1951	Doris Hart, Shirley Fry	
	d. Beryl Bartlett, Barbara Scofield	10–8, 6–3
1952	Doris Hart, Shirley Fry	
	d. Hazel Redick-Smith, Julie Wipplinger	7–5, 6–1
1953	Doris Hart, Shirley Fry	
	d. Maureen Connolly, Julia Sampson	6–4, 6–3
1954	Maureen Connolly, Nell Hall Hopman	
	d. Maude Galtier, Suzanne Schmitt	7–5, 4–6, 6–0
1955	Beverly Baker Fleitz, Darlene Hard	
	d. Shirley Bloomer, Pat Ward	7–5, 6–8, 13–11
1956	Angela Buxton, Althea Gibson	
	d. Darlene Hard, Dorothy Head Knode	6–8, 8–6, 6–1
1957	Shirley Bloomer, Darlene Hard	
	d. Yola Ramirez, Rosie Reyes	7–5, 4–6, 7–5
1958	Rosie Reyes, Yola Ramirez	
	d. Mary Hawton, Thelma Coyne Long	6–4, 7–5
1959	Sandra Reynolds, Renee Schuurman	
	d. Yola Ramirez, Rosie Reyes	2–6, 6–0, 6–1
1960	Maria Bueno, Darlene Hard	
	d. Pat Ward Hales, Ann Haydon	6–2, 7–5
1961	Sandra Reynolds, Renee Schuurman	
	d. Maria Bueno, Darlene Hard	default
1962	Sandra Reynolds Price, Renee Schuurman	
	d. Justina Bricka, Margaret Smith	6–4, 6–4
1963	Ann Haydon Jones, Renee Schuurmann	
	d. Robyn Ebbern, Margaret Smith	7–5, 6–4
1964	Margaret Smith, Lesley Turner	
	d. Norma Baylon, Helga Schultze	6–3, 6–1
1965	Margaret Smith, Lesley Turner	
	d. Francoise Durr, Jeanine Lieffrig	6–3, 6–1
1966	Margaret Smith, Judy Tegart	
	d. Jill Blackman, Fay Toyne	4–6, 6–1, 6–1
1967	Francoise Durr, Gail Sherriff	
	d. Annette Van Zyl, Pat Walkden	6–2, 6–2
1968	Francoise Durr, Ann Haydon Jones	
	d. Rosemary Casals, Billie Jean King	7–5, 4–6, 6–4
1969	Francoise Durr, Ann Haydon Jones	
	d. Margaret Smith, Nancy Richey	6–0, 4–6, 7–5
1970	Gail Sherriff Chanfreau, Francoise Durr	
	d. Rosemary Casals, Billie Jean King	6–1, 3–6, 6–3

Year	Final Round Results	Scores
1971	Gail Sherriff Chanfreau, Francoise Durr	
	d. Helen Gourlay, Kerry Harris	6–4, 6–1
1972	Billie Jean King, Betty Stove	
	d. Winnie Shaw, Christine Truman	6–1, 6–2
1973	Margaret Smith Court, Virginia Wade	
	d. Francoise Durr, Betty Stove	6–2, 6–3
1974	Chris Evert, Olga Morozova	
	d. Gail Sherriff Chanfreau, Katja Ebbinghaus	6–4, 2–6, 6–1
1975	Chris Evert, Martina Navratilova	
	d. Julie Anthony, Olga Morozova	6–3, 6–2
1976	Fiorella Bonicelli, Gail Sherriff Lovera	
	d. Kathleen Harter, Helga Niessen Masthoff	6–4, 1–6, 6–3
1977	Regina Marsikova, Pam Teeguarden	
	d. Rayni Fox, Helen Gourlay	5–7, 6–4, 6–2
1978	Mima Jausovec, Virginia Ruzici	
	d. Lesley Turner Bowery, Gail Sherriff Lovera	5–7, 6–4, 8–6
1979	Betty Stove, Wendy Turnbull	
	d. Francoise Durr, Virginia Wade	3–6, 7–5, 6–4
1980	Kathy Jordan, Anne Smith	
	d. Ivanna Madruga, Adriana Villagran	6–1, 6–0
1981	Rosalyn Fairbank, Tanya Harford	
	d. Candy Reynolds, Paula Smith	6–1, 6–3
1982	Martina Navratilova, Anne Smith	
	d. Rosemary Casals, Wendy Turnbull	6–3, 6–4
1983	Rosalyn Fairbank, Candy Reynolds	
	d. Kathy Jordan, Anne Smith	5–7, 7–5, 6–2
1984	Martina Navratilova, Pam Shriver	
	d. Claudia Kohde Kilsch, Hana Mandlikova	5–7, 6–3, 6–2
1985	Martina Navratilova, Pam Shriver	
	d. Claudia Kohde Kilsch, Helena Sukova	4–6, 6–2, 6–2
1986	Martina Navratilova, Andrea Temesvari	
	d. Steffi Graf, Gabriela Sabatini	6–1, 6–2
1987	Martina Navratilova, Pam Shriver	
	d. Steffi Graf, Gabriela Sabatini	6–2, 6–1
1988	Martina Navratilova, Pam Shriver	
	d. Claudia Kohde Kilsch, Helena Sukova	6–2, 7–5
1989	Larisa Savchenko, Natasha Zvereva	
	d. Steffi Graf, Gabriela Sabatini	6–4, 6–4
1990	Jana Novotna, Helena Sukova	
	d. Larisa Savchenko, Natasha Zvereva	6–4, 7–5
1991	Gigi Fernandez, Jana Novotna	
	d. Larisa Savchenko, Natasha Zvereva	6–4, 6–0
1992	Gigi Fernandez, Natasha Zvereva	
	d. Conchita Martinez, Arantxa Sanchez-Vicario	6–3, 6–2
1993	Gigi Fernandez, Natasha Zvereva	
	d. Larisa Savchenko Neiland, Jana Novotna	6–3, 7–5
1994	Gigi Fernandez, Natasha Zvereva	
	d. Lindsay Davenport, Lisa Raymond	6–2, 6–2

Year	Final Round Results	Scores
1995	Gigi Fernandez, Natasha Zvereva	
	d. Jana Novotna, Arantxa Sanchez-Vicario	6–7, 6–4, 7–5
1996	Lindsay Davenport, Mary Joe Fernandez	
	d. Gigi Fernandez, Natasha Zvereva	6–2, 6–1
1997	Gigi Fernandez, Natasha Zvereva	
	d. Mary Joe Fernandez, Lisa Raymond	6–2, 6–3
1998	Martina Hingis, Jana Novotna	
	d. Lindsay Davenport, Natasha Zvereva	6–1, 7–6 (4)
1999	Serena Williams, Venus Williams	
	d. Martina Hingis, Anna Kournikova	6–3, 6–7 (2), 8–6
2000	Martina Hingis, Mary Pierce	
	d. Virginia Ruano Pascual, Paola Suarez	6–2, 6–4
2001	Virginia Ruano Pascual, Paola Suarez	
	d. Jelena Dokic, Conchita Martinez	6–2, 6–1
2002	Virginia Ruano Pascual, Paola Suarez	
	d. Lisa Raymond, Rennae Stubbs	6–4, 6–2
2003	Kim Clijsters, Ai Sugiyama	
	d. Virginia Ruano Pascual, Paola Suarez	6–7 (5), 6–2, 9–7
2004	Virginia Ruano Pascual, Paola Suarez	
	d. Svetlana Kuznetsova, Elena Likhovtseva	6–0, 6–3
2005	Virginia Ruano Pascual, Paola Suarez	
	d. Cara Black, Liezel Huber	4–6, 6–3, 6–3
2006	Lisa Raymond, Samantha Stosur	
	d. Daniela Hantuchova, Ai Sugiyama	6–3, 6–2
2007	Alicia Molik, Mara Santangelo	
	d. Katarina Srebotnik, Ai Sugiyama	7–6 (5), 6–4
2008	Anabel Medina Garrigues, Virginia Ruano Pascual	
	d. Casey Dellacqua, Francesca Schiavone	2–6, 7–5, 6–4

Mixed Doubles

Year	Final Round Results	Scores
1925	Suzanne Lenglen, Jacques Brugnon	
	d. Didi Vlasto, Henri Cochet	6–2, 6–2
1926	Suzanne Lenglen, Jacques Burgnon	
	d. Mme. LeBesnerais, Jean Borotra	6–4, 6–3
1927	Marguerite Broquedis Bordes, Jean Borotra	
	d. Lili de Alvarez, Bill Tilden	6–4, 2–6, 6–2
1928	Eileen Bennett, Henri Cochet	
	d. Helen Wills, Frank Hunter	3–6, 6–3, 6–3
1929	Eileen Bennett, Henri Cochet	
	d. Helen Wills, Frank Hunter	6–3, 6–2
1930	Cilly Aussem, Bill Tilden	
	d. Eileen Bennett Whittingstall, Henri Cochet	6–4, 6–4
1931	Betty Nuthall, Pat Spence	
	d. Dorothy Shepherd Barron, Henry "Bunny" Austin	6–3, 5–7, 6–3
1932	Betty Nuthall, Fred Perry	
	d. Helen Wills Moody, Sidney Wood	6–4, 6–2
1933	Margaret Scriven, Jack Crawford	
	d. Betty Nuthall, Fred Perry	6–2, 6–3

Year	Final Round Results	Scores
1934	Colette Rosambert, Jean Borotra	
	d. Elizabeth Ryan, Adrian Quist	6–2, 6–4
1935	Lolette Payot, Marcel Bernard	
	d. Sylvie Jung Henrotin, Martin Legeay	4–6, 6–2, 6–4
1936	Adeline York, Marcel Bernard	
	d. Sylvie Jung Henrotin, Martin Legeay	7–5, 6–8, 6–3
1937	Simone Passemard Mathieu, Yvon Petra	
	d. M. Horne, R. Journu	7–5, 7–5
1938	Simone Passemard Mathieu, Dragutin Mitic	
	d. Nancye Wynne, Christian Boussus	2–6, 6–3, 6–4
1939	Sarah Palfrey Fabyan, Elwood Cooke	
	d. Simone Passemard Mathieu, Franjo Kukuljevic	4–6, 6–1, 7–5
1940–1945	Not held because of World War II	
1946	Pauline Betz, J.E. "Budge" Patty	
	d. Dorothy Bundy, Tom Brown	7–5, 9–7
1947	Sheila Piercey Summers, Eric Sturgess	
	d. Jadwiga Jedrzejowska, Christian Caralulis	6–0, 6–0
1948	Patricia Canning Todd, Jaroslav Drobny	
	d. Doris Hart, Frank Sedgman	6–3, 3–6, 6–3
1949	Sheila Piercey Summers, Eric Sturgess	
	d. Jean Quertier, Gerry Oakley	6–1, 6–1
1950	Barbara Scofield, Enrique Morea	
	d. Patricia Canning Todd, Bill Talbert	default
1951	Doris Hart, Frank Sedgman	
	d. Thelma Coyne Long, Mervyn Rose	7–5, 6–2
1952	Doris Hart, Frank Sedgman	
	d. Shirley Fry, Eric Sturgess	6–8, 6–3, 6–3
1953	Doris Hart, Vic Seixas	
	d. Maureen Connolly, Mervyn Rose	4–6, 6–4, 6–0
1954	Maureen Connolly, Lew Hoad	
	d. J. Patorni, Rex Hartwig	6–4, 6–3
1955	Darlene Hard, Gordon Forbes	
	d. Jenny Staley, Luis Ayala	5–7, 6–1, 6–2
1956	Thelma Coyne Long, Luis Ayala	
	d. Doris Hart, Bob Howe	4–6, 6–4, 6–1
1957	Vera Puzejova, Jiri Javorsky d. Edda Buding, Luis Ayala	6–3, 6–4
1958	Shirley Bloomer, Nicola Pietrangeli	
	d. Lorraine Coghlan, Bob Howe	9–7, 6–8, 6–2
1959	Yola Ramirez, Billy Knight	
	d. Renee Schuurman, Rod Laver	6–4, 6–4
1960	Maria Bueno, Bob Howe	
	d. Ann Haydon, Roy Emerson	1–6, 6–1, 6–2
1961	Darlene Hard, Rod Laver d. Vera Puzejova, Jiri Javorsky	6–0, 2–6, 6–3
1962	Renee Schuurman, Bob Howe	
	d. Lesley Turner, Fred Stolle	3–6, 6–4, 6–4
1963	Margaret Smith, Ken Fletcher	
	d. Lesley Turner, Fred Stolle	6–1, 6–2
1964	Margaret Smith, Ken Fletcher	
	d. Lesley Turner, Fred Stolle	6–3, 6–4

Year	Final Round Results	Scores
1965	Margaret Smith, Ken Fletcher	
	d. Maria Bueno, John Newcombe	6–4, 6–4
1966	Annette Van Zyl, Frew McMillan	
	d. Ann Haydon Jones, Clark Graebner	1–6, 6–3, 6–2
1967	Billie Jean King, Owen Davidson	
	d. Ann Haydon Jones, Ion Tiriac	6–3, 6–1
1968	Francoise Durr, Jean Claude Barclay	
	d. Billie Jean King, Owen Davidson	6–1, 6–4
1969	Margaret Smith Court, Marty Riessen	
	d. Francoise Durr, Jeanne Claude Barclay	7–5, 6–4
1970	Billie Jean King, Bob Hewitt	
	d. Francoise Durr, Jean Claude Barclay	3–6, 6–3, 6–2
1971	Francoise Durr, Jean Claude Barclay	
	d. Winnie Shaw, Tomas Lejus	6–2, 6–4
1972	Evonne Goolagong, Kim Warwick	
	d. Francoise Durr, Jean Claude Barclay	6–2, 6–4
1973	Francoise Durr, Jean Claude Barclay	
	d. Betty Stove, Patrice Dominguez	6–1, 6–4
1974	Martina Navratilova, Ivan Molina	
	d. Rosie Reyes Darmon, Marcelo Lara	6–3, 6–3
1975	Fiorella Bonicelli, Tom Koch	
	d. Pam Teeguarden, Jaime Fillol	6–4, 7–6
1976	Ilana Kloss, Kim Warwick	
	d. Delina Boshoff, Colin Dowdeswell	5–7, 7–6, 6–2
1977	Mary Carillo, John McEnroe	
	d. Florenta Mihai, Ivan Molina	7–6, 6–3
1978	Renata Tomanova, Pavel Slozil	
	d. Virginia Ruzici, Patrice Dominguez	7–6, retired
1979	Wendy Turnbull, Bob Hewitt	
	d. Virginia Ruzici, Ion Tiriac	6–3, 2–6, 6–3
1980	Anne Smith, Billy Martin	
	d. Renata Tomanova, Stanislav Birner	2–6, 6–4, 8–6
1981	Andrea Jaeger, Jimmy Arias	
	d. Betty Stove, Fred McNair	7–6, 6–4
1982	Wendy Turnbull, John Lloyd	
	d. Claudia Monteiro, Cassio Motta	6–2, 7–6
1983	Barbara Jordan, Eliot Teltscher	
	d. Lesley Allen, Charles Strode	6–2, 6–3
1984	Anne Smith, Dick Stockton	
	d. Anne Minter, Laurie Warder	6–2, 6–4
1985	Martina Navratilova, Heinz Gunthardt	
	d. Paula Smith, Francisco Gonzalez	2–6, 6–3, 6–2
1986	Kathy Jordan, Ken Flach	
	d. Rosalyn Fairbank, Mark Edmondson	3–6, 7–6 (3), 6–3
1987	Pam Shriver, Emilio Sanchez	
	d. Lori McNeil, Sherwood Stewart	6–3, 7–6 (4)
1988	Lori McNeil, Jorge Lozano	
	d. Brenda Schultz, Michiel Schapers	7–5, 6–2

Year	Final Round Results	Scores
1989	Manon Bollegaaff, Tom Nijssen	
	d. Arantxa Sanchez-Vicario, Horacio de la Pena	6–3, 6–7 (3), 6–2
1990	Arantxa Sanchez-Vicario, Jorge Lozano	
	d. Nicole Provis, Danie Visser	7–6 (5), 7–6 (8)
1991	Helena Sukova, Cyril Suk	
	d. Caroline Vis, Paul Haarhuis	3–6, 6–4, 6–1
1992	Arantxa Sanchez-Vicario, Mark Woodforde	
	d. Lori McNeil, Bryan Shelton	6–2, 6–3
1993	Eugenia Maniokova, Andrei Olhovskiy	
	d. Elna Reinach, Danie Visser	6–2, 4–6, 6–4
1994	Kristie Boggert, Menno Oosting	
	d. Larisa Savchenko Neiland, Andrei Olhovskiy	7–5, 3–6, 7–5
1995	Larisa Savchenko Neiland, Mark Woodforde	
	d. Jill Hetherington, John-Laffnie de Jager	7–6 (8), 7–6 (4)
1996	Patricia Tarabini, Javier Frana	
	d. Nicole Arendt, Luke Jensen	6–2, 6–2
1997	Rika Hiraki, Mahesh Bhupathi	
	d. Lisa Raymond, Patrick Galbraith	6–4, 6–1
1998	Venus Williams, Justin Gimelstob	
	d. Serena Williams, Luis Lobo	6–4, 6–4
1999	Katarina Srebotnik, Piet Norval	
	d. Larisa Savchenko Neiland, Rick Leach	6–3, 3–6, 6–3
2000	Mariaan DeSwardt, David Adams	
	d. Rennae Stubbs, Todd Woodbridge	6–3, 3–6, 6–3
2001	Virginia Ruano Pascual, Tomas Carbonell	
	d. Paola Suarez, Jamie Oncins	7–5, 6–3
2002	Cara Black, Wayne Black	
	d. Elena Bovina, Mark Knowles	6–3, 6–3
2003	Lisa Raymond, Mike Bryan	
	d. Elena Likhovtseva, Mahesh Bhupathi	6–3, 6–4
2004	Tatiana Golovin, Richard Gasquet	
	d. Cara Black, Wayne Black	6–3, 6–4
2005	Daniela Hantuchova, Fabrice Santoro	
	d. Martina Navratilova, Leander Paes	3–6, 6–3, 6–2
2006	Katarina Srebotnik, Nenad Zimonjic	
	d. Elena Likhovtseva, Daniel Nestor	6–3, 6–4
2007	Nathalie Dechy, Andy Ram	
	d. Katarina Srebotnik, Nenad Zimonjic	7–5, 6–3
2008	Victoria Azarenka, Bob Bryan	
	d. Katarina Srebotnik, Nenad Zimonjic	6–2, 7–6 (4)

The Wimbledon Championships

Considered by many to be the grandest and most elite of the Grand Slams, this tournament is the only major tennis event which is played on natural grass. It is held on the grounds of the All England Lawn Tennis Club located on Church Road in the London suburb of Wimbledon. From 1877 to 1921, the tournament was played at the "old Wimbledon" site on Worple Road not far from the present day venue.

Singles competition for women began in 1884, while doubles and mixed doubles started in 1913. In 1968, the Wimbledon Championships became an open tournament, as both amateurs and professionals competed in this prestigious tournament for the first time. Major changes have taken place recently at the club including the awarding of equal prize money for both men and women competitors; the implementation of Hawk-Eye, an electronic computer line reviewing system; and the installation of big screen TV monitors around the grounds. A retractable roof is scheduled to be in place on Centre Court in 2009. Wimbledon has preserved part of the traditional scoring system, however, by eliminating the tiebreaker in the third set of a women's match and the fifth set of a men's match. A player still needs to win those sets by two games.

In 1879, two years after the men's lawn tennis championship event began, one of the club's members proposed a competitive cup for women players. The idea was adamantly opposed by members of the club. It wasn't until 1884 that the first ladies' event was held at Wimbledon. It was a separate event not started until the men had completed their championship. From 1884 to 1921, the women's singles championship was decided on a challenge-round system in which the previous year's winner stood out until the winner of the so-called All-Comers' event qualified to challenge the defending champion. In those years when the previous year's winner did not compete, the title was decided in the challenge round.

The women were not enthusiastic about playing at Wimbledon in 1884. Only a dozen women players showed up for the first tournament. Their numbers declined year by year and by 1890 there were only 4 competitors. Today hundreds of female players from around the world compete for the 128 cherished spots in each year's Wimbledon singles draw.

Women's Singles

Year	Final Round Results	Scores
1884	Maud Watson d. Lilian Watson	6–8, 6–3, 6–3
1885	Maud Watson d. Blanche Bingley	6–1, 7–5
1886	Blanche Bingley d. Maud Watson	6–3, 6–3
1887	Lottie Dod d. Blanche Bingley Hillyard	6–2, 6–0
1888	Lottie Dod d. Blanche Bingley Hillyard	6–3, 6–3
1889	Blanche Bingley Hillyard d. Lena Rice	4–6, 8–6, 6–4
1890	Lena Rice d. M. Jacks	6–4, 6–1
1891	Lottie Dod d. Blanche Bingley Hillyard	6–2, 6–1
1892	Lottie Dod d. Blanche Bingley Hillyard	6–1, 6–1
1893	Lottie Dod d. Blanche Bingley Hillyard	6–8, 6–1, 6–4
1894	Blanche Bingley Hillyard d. Edith Austin	6–1, 6–1
1895	Charlotte Cooper d. Helen Jackson	7–5, 8–6
1896	Charlotte Cooper d. Alice Simpson Pickering	6–2, 6–3
1897	Blanche Bingley Hillyard d. Charlotte Cooper	5–7, 7–5, 6–2
1898	Charlotte Cooper d. Louise Martin	6–4, 6–4
1899	Blanche Bingley Hillyard d. Charlotte Cooper	6–2, 6–3
1900	Blanche Bingley Hillyard d. Charlotte Cooper	4–6, 6–4, 6–4
1901	Charlotte Cooper Sterry d. Blanche Bingley Hillyard	6–2, 6–2
1902	Muriel Robb d. Charlotte Cooper Sterry	7–5, 6–1
1903	Dorothea Douglass d. Ethel Thomson	4–6, 6–4, 6–2

Year	*Final Round Results*	*Scores*
1904	Dorothea Douglass d. Charlotte Cooper Sterry	6–0, 6–3
1905	May Sutton d. Dorothea Douglass	6–3, 6–4
1906	Dorothea Douglass d. May Sutton	6–3, 9–7
1907	May Sutton d. Dorothea Douglass Lambert Chambers	6–1, 6–4
1908	Charlotte Cooper Sterry d. Agnes Morton	6–4, 6–4
1909	Dora Boothby d. Agnes Morton	6–4, 4–6, 8–6
1910	Dorothea Douglass Lambert Chambers d. Dora Boothby	6–2, 6–2
1911	Dorothea Douglass Lambert Chambers d. Dora Boothby	6–0, 6–0
1912	Ethel Thomson Larcombe d. Charlotte Cooper Sterry	6–3, 6–1
1913	Dorothea Douglass Lambert Chambers d. Winifred Slocock McNair	6–0, 6–4
1914	Dorothea Douglass Lambert Chambers d. Ethel Thomson Larcombe	7–5, 6–4
1915–1918	Not held because of World War I	
1919	Suzanne Lenglen d. Dorothea Douglass Lambert Chambers	10–8, 4–6, 9–7
1920	Suzanne Lenglen d. Dorothea Douglass Lambert Chambers	6–3, 6–0
1921	Suzanne Lenglen d. Elizabeth Ryan	6–2, 6–0
1922	Suzanne Lenglen d. Molla Bjurstedt Mallory	6–2, 6–0
1923	Suzanne Lenglen d. Kitty McKane	6–2, 6–2
1924	Kitty McKane d. Helen Wills	4–6, 6–4, 6–4
1925	Suzanne Lenglen d. Joan Fry	6–2, 6–0
1926	Kitty McKane Godfree d. Lili de Alvarez	6–2, 4–6, 6–3
1927	Helen Wills d. Lili de Alvarez	6–2, 6–4
1928	Helen Wills d. Lili de Alvarez	6–2, 6–3
1929	Helen Wills d. Helen Jacobs	6–1, 6–2
1930	Helen Wills Moody d. Elizabeth Ryan	6–2, 6–2
1931	Cilly Aussem d. Hilde Krahwinkel	6–2, 7–5
1932	Helen Wills Moody d. Helen Jacobs	6–3, 6–1
1933	Helen Wills Moody d. Dorothy Round	6–4, 6–8, 6–3
1934	Dorothy Round d. Helen Jacobs	6–2, 5–7, 6–3
1935	Helen Wills Moody d. Helen Jacobs	6–3, 3–6, 7–5
1936	Helen Jacobs d. Hilde Krahwinkel Sperling	6–2, 4–6, 7–5
1937	Dorothy Round d. Jadwiga Jedrzejowska	6–2, 2–6, 7–5
1938	Helen Wills Moody d. Helen Jacobs	6–4, 6–0
1939	Alice Marble d. Kay Stammers	6–2, 6–0
1940–1945	Not held because of World War II	
1946	Pauline Betz d. Louise Brough	6–2, 6–4
1947	Margaret Osborne d. Doris Hart	6–2, 6–4
1948	Louise Brough d. Doris Hart	6–3, 8–6
1949	Louise Brough d. Margaret Osborne duPont	10–8, 1–6, 10–8
1950	Louise Brough d. Margaret Osborne duPont	6–1, 3–6, 6–1
1951	Doris Hart d. Shirley Fry	6–1, 6–0
1952	Maureen Connolly d. Louise Brough	7–5, 6–3
1953	Maureen Connolly d. Doris Hart	8–6, 7–5
1954	Maureen Connolly d. Louise Brough	6–2, 7–5

Year	Final Round Results	Scores
1955	Louise Brough d. Beverly Baker Fleitz	7–5, 8–6
1956	Shirley Fry d. Angela Buxton	6–3, 6–1
1957	Althea Gibson d. Darlene Hard	6–3, 6–2
1958	Althea Gibson d. Angela Mortimer	8–6, 6–2
1959	Maria Bueno d. Darlene Hard	6–4, 6–3
1960	Maria Bueno d. Sandra Reynolds	8–6, 6–0
1961	Angela Mortimer d. Christine Truman	4–6, 6–4, 7–5
1962	Karen Hantze Susman d. Vera Sukova	6–4, 6–4
1963	Margaret Smith d. Billie Jean King	6–3, 6–4
1964	Maria Bueno d. Margaret Smith	6–4, 7–9, 6–3
1965	Margaret Smith d. Maria Bueno	6–4, 7–5
1966	Billie Jean King d. Maria Bueno	6–3, 3–6, 6–1
1967	Billie Jean King d. Ann Haydon Jones	6–3, 6–4
1968	Billie Jean King d. Judy Tegart	9–7, 7–5
1969	Ann Haydon Jones d. Billie Jean King	3–6, 6–3, 6–2
1970	Margaret Smith Court d. Billie Jean King	14–12, 11–9
1971	Evonne Goolagong d. Margaret Smith Court	6–4, 6–1
1972	Billie Jean King d. Evonne Goolagong	6–3, 6–3
1973	Billie Jean King d. Chris Evert	6–0, 7–5
1974	Chris Evert d. Olga Morozova	6–0, 6–4
1975	Billie Jean King d. Evonne Goolagong Cawley	6–0, 6–1
1976	Chris Evert d. Evonne Goolagong Cawley	6–3, 4–6, 8–6
1977	Virginia Wade d. Betty Stove	4–6, 6–3, 6–1
1978	Martina Navratilova d. Chris Evert	2–6, 6–4, 7–5
1979	Martina Navratilova d. Chris Evert	6–4, 6–4
1980	Evonne Goolagong Cawley d. Chris Evert	6–1, 7–6 (4)
1981	Chris Evert d. Hana Mandlikova	6–2, 6–2
1982	Martina Navratilova d. Chris Evert	6–1, 3–6, 6–2
1983	Martina Navratilova d. Andrea Jaeger	6–0, 6–3
1984	Martina Navratilova d. Chris Evert	7–6 (5), 6–2
1985	Martina Navratilova d. Chris Evert	4–6, 6–3, 6–2
1986	Martina Navratilova d. Hana Mandlikova	7–6 (1), 6–3
1987	Martina Navratilova d. Steffi Graf	7–5, 6–3
1988	Steffi Graf d. Martina Navratilova	5–7, 6–2, 6–1
1989	Steffi Graf d. Martina Navratilova	6–2, 6–7 (1), 6–1
1990	Martina Navratilova d. Zina Garrison	6–4, 6–1
1991	Steffi Graf d. Gabriela Sabatini	6–4, 3–6, 8–6
1992	Steffi Graf d. Monica Seles	6–2, 6–1
1993	Steffi Graf d. Jana Novotna	7–6 (6), 1–6, 6–4
1994	Conchita Martinez d. Martina Navratilova	6–4, 3–6, 6–3
1995	Steffi Graf d. Arantxa Sanchez-Vicario	4–6, 6–1, 7–5
1996	Steffi Graf d. Arantxa Sanchez-Vicario	6–3, 7–5
1997	Martina Hingis d. Jana Novotna	2–6, 6–3, 6–3
1998	Jana Novotna d. Nathalie Tauziat	6–4, 7–6 (2)
1999	Lindsay Davenport d. Steffi Graf	6–7 (3), 6–4, 6–3
2000	Venus Williams d. Lindsay Davenport	6–3, 7–6 (3)
2001	Venus Williams d. Justin Henin	6–1, 3–6, 6–0
2002	Serena Williams d. Venus Williams	7–5, 6–3
2003	Serena Williams d. Venus Williams	4–6, 6–4, 6–2

Year	Final Round Results	Scores
2004	Maria Sharapova d. Serena Williams	6–1, 6–4
2005	Venus Williams d. Lindsay Davenport	4–6, 7–6 (4), 9–7
2006	Amelia Mauresmo d. Justine Henin	2–6, 6–3, 6–4
2007	Venus Williams d. Marion Bartoli	6–4, 6–1
2008	Venus Williams d. Serena Williams	7–5, 6–4

Women's Doubles

Year	Final Round Results	Scores
1913	Winifred Slocock McNair, Dora Boothby d. Charlotte Cooper Sterry, Dorothea Douglass Lambert Chambers	4–6, 2–4, retired
1914	Agnes Morton, Elizabeth Ryan d. Edith Boucher Hannam, Ethel Thompson Larcombe	6–1, 6–3
1915–1918	Not held because of World War I	
1919	Suzanne Lenglen, Elizabeth Ryan d. Dorothea Douglass Lambert Chambers, Ethel Thompson Larcombe	4–6, 7–5, 6–3
1920	Suzanne Lenglen, Elizabeth Ryan d. Dorothea Douglass Lambert Chambers, Ethel Thompson Larcombe	6–4, 6–0
1921	Suzanne Lenglen, Elizabeth Ryan d. Geraldine Ramsey Beamish, Irene Peacock	6–1, 6–2
1922	Suzanne Lenglen, Elizabeth Ryan d. Kitty McKane, Margaret McKane Stocks	6–0, 6–4
1923	Suzanne Lenglen, Elizabeth Ryan d. Joan Austin, Evelyn Colyer	6–3, 6–1
1924	Hazel Hotchkiss Wightman, Helen Wills d. Phyllis Howkins Covell, Kitty McKane	6–4, 6–4
1925	Suzanne Lenglen, Elizabeth Ryan d. Kathleen Lidderdale Bridge, Mary McIlquham	6–2, 6–2
1926	Mary K. Browne, Elizabeth Ryan d. Kitty McKane Godfree, Evelyn Colyer	6–1, 6–1
1927	Helen Wills, Elizabeth Ryan d. Bobbie Heine, Irene Peacock	6–3, 6–2
1928	Peggy Saunders, Phoebe Holcroft Watson d. Eileen Bennett, Ermyntrude Harvey	6–2, 6–3
1929	Peggy Saunders Michell, Phoebe Holcroft Watson d. Phyllis Howkins Covell, Dorothy Shepherd Barron	6–4, 8–6
1930	Helen Wills Moody, Elizabeth Ryan d. Edith Cross, Sarah Palfrey	6–2, 9–7
1931	Dorothy Shepherd Barron, Phyllis Mudford d. Doris Metaxa, Josane Sigart	3–6, 6–3, 6–4
1932	Doris Metaxa, Josane Sigart d. Helen Jacobs, Elizabeth Ryan	6–4, 6–3
1933	Simone Passemard Mathieu, Elizabeth Ryan d. Freda James, Adeline Yorke	6–2, 9–11, 6–4

Year	Final Round Results	Scores
1934	Simone Passemard Mathieu, Elizabeth Ryan d. Dorothy Burke Andrus, Sylvie Jung Henrotin	6–3, 6–3
1935	Freda James, Kay Stammers d. Simone Passemard Mathieu, Hilde Krahwinkel Sperling	6–1, 6–4
1936	Freda James, Kay Stammers d. Sarah Palfrey Fabyan, Helen Jacobs	6–2, 6–1
1937	Simone Passemard Mathieu, Adeline Yorke d. Phyllis Mudford King, Elsie Goldsack Pittman	6–3, 6–3
1938	Sarah Palfrey Fabyan, Alice Marble d. Simone Passemard Mathieu, Adeline Yorke	6–2, 6–3
1939	Sarah Palfrey Fabyan, Alice Marble d. Helen Jacobs, Adeline Yorke	6–1, 6–0
1940–1945	Not held because of World War II	
1946	Louise Brough, Margaret Osborne d. Pauline Betz, Doris Hart	6–3, 2–6, 6–3
1947	Doris Hart, Patricia Canning Todd d. Louise Brough, Margaret Osborne	3–6, 6–4, 7–5
1948	Louise Brough, Margaret Osborne duPont d. Doris Hart, Patricia Canning Todd	6–3, 3–6, 6–3
1949	Louise Brough, Margaret Osborne duPont d. Gertrude Moran, Patricia Canning Todd	8–6, 7–5
1950	Louise Brough, Margaret Osborne duPont d. Shirley Fry, Doris Hart	6–4, 5–7, 6–1
1951	Shirley Fry, Doris Hart d. Louise Brough, Margaret Osborne duPont	6–3, 13–11
1952	Shirley Fry, Doris Hart d. Louise Brough, Maureen Connolly	8–6, 6–3
1953	Shirley Fry, Doris Hart d. Maureen Connolly, Julia Sampson	6–0, 6–0
1954	Louise Brough, Margaret Osborne duPont d. Shirley Fry, Doris Hart	4–6, 9–7, 6–3
1955	Angela Mortimer, Anne Shilcock d. Shirley Bloomer, Pat Ward	7–5, 6–1
1956	Angela Buxton, Althea Gibson d. Fay Muller, Daphne Seeney	6–1, 8–6
1957	Althea Gibson, Darlene Hard d. Mary Hawton, Thelma Coyne Long	6–1, 6–2
1958	Maria Bueno, Althea Gibson d. Margaret Osborne duPont, Margaret Varner	6–3, 7–5
1959	Jeanne Arth, Darlene Hard d. Beverly Baker Fleitz, Christine Truman	2–6, 6–2, 6–3
1960	Maria Bueno, Darlene Hard d. Sandra Reynolds, Renee Schuurman	6–4, 6–0
1961	Karen Hantze, Billie Jean King d. Jan Lehane, Margaret Smith	6–3, 6–4
1962	Billie Jean King, Karen Hantze d. Sandra Reynolds Price, Renee Schuurma	5–7, 6–3, 7–5

Year	Final Round Results	Scores
1963	Maria Bueno, Darlene Hard	
	d. Robyn Ebbern, Margaret Smith	8–6, 9–7
1964	Margaret Smith, Lesley Turner	
	d. Billie Jean King, Karen Hantze Susman	7–5, 6–2
1965	Maria Bueno, Billie Jean King	
	d. Francoise Durr, Jeanine Lieffrig	6–2, 7–5
1966	Maria Bueno, Nancy Richey	
	d. Margaret Smith, Judy Tegart	6–3, 4–6, 6–4
1967	Rosie Casals, Billie Jean King	
	d. Maria Bueno Nancy Richey	9–11, 6–4, 6–2
1968	Rosie Casals, Billie Jean King	
	d. Francoise Durr, Ann Haydon Jones	3–6, 6–4, 7–5
1969	Margaret Smith Court, Judy Tegart	
	d. Patty Hogan, Peggy Michel	9–7, 6–2
1970	Rosie Casals, Billie Jean King	
	d. Francoise Durr, Virginia Wade	6–2, 6–3
1971	Rosie Casals, Billie Jean King	
	d. Margaret Smith Court, Evonne Goolagong	6–3, 6–2
1972	Billie Jean King, Betty Stove	
	d. Judy Tegart, Francoise Durr	6–2, 4–6, 6–3
1973	Rosie Casals, Billie Jean King	
	d. Francoise Durr, Betty Stove	6–1, 4–6, 7–5
1974	Evonne Goolagong, Peggy Michel	
	d. Helen Gourlay, Karen Krantzcke	2–6, 6–4, 6–3
1975	Ann Kiyomura, Kazuko Sawamatsu	
	d. Francoise Durr, Betty Stove	7–5, 1–6, 7–5
1976	Chris Evert, Martina Navratilova	
	d. Billie Jean King, Betty Stove	6–1, 3–6, 7–5
1977	Helen Gourlay Cawley, JoAnne Russell	
	d. Martina Navratilova, Betty Stove	6–3, 6–3
1978	Kerry Melville Reid, Wendy Turnbull	
	d. Mima Jausovec, Virginia Ruzici	4–6, 9–8 (10), 6–3
1979	Billie Jean King, Martina Navratilova	
	d. Betty Stove, Wendy Turnbull	5–7, 6–3, 6–2
1980	Kathy Jordon, Anne Smith	
	d. Rosie Casals, Wendy Turnbull	4–6, 7–5, 6–1
1981	Martina Navratilova, Pam Shriver	
	d. Kathy Jordan, Anne Smith	6–3, 7–6 (6)
1982	Martina Navratilova, Pam Shriver	
	d. Kathy Jordan, Anne Smith	6–4, 6–1
1983	Martina Navratilova, Pam Shriver	
	d. Rosie Casals, Wendy Turnbull	6–2, 6–2
1984	Martina Navratilova, Pam Shriver	
	d. Kathy Jordan, Anne Smith	6–3, 6–4
1985	Kathy Jordan, Elizabeth Sayers Smylie	
	d. Martina Navratilova, Pam Shriver	5–7, 6–3, 6–4
1986	Martina Navratilova, Pam Shriver	
	d. Hana Mandlikova, Wendy Turnbull	6–1, 6–3

Year	Final Round Results	Scores
1987	Claudia Kohde-Kilsch, Helena Sukova	
	d. Betsy Nagelsen, Elizabeth Sayers Smylie	7–5, 7–5
1988	Steffi Graf, Gabriela Sabatini	
	d. Larisa Savchenko, Natasha Zvereva	6–3, 1–6, 12–10
1989	Jana Novotna, Helena Sukova	
	d. Larisa Savchenko, Natasha Zvereva	6–1, 6–2
1990	Jana Novotna, Helena Sukova	
	d. Kathy Jordan, Elizabeth Sayers Smylie	6–3, 6–4
1991	Larisa Savchenko, Natasha Zvereva	
	d. Gigi Fernandez, Jana Novotna	6–4, 3–6, 6–4
1992	Gigi Fernandez, Natasha Zvereva	
	d. Jana Novotna, Larisa Savchenko Neiland	6–4, 6–1
1993	Gigi Fernandez, Natasha Zvereva	
	d. Jana Novotna, Larisa Savchenko Neiland	6–4, 6–7 (4), 6–4
1994	Gigi Fernandez, Natasha Zvereva	
	d. Jana Novotna, Arantxa Sanchez-Vicario	6–4, 6–1
1995	Jana Novotna, Arantxa Sanchez-Vicario	
	d. Gigi Fernandez, Natasha Zvereva	5–7, 7–5, 6–4
1996	Martina Hingis, Helena Sukova	
	d. Meredith McGrath, Larisa Savchenko Neiland	5–7, 7–5, 6–1
1997	Gigi Fernandez, Natasha Zvereva	
	d. Manon Bellegraf, Nicole Arendt	7–6 (4), 6–4
1998	Martina Hingis, Jana Novotna	
	d. Lindsay Davenport, Natasha Zvereva	6–3, 3–6, 8–6
1999	Lindsay Davenport, Corina Morariu	
	d. Mariaan DeSwardt, Elena Tatarkova	6–4, 6–4
2000	Serena Williams, Venus Williams	
	d. Julie Halard-Decugis, Ai Sugiyama	6–3, 6–2
2001	Lisa Raymond, Rennae Stubbs	
	d. Kim Clijsters, Ai Sugiyama	6–4, 6–3
2002	Serena Williams, Venus Williams	
	d. Virginia Ruano Pascual, Paola Suarez	6–2, 7–5
2003	Kim Clijsters, Ai Sugiyama	
	d. Virginia Ruano Pascual, Paola Suarez	6–4, 6–4
2004	Cara Black, Rennae Stubbs	
	d. Liezel Huber, Ai Sugiyama	6–3, 7–6 (5)
2005	Cara Black, Liezel Huber	
	d. Svetlana Kuznetsova, Amelie Mauresmo	6–2, 6–1
2006	Zi Yan, Jie Zheng	
	d. Virginia Ruano Pascual, Paola Suarez	6–3, 3–6, 6–2
2007	Cara Black, Liezel Huber	
	d. Ai Sugiyama, Katarina Srebotnik	3–6, 6–3, 6–2
2008	Serena Williams, Venus Williams	
	d. Lisa Raymond, Samantha Stosur	6–2, 6–2

Mixed Doubles

Year	Final Round Results	Scores
1913	Agnes Daniell Tuckey, J. Hope Crisp	
	d. Ethel Thompson Larcombe, James Parke	3–6, 5–3 (retired)

Year	Final Round Results	Scores
1914	Ethel Thompson Larcombe, Cecil Parke	
	d. Marguerite Broquedis, Tony Wilding	4–6, 6–4, 6–2
1915–1918	Not held because of World War I	
1919	Elizabeth Ryan, Randolph Lycett	
	d. Dorothea Douglass Lambert Chambers,	
	Albert Prebble	6–0, 6–0
1920	Suzanne Lenglen, Gerald Patterson	
	d. Elizabeth Ryan, Randolph Lycett	7–5, 6–3
1921	Elizabeth Ryan, Randolph Lycett	
	d. Phyllis Howkins, Max Woosnam	6–3, 6–1
1922	Suzanne Lenglen, Pat O'Hara Wood	
	d. Elizabeth Ryan, Randolph Lycett	6–4, 6–3
1923	Elizabeth Ryan, Randolph Lycett	
	d. Dorothy Shepherd Barron, Lewis Deane	6–4, 7–5
1924	Kitty McKane, J. Brian Gilbert	
	d. Dorothy Shephard Barron, Leslie Godfree	6–3, 3–6, 6–3
1925	Suzanne Lenglen, Jean Borotra	
	d. Elizabeth Ryan, Umberto de Morpurgo	6–3, 6–3
1926	Kitty McKane Godfree, Leslie Godfree	
	d. Mary K. Browne, Howard Kinsey	6–3, 6–4
1927	Elizabeth Ryan, Frank Hunter	
	d. Kitty McKane Godfree, Leslie Godfree	8–6, 6–0
1928	Elizabeth Ryan, Pat Spence	
	d. Daphne Akhurst, Jack Crawford	7–5, 6–4
1929	Helen Wills, Frank Hunter d. Joan Fry, Ian Collins	6–1, 6–4
1930	Elizabeth Ryan, Jack Crawford	
	d. Hilde Krahwinkel, Daniel Prenn	6–1, 6–3
1931	Anna McCune Harper, George Lott	
	d. Joan Ridley, Ian Collins	6–3, 1–6, 6–1
1932	Elizabeth Ryan, Enrique Maier	
	d. Josane Sigart, Harry Hopman	7–5, 6–2
1933	Hilde Krahwinkel, Gottfried von Cramm	
	d. Mary Heeley, Norman Farquharson	7–5, 8–6
1934	Dorothy Round, Ryuki Miki	
	d. Dorothy Shepherd Barron, Henry "Bunny" Austin	3–6, 6–4, 6–0
1935	Dorothy Round, Fred Perry	
	d. Nell Hall Hopman, Harry Hopman	7–5, 4–6, 6–2
1936	Dorothy Round, Fred Perry	
	d. Sarah Palfrey Fabyan, Don Budge	7–9, 7–5, 6–4
1937	Alice Marble, Don Budge	
	d. Simone Passemard Mathieu, Yvon Petra	6–4, 6–1
1938	Alice Marble, Don Budge	
	d. Sarah Palfrey Fabyan, Henner Henkel	6–1, 6–4
1939	Alice Marble, Bobby Riggs	
	d. Nina Brown, Frank Wilde	9–7, 6–1
1940–1945	Not held because of World War II	
1946	Louise Brough, Tom Brown	
	d. Dorothy Bundy, Goeff Brown	6–4, 6–4

Year	*Final Round Results*	*Scores*
1947	Louise Brough, John Bromwich	
	d. Nancye Wynne Bolton, Colin Long	1–6, 6–4, 6–2
1948	Louise Brough, John Bromwich	
	d. Doris Hart, Frank Sedgman	6–2, 3–6, 6–3
1949	Sheila Piercey Summers, Eric Sturgess	
	d. Louise Brough, John Bromwich	9–7, 9–11, 7–5
1950	Louise Brough, Eric Sturgess	
	d. Pat Canning Todd, Geoff Brown	11–9, 1–6, 6–4
1951	Doris Hart, Frank Sedgman	
	d. Nancye Wynne Bolton, Mervyn Rose	7–5, 6–2
1952	Doris Hart, Frank Sedgman	
	d. Thelma Coyne Long, Enrique Morea	4–6, 6–3, 6–4
1953	Doris Hart, Vic Seixas d. Shirley Fry, Enrique Morea	9–7, 7–5
1954	Doris Hart, Vic Seixas	
	d. Margaret Osborne duPont, Ken Rosewall	5–7, 6–4, 6–3
1955	Doris Hart, Vic Seixas	
	d. Louise Brough, Enrique Morea	8–6, 2–6, 6–3
1956	Shirley Fry, Vic Seixas	
	d. Althea Gibson, Gardnar Mulloy	2–6, 6–2, 7–5
1957	Darlene Hard, Mervyn Rose	
	d. Althea Gibson, Neale Fraser	6–4, 7–5
1958	Lorraine Coghlan, Bob Howe	
	d. Althea Gibson, Kurt Nielsen	6–3, 13–11
1959	Darlene Hard, Rod Laver d. Maria Bueno, Neale Fraser	6–4, 6–3
1960	Darlene Hard, Rod Laver d. Maria Bueno, Bob Howe	13–11, 3–6, 8–6
1961	Lesley Turner, Fred Stolle d. Edda Buding, Bob Howe	11–9, 6–2
1962	Margaret Osborne duPont, Neale Fraser	
	d. Ann Haydon, Dennis Ralston	2–6, 6–3, 13–11
1963	Margaret Smith, Ken Fletcher	
	d. Darlene Hard, Bob Hewitt	11–9, 6–4
1964	Lesley Turner, Fred Stolle	
	d. Margaret Smith, Ken Fletcher	6–4, 6–4
1965	Margaret Smith, Ken Fletcher	
	d. Judy Tegart, Tony Roche	12–10, 6–3
1966	Margaret Smith, Ken Fletcher	
	d. Billie Jean King, Dennis Ralston	4–6, 6–3, 6–3
1967	Billie Jean King, Owen Davidson	
	d. Maria Bueno, Ken Fletcher	7–5, 6–2
1968	Margaret Smith Court, Ken Fletcher	
	d. Olga Morozova, Alex Metreveli	6–1, 14–12
1969	Ann Haydon Jones, Fred Stolle	
	d. Judy Tegart, Tony Roche	6–3, 6–2
1970	Rosemary Casals, Ilie Nastase	
	d. Olga Morozova, Alex Metreveli	6–3, 4–6, 9–7
1971	Billie Jean King, Owen Davidson	
	d. Margaret Smith Court, Martin Riessen	3–6, 6–2, 15–13
1972	Rosemary Casals, Ilie Nastase	
	d. Evonne Goolagong, Kim Warwick	6–4, 6–4

Year	Final Round Results	Scores
1973	Billie Jean King, Owen Davidson	
	d. Janet Newberry, Raul Ramirez	6–3, 6–2
1974	Billie Jean King, Owen Davidson	
	d. Lesley Charles, Mark Farrell	6–3, 9–7
1975	Margaret Smith Court, Martin Riessen	
	d. Betty Stove, Allan Stone	6–4, 7–5
1976	Francoise Durr, Tony Roche	
	d. Rosemary Casals, Dick Stockton	6–3, 2–6, 7–5
1977	Greer Stevens, Bob Hewitt	
	d. Betty Stove, Frew McMillan	3–6, 7–5, 6–4
1978	Betty Stove, Frew McMillan	
	d. Billie Jean King, Ray Ruffels	6–2, 6–2
1979	Greer Stevens, Bob Hewitt	
	d. Betty Stove, Frew McMillan	7–5, 7–6 (7)
1980	Tracy Austin, John Austin	
	d. Dianne Fromholtz, Mark Edmondson	4–6, 7–6 (6), 6–3
1981	Betty Stove, Frew McMillan	
	d. Tracy Austin, John Austin	4–6, 7–6 (2), 6–3
1982	Anne Smith, Kevin Curren	
	d. Wendy Turnbull, John Lloyd	2–6, 6–3, 7–5
1983	Wendy Turnbull, John Lloyd	
	d. Billie Jean King, Steve Denton	6–7 (5), 7–6 (5), 7–5
1984	Wendy Turnbull, John Lloyd	
	d. Kathy Jordan, Steve Denton	6–3, 6–3
1985	Martina Navratilova, Paul McNamee	
	d. Elizabeth Sayers Smylie, John Fitzgerald	7–5, 4–6, 6–2
1986	Kathy Jordan, Ken Flach	
	d. Martina Navratilova, Heinz Gunthardt	6–3, 7–6 (7)
1987	Jo Durie, Jeremy Bates d. Nicole Provis, Darren Cahill	7–6 (10), 6–3
1988	Zina Garrison, Sherwood Stewart	
	d. Gretchen Rush Magers, Kelly Jones	6–1, 7–6 (3)
1989	Jana Novotna, Jim Pugh	
	d. Jenny Byrne, Mark Kratzmann	6–4, 5–7, 6–4
1990	Zina Garrison, Rick Leach	
	d. Elizabeth Sayers Smylie, John Fitzgerald	7–5, 6–2
1991	Elizabeth Sayers Smylie, John Fitzgerald	
	d. Natasha Zvereva, Jim Pugh	7–6 (4), 6–2
1992	Larisa Savchenko Neiland, Cyril Suk	
	d. Miriam Oremans, Jacco Eltingh	7–6 (2), 6–2
1993	Martina Navratilova, Mark Woodforde	
	d. Manon Bollegraf, Tom Nijssen	6–3, 6–4
1994	Helena Sukova, Todd Woodbridge	
	d. Lori McNeil, T.J. Middleton	3–6, 7–5, 6–3
1995	Martina Navratilova, Jonathan Stark	
	d. Gigi Fernandez, Cyril Suk	6–4, 6–4
1996	Helena Sukova, Cyril Suk	
	d. Larisa Savchenko Neiland, Mark Woodforde	1–6, 6–3, 6–2
1997	Helena Sukova, Cyril Suk	
	d. Larisa Savchenko Neiland, Andrei Olhovskiy	4–6, 6–3, 6–4

Year	Final Round Results	Scores
1998	Serena Williams, Max Mirnyi	
	d. Mirjana Lucic, Mahesh Bhupathi	6–4, 6–4
1999	Lisa Raymond, Leander Paes	
	d. Anna Kournikova, Jonas Bjorkman	6–4, 3–6, 6–3
2000	Kimberly Po, Donald Johnson	
	d. Kim Clijsters, Lleyton Hewitt	6–4, 7–6 (3)
2001	Daniela Hantuchova, Leos Friedl	
	d. Liezel Huber, Mike Bryan	4–6, 6–3, 6–2
2002	Elena Likhovtseva, Mahesh Bhupathi	
	d. Daniela Hantuchova, Kevin Ullyett	6–2, 1–6, 6–1
2003	Martina Navratilova, Leander Paes	
	d. Anastassia Rodionova, Andy Ram	6–3, 6–3
2004	Cara Black, Wayne Black	
	d. Alicia Molik, Todd Woodbridge	3–6, 7–6 (8), 6–4
2005	Mary Pierce, Mahesh Bhupathi	
	d. Tatiana Perebiynis, Paul Hanley	6–4, 6–2
2006	Vera Zvonareva, Andy Ram	
	d. Venus Williams, Bob Bryan	6–3, 6–2
2007	Jelena Jankovic, Jamie Murray	
	d. Alicia Molik, Jonas Bjorkman	6–4, 3–6, 6–1
2008	Samantha Stosur, Bob Bryan	
	d. Katarina Srebotnik, Mike Bryan	7–5, 6–4

The United States Championships

The United States Championships date back to 1881, when the first men's tournament was played at the Newport Casino in Newport, Rhode Island. The women's championships in singles and doubles began at the Philadelphia Cricket Club in 1887 and 1889 respectively. Mixed doubles competition began in 1892. The women's and mixed doubles championships remained at the Philadelphia Cricket Club until 1921, when the singles and doubles events were moved to Forest Hills. The mixed doubles moved to the Longwood Cricket Club in Boston, where it was played along with the men's doubles. Until 1919, the defending champion did not have to play through the early rounds of the tournament. She stood by as the other competitors played in an elimination tourney called the All-Comers to determine who would meet the defending champion in the finals.

In 1935 the men's and women's singles championships were both played at Forest Hills, but the women's doubles moved to Longwood to join the men's doubles and mixed doubles events. From 1942 to 1945 all five events were played at Forest Hills. In 1946, the women's doubles moved back to Longwood.

The U.S. Championships was a segregated event before Althea Gibson broke the color barrier. On August 28, 1950, she made her historic debut by defeating Barbara Knapp 6–2, 6–2. Gibson was eliminated, however, in the next round. Gibson became the first black champion at Forest

Hills in 1957 when she defeated Louise Brough in the finals 6–3, 6–2. She successfully defended her American title in 1958.

The first U.S. Open was played at Forest Hills in 1968 when amateur and professional tennis players competed together for the first time in an American tournament. But the USTA decided to maintain a second tournament to crown an amateur national champion. The twin tournament format was abandoned after the 1969 season. The championships were played on grass until 1975, when the court surface at Forest Hills was changed to red clay. The U.S. Open moved to its current home, Flushing Meadows, in 1978. Since 1978, the tournament has been played on a hard, asphalt-like composition called Deco Turf II at Flushing Meadows in New York. In 2005, the USTA changed the tennis court color from green to blue to allow for a better viewer image during television broadcasts. In 2006, the U.S. Open became the first Grand Slam tournament in history to use electronic review technology and on-court player challenges.

Women's Singles

Year	Final Round Results	Scores
1887	Ellen Hansell d. Laura Knight	6–1, 6–0
1888	Bertha Townsend d. Ellen Hansell	6–3, 6–5
1889	Bertha Townsend d. Lida Voorhees	7–5, 6–2
1890	Ellen Roosevelt d. Bertha Townsend	6–2, 6–2
1891	Mabel Cahill d. Ellen Roosevelt	6–4, 6–1, 4–6, 6–3
1892	Mabel Cahill d. Elisabeth Moore	5–7, 6–3, 6–4, 4–6, 6–2
1893	Aline Terry d. Augusta Schultz	6–1, 6–3
1894	Helena Hellwig d. Aline Terry	7–5, 3–6, 6–0, 3–6, 6–3
1895	Juliette Atkinson d. Helena Hellwig	6–4, 6–1, 6–2
1896	Elisabeth Moore d. Juliette Atkinson	6–4, 4–6, 6–2, 6–2
1897	Juliette Atkinson d. Elisabeth Moore	6–3, 6–3, 4–6, 3–6, 6–3
1898	Juliette Atkinson d. Marion Jones	6–3, 5–7, 6–4, 2–6, 7–5
1899	Marion Jones d. Maud Banks	6–1, 6–1, 7–5
1900	Myrtle McAteer d. Edith Parker	6–2, 6–2, 6–0
1901	Elisabeth Moore d. Myrtle McAteer	6–4, 3–6, 7–5, 2–6, 6–2
1902	Marion Jones d. Elisabeth Moore	6–1, 1–0 retired
1903	Elisabeth Moore d. Marion Jones	7–5, 8–6
1904	May Sutton d. Elisabeth Moore	6–1, 6–2
1905	Elisabeth Moore d. Helen Homans	6–4, 5–7, 6–1
1906	Helen Homans d. Maud Barger Wallach	6–4, 6–3
1907	Evelyn Sears d. Carrie Neely	6–3, 6–2
1908	Maud Barger Wallach d. Evelyn Sears	6–2, 1–6, 6–3
1909	Hazel Hotchkiss d. Maud Barger Wallach	6–0, 6–1
1910	Hazel Hotchkiss d. Louise Hammond	6–4, 6–2
1911	Hazel Hotchkiss d. Florence Sutton	8–10, 6–1, 9–7
1912	Mary K. Browne d. Eleonora Sears	6–4, 6–2
1913	Mary K. Browne d. Dorothy Green	6–2, 7–5

Year	Final Round Results	Scores
1914	Mary K. Browne d. Marie Wagner	6–2, 1–6, 6–1
1915	Molla Bjurstedt d. Hazel Hotchkiss Wightman	4–6, 6–2, 6–0
1916	Molla Bjurstedt d. Louise Hammond Raymond	6–0, 6–1
1917	Molla Bjurstedt d. Marion Vanderhoef	4–6, 6–0, 6–2
1918	Molla Bjurstedt d. Eleanor Goss	6–4, 6–3

1918 was the last year the Singles Championship was decided by the challenge round system in which the defending champion played only one match, waiting for a challenger to emerge from the All-Comers tournament.

Year	Final Round Results	Scores
1919	Hazel Hotchkiss Wightman d. Marion Zinderstein	6–1, 6–2
1920	Molla Bjurstedt Mallory d. Marion Zinderstein	6–3, 6–1
1921	Molla Bjurstedt Mallory d. Mary K. Browne	4–6, 6–4, 6–2
1922	Molla Bjurstedt Mallory d. Helen Wills	6–3, 6–1
1923	Helen Wills d. Molla Bjurstedt Mallory	6–2, 6–1
1924	Helen Wills d. Molla Bjurstedt Mallory	6–1, 6–3
1925	Helen Wills d. Kathleen McKane	3–6, 6–0, 6–2
1926	Molla Bjurstedt Mallory d. Elizabeth Ryan	4–6, 6–4, 9–7
1927	Helen Wills d. Betty Nuthall	6–1, 6–4
1928	Helen Wills d. Helen Jacobs	6–2, 6–1
1929	Helen Wills d. Phoebe Holcroft Watson	6–4, 6–2
1930	Betty Nuthall d. Anna McCune Harper	6–1, 6–4
1931	Helen Wills Moody d. Eileen Bennett Whitingstall	6–4, 6–1
1932	Helen Jacobs d. Carolin Babcock	6–2, 6–2
1933	Helen Jacobs d. Helen Wills Moody	8–6, 3–6, 3–0, retired
1934	Helen Jacobs d. Sarah Palfrey	6–1, 6–4
1935	Helen Jacobs d. Sarah Palfrey Fabyan	6–2, 6–4
1936	Alice Marble d. Helen Jacobs	4–6, 6–3, 6–2
1937	Anita Lizana d. Jadwiga Jedrzejowska	6–4, 6–2
1938	Alice Marble d. Nancye Wynne Bolton	6–0, 6–3
1939	Alice Marble d. Helen Jacobs	6–0, 8–10, 6–4
1940	Alice Marble d. Helen Jacobs	6–2, 6–3
1941	Sarah Palfrey Cooke d. Pauline Betz	7–5, 6–2
1942	Pauline Betz d. Louise Brough	4–6, 6–1, 6–4
1943	Pauline Betz d. Louise Brough	6–3, 5–7, 6–3
1944	Pauline Betz d. Margaret Osborne	6–3, 8–6
1945	Sarah Palfrey Cooke d. Pauline Betz	3–6, 8–6, 6–4
1946	Pauline Betz d. Doris Hart	11–9, 6–3
1947	Louise Brough d. Margaret Osborne	8–6, 4–6, 6–1
1948	Margaret Osborne duPont d. Louise Brough	4–6, 6–4, 15–13
1949	Margaret Osborne duPont d. Doris Hart	6–4, 6–1
1950	Margaret Osborne duPont d. Doris Hart	6–3, 6–3
1951	Maureen Connolly d. Shirley Fry	6–3, 1–6, 6–4
1952	Maureen Connolly d. Doris Hart	6–3, 7–5
1953	Maureen Connolly d. Doris Hart	6–2, 6–4
1954	Doris Hart d. Louise Brough	6–8, 6–1, 8–6
1955	Doris Hart d. Patricia Ward	6–4, 6–2
1956	Shirley Fry d. Althea Gibson	6–3, 6–4
1957	Althea Gibson d. Louise Brough	6–3, 6–2
1958	Althea Gibson d. Darlene Hard	3–6, 6–1, 6–2
1959	Maria Bueno d. Christine Truman	6–1, 6–4

Year	Final Round Results	Scores
1960	Darlene Hard d. Maria Bueno	6–4, 10–12, 6–4
1961	Darlene Hard d. Ann Haydon	6–3, 6–4
1962	Margaret Smith d. Darlene Hard	9–7, 6–4
1963	Maria Bueno d. Margaret Smith	7–5, 6–4
1964	Maria Bueno d. Carole Caldwell Graebner	6–1, 6–0
1965	Margaret Smith d. Billie Jean King	8–6, 7–5
1966	Maria Bueno d. Nancy Richey	6–3, 6–1
1967	Billie Jean King d. Ann Haydon Jones	11–9, 6–4
1968	Margaret Smith Court d. Maria Bueno (United States Lawn Tennis Association Championship, amateur)	6–2, 6–2
1968	Virginia Wade d. Billie Jean King (U.S. Open Championship, professional)	6–4, 6–2
1969	Margaret Smith Court d. Virginia Wade (United States Lawn Tennis Association Championship, amateur)	4–6, 6–3, 6–0
1969	Margaret Smith Court d. Nancy Richey (U.S. Open Championship, professional)	6–2, 6–2
1970	Margaret Smith Court d. Rosemary Casals	6–2, 2–6, 6–1
1971	Billie Jean King d. Rosemary Casals	6–4, 7–6 (2)
1972	Billie Jean King d. Kerry Melville	6–3, 7–5
1973	Margaret Smith Court d. Evonne Goolagong	7–6 (2), 5–7, 6–2
1974	Billie Jean King d. Evonne Goolagong	3–6, 6–3, 7–5
1975	Chris Evert d. Evonne Goolagong	5–7, 6–4, 6–2
1976	Chris Evert d. Evonne Goolagong	6–3, 6–0
1977	Chris Evert d. Wendy Turnbull	7–6 (3), 6–2
1978	Chris Evert d. Pam Shriver	7–5, 6–4
1979	Tracy Austin d. Chris Evert	6–4, 6–3
1980	Chris Evert d. Hana Mandlikova	5–7, 6–1, 6–1
1981	Tracy Austin d. Martina Navratilova	1–6, 7–6 (4), 7–6 (1)
1982	Chris Evert d. Hana Mandlikova	6–3, 6–1
1983	Martina Navratilova d. Chris Evert	6–1, 6–3
1984	Martina Navratilova d. Chris Evert	4–6, 6–4, 6–4
1985	Hana Mandlikova d. Martina Navratilova	7–6 (3), 1–6, 7–6 (2)
1986	Martina Navratilova d. Helena Sukova	6–3, 6–2
1987	Martina Navratilova d. Steffi Graf	7–6 (4), 6–1
1988	Steffi Graf d. Gabriela Sabatini	6–3, 3–6, 6–1
1989	Steffi Graf d. Martina Navratilova	3–6, 7–5, 6–1
1990	Gabriela Sabatini d. Steffi Graf	6–2, 7–6 (4)
1991	Monica Seles d. Martina Navratilova	7–6 (1), 6–1
1992	Monica Seles d. Arantxa Sanchez-Vicario	6–3, 6–3
1993	Steffi Graf d. Helena Sukova	6–3, 6–3
1994	Arantxa Sanchez-Vicario d. Steffi Graf	1–6, 7–6 (3), 6–4
1995	Steffi Graf d. Monica Seles	7–6 (6), 0–6, 6–3
1996	Steffi Graf d. Monica Seles	7–5, 6–3
1997	Martina Hingis d. Venus Williams	6–0, 6–4
1998	Lindsay Davenport d. Martina Hingis	6–3, 7–5
1999	Serena Williams d. Martina Hingis	6–3, 7–6 (4)
2000	Venus Williams d. Lindsay Davenport	6–4, 7–5

Year	Final Round Results	Scores
2001	Venus Williams d. Serena Williams	6–2, 6–4
2002	Serena Williams d. Venus Williams	6–4, 6–3
2003	Justine Henin d. Kim Clijsters	7–5, 6–1
2004	Svetlana Kuznetsova d. Elena Dementieva	6–3, 7–5
2005	Kim Clijsters d. Mary Pierce	6–3, 6–1
2006	Maria Sharapova d. Justine Henin	6–4, 6–4
2007	Justine Henin d. Svetlana Kuznetsova	6–1, 6–2
2008	Serena Williams d. Jelena Jankovic	6–4, 7–5

Women's Doubles

Year	Final Round Results	Scores
1889	Margarette Ballard, Bertha Townsend d. Marion Wright, Laura Knight	6–0, 6–2
1890	Ellen Roosevelt, Grace Roosevelt d. Bertha Townsend, Margarette Ballard	6–1, 6–2
1891	Mabel Cahill, Emma Leavitt Morgan d. Grace Roosevelt, Ellen Roosevelt	2–6, 8–6, 6–4
1892	Mabel Cahill, Adeline McKinlay d. Helen Day Harris, Amy Williams	6–1, 6–3
1893	Aline Terry, Hattie Butler d. Augusta Shultz, Miss Stone	6–4, 6–3
1894	Helen Hellwig, Juliette Atkinson d. Annabella Wistar, Amy Williams	6–4, 8–6, 6–2
1895	Helen Hellwig, Juliette Atkinson d. Elisabeth Moore, Amy Williams	6–2, 6–2, 12–10
1896	Elisabeth Moore, Juliette Atkinson d. Annabella Wistar, Amy Williams	6–4, 7–5
1897	Juliette Atkinson, Kathleen Atkinson d. Mrs. F. Edwards, Elizabeth Rastall	6–2, 6–1, 6–1
1898	Juliette Atkinson, Kathleen Atkinson d. Marie Wimer, Carrie Neely	6–1, 2–6, 4–6, 6–1, 6–2
1899	Jane Craven, Myrtle McAteer d. Maud Banks, Elizabeth Rastall	6–1, 6–1, 7–5
1900	Edith Parker, Hallie Champlin d. Marie Wimer, Myrtle McAteer	9–7, 6–2, 6–2
1901	Juliette Atkinson, Myrtle McAteer d. Marion Jones, Elisabeth Moore	default
1902	Juliette Atkinson, Marion Jones d. Maud Banks, Nona Closterman	6–2, 7–5
1903	Elisabeth Moore, Carrie Neely d. Miriam Hall, Marion Jones	6–4, 6–1, 6–1
1904	May Sutton, Miriam Hall d. Elisabeth Moore, Carrie Neely	3–6, 6–3, 6–3
1905	Helen Homans, Carrie Neely d. Marjorie Oberteuffer, Virginia Maule	6–0, 6–1
1906	Ann Burdette Coe, Mrs. D. Platt d. Helen Homans, Clover Boldt	6–4, 6–4
1907	Marie Wimer, Carrie Neely d. Edna Wildey, Natalie Wildey	6–1, 2–6, 6–4

Year	Final Round Results	Scores
1908	Evelyn Sears, Margaret Curtis	
	d. Carrie Neely, Marion Steever	6–3, 5–7, 9–7
1909	Hazel Hotchkiss, Edith Rotch	
	d. Dorothy Green, Lois Moyes	6–1, 6–1
1910	Hazel Hotchkiss, Edith Rotch	
	d. Adelaide Browning, Edna Wildey	6–4, 6–4
1911	Hazel Hotchkiss, Eleonora Sears	
	d. Dorothy Green, Florence Sutton	6–4, 4–6, 6–2
1912	Dorothy Green, Mary K. Browne	
	d. Maud Barger Wallach, Mrs. Frederick Schmitz	6–2, 5–7, 6–0
1913	Mary K. Browne, Louise Williams	
	d. Dorothy Green, Edna Wildey	12–10, 2–6, 6–3
1914	Mary K. Browne, Louise Williams	
	d. Louise Hammond Raymond, Edna Wildey	8–6, 6–2
1915	Hazel Hotchkiss Wightman, Eleonora Sears	
	d. Helen Homans McLean, Mrs. G. L. Chapman	10–8, 6–2
1916	Molla Bjurstedt, Eleonora Sears	
	d. Louise Hammond Raymond, Edna Wildey	4–6, 6–2, 10–8
1917	Molla Bjurstedt, Eleonora Sears	
	d. Phyllis Walsh, Mrs. Robert LeRoy	6–2, 6–4
1918	Marion Zinderstein, Eleanor Goss	
	d. Molla Bjurstedt, Mrs. Johan Rogge	7–5, 8–6
1919	Marion Zinderstein, Eleanor Goss	
	d. Eleanora Sears, Hazel Hotchkiss Wightman	10–8, 9–7
1920	Marion Zinderstein, Eleanor Goss	
	d. Eleanor Tennant, Helen Baker	6–3, 6–1
1921	Mary K. Browne, Mrs. R. H. Williams	
	d. Helen Gilleaudeau, Mrs. L. G. Morris	6–3, 6–2
1922	Marion Zinderstein Jessup, Helen Wills	
	d. Edith Sigourney, Molla Bjurstedt Mallory	6–4, 7–9, 6–3
1923	Kathleen McKane, Phyllis Hawkins Covell	
	d. Hazel Hotchkiss Wightman, Eleanor Goss	2–6, 6–2, 6–1
1924	Hazel Hotchkiss Wightman, Helen Wills	
	d. Eleanor Goss, Marion Zinderstein Jessup	6–4, 6–3
1925	Mary K. Browne, Helen Wills	
	d. May Sutton Bundy, Elizabeth Ryan	6–4, 6–3
1926	Elizabeth Ryan, Eleanor Goss	
	d. Mary K. Browne, Charlotte Hosmer Chapin	3–6, 6–4, 12–10
1927	Kathleen McKane Godfree, Ermyntrude Harvey	
	d. Betty Nuthall Joan Fry	6–1, 4–6, 6–4
1928	Hazel Hotchkiss Wightman, Helen Wills	
	d. Edith Cross, Anna McCune Harper	6–2, 6–2
1929	Phoebe Watson, Peggy S. Michell	
	d. Phyllis Hawkins Covell,	
	Dorothy Shepherd Barron	2–6, 6–3, 6–4
1930	Betty Nuthall, Sarah Palfrey	
	d. Edith Cross, Anna McCune Harper	3–6, 6–3, 7–5
1931	Betty Nuthall, Eileen B.Whittingstall	
	d. Helen Jacobs, Dorothy Round	6–2, 6–4

Year	Final Round Results	Scores
1932	Helen Jacobs, Sarah Palfrey	
	d. Edith Cross, Anna McCune Harper	3–6, 6–3, 7–5
1933	Betty Nuthall, Freda James	
	d. Helen Wills Moody, Elizabeth Ryan	default
1934	Helen Jacobs, Sarah Palfrey	
	d. Carolin Babcock, Dorothy Andrus	4–6, 6–3, 6–4
1935	Helen Jacobs, Sarah Palfrey Fabyan	
	d. Carolin Babcock, Dorothy Andrus	6–4, 6–2
1936	Marjorie Gladman Van Ryn, Carolin Babcock	
	d. Helen Jacobs, Sarah Palfrey Fabyan	9–7, 2–6, 6–4
1937	Sarah Palfrey Fabyan, Alice Marble	
	d. Marjorie Gladman Van Ryn, Carolin Babcock	7–5, 6–4
1938	Sarah Palfrey Fabyan, Alice Marble	
	d. Simone Passemard Mathieu,	
	Jadwiga Jedrzejowska	6–8, 6–4, 6–3
1939	Sarah Palfrey Fabyan, Alice Marble	
	d. Kay Stammers, Freda Hammersley	7–5, 8–6
1940	Sarah Palfrey Fabyan, Alice Marble	
	d. Dorothy Bundy, Marjorie Gladman Van Ryn	6–4, 6–3
1941	Sarah Palfrey Fabyan, Margaret Osborne	
	d. Dorothy Bundy, Pauline Betz	3–6, 6–1, 6–4
1942	Louise Brough, Margaret Osborne	
	d. Pauline Betz, Doris Hart	2–6, 7–5, 6–0
1943	Louise Brough, Margaret Osborne	
	d. Pauline Betz, Doris Hart	6–1, 6–3
1944	Louise Brough, Margaret Osborne	
	d. Pauline Betz, Doris Hart	4–6, 6–4, 6–3
1945	Louise Brough, Margaret Osborne	
	d. Pauline Betz, Doris Hart	6–3, 6–3
1946	Louise Brough, Margaret Osborne	
	d. Patricia Canning Todd, Mary Prentiss	6–1, 6–3
1947	Louise Brough, Margaret Osborne	
	d. Patricia Canning Todd, Doris Hart	5–7, 6–3, 7–5
1948	Louise Brough, Margaret Osborne duPont	
	d. Patricia Canning Todd, Doris Hart	6–4, 8–10, 6–1
1949	Louise Brough, Margaret Osborne duPont	
	d. Doris Hart, Shirley Fry	6–4, 10–8
1950	Louise Brough, Margaret Osborne duPont	
	d. Doris Hart, Shirley Fry	6–2, 6–3
1951	Shirley Fry, Doris Hart	
	d. Nancy Chaffee, Patricia Canning Todd	6–4, 6–2
1952	Shirley Fry, Doris Hart	
	d. Louise Brough, Maureen Connolly	10–8, 6–4
1953	Shirley Fry, Doris Hart	
	d. Louise Brough, Margaret Osborne duPont	6–2, 7–9, 9–7
1954	Shirley Fry, Doris Hart	
	d. Louise Brough. Margaret Osborne duPont	6–4, 6–4
1955	Louise Brough, Margaret Osborne duPont	
	d. Doris Hart, Shirley Fry	6–3, 1–6, 6–3

Year	Final Round Results	Scores
1956	Louise Brough, Margaret Osborne duPont	
	d. Betty Pratt, Shirley Fry	6–3, 6–0
1957	Louise Brough, Margaret Osborne duPont	
	d. Althea Gibson, Darlene Hard	6–2, 7–5
1958	Jeanne Arth, Darlene Hard	
	d. Althea Gibson, Maria Bueno	2–6, 6–3, 6–4
1959	Jeanne Arth, Darlene Hard	
	d. Maria Bueno, Sally Moore	6–2, 6–3
1960	Maria Bueno, Darlene Hard	
	d. Ann Haydon, Deidre Catt	6–1, 6–1
1961	Darlene Hard, Lesley Turner	
	d. Edda Buding, Yola Ramirez	6–4, 5–7, 6–0
1962	Darlene Hard, Maria Bueno	
	d. Karen Hantze Susman, Billie Jean King	4–6, 6–3, 6–2
1963	Robyn Ebbern, Margaret Smith	
	d. Darlene Hard, Maria Bueno	4–6, 10–8, 6–3
1964	Billie Jean King, Karen Hantze Susman	
	d. Margaret Smith, Lesley Turner	3–6, 6–2, 6–4
1965	Carole Caldwell Graebner, Nancy Richey	
	d. Billie Jean King, Karen Hantze Susman	6–4, 6–4
1966	Maria Bueno, Nancy Richey	
	d. Billie Jean King, Rosemary Casals	6–3, 6–4
1967	Rosemary Casals, Billie Jean King	
	d. Mary Ann Eisel, Donna Floyd Fales	4–6, 6–3, 6–4
1968	Maria Bueno, Margaret Smith Court	
	d. Virginia Wade, Joyce Barclay Williams	6–3, 7–5
	(U.S. Lawn Tennis Association Championship, amateur)	
1968	Maria Bueno, Margaret Smith Court	
	d. Billie Jean King, Rosemary Casals	4–6, 9–7, 8–6
	(U.S. Open Championship, professional)	
1969	Virginia Wade, Margaret Court Smith	
	d. Mary Ann Eisel Curtis, Valerie Ziegenfuss	6–1, 6–3
	(U.S. Lawn Tennis Association Championship, amateur)	
1969	Francoise Durr, Darlene Hard	
	d. Margaret Smith Court, Virginia Wade	0–6, 6–4, 6–4
	(U.S. Open Championship, professional)	
1970	Margaret Smith Court, Judy Tegart Dalton	
	d. Rosemary Casals, Virginia Wade	6–3, 6–4
1971	Rosemary Casals, Judy Tegart Dalton	
	d. Gail Sherriff Chanfreau, Francoise Durr	6–3, 6–3
1972	Francoise Durr, Betty Stove	
	d. Margaret Smith Court, Virginia Wade	6–3, 1–6, 6–3
1973	Margaret Smith Court, Virginia Wade	
	d. Billie Jean King, Rosemary Casals	3–6, 6–3, 7–5
1974	Rosemary Casals, Billie Jean King	
	d. Francoise Durr, Betty Stove	7–6 (4), 6–7 (2), 6–4

Year	Final Round Results	Scores
1975	Margaret Smith Court, Virginia Wade	
	d. Billie Jean King, Rosemary Casals	7–5, 2–6, 7–5
1976	Delina Boshoff, Ilana Kloss	
	d. Olga Morozova, Virginia Wade	6–1, 6–4
1977	Martina Navratilova, Betty Stove	
	d. Renee Richards, Bettyann Stuart	6–1, 7–6
1978	Billie Jean King, Martina Navratilova	
	d. Kerry Melville Reid, Wendy Turnbull	7–6 (7), 6–4
1979	Betty Stove, Wendy Turnbull	
	d. Billie Jean King, Martina Navratilova	7–5, 6–3
1980	Billie Jean King, Martina Navratilova	
	d. Pam Shriver, Betty Stove	7–6 (2), 7–5
1981	Anne Smith, Kathy Jordan	
	d. Rosemary Casals, Wendy Turnbull	6–3, 6–3
1982	Rosemary Casals, Wendy Turnbull	
	d. Sharon Walsh, Barbara Potter	6–4, 6–4
1983	Martina Navratilova, Pam Shriver	
	d. Rosalyn Fairbank, Candy Reynolds	6–7 (4), 6–1, 6–3
1984	Martina Navratilova, Pam Shriver	
	d. Anne Hobbs, Wendy Turnbull	6–2, 6–4
1985	Claudia Kohde-Kilsch, Helena Sukova	
	d. Martina Navratilova, Pam Shriver	6–7, 6–2, 6–3
1986	Martina Navratilova, Pam Shriver	
	d. Hana Mandlikova, Wendy Turnbull	6–4, 3–6, 6–3
1987	Martina Navratilova, Pam Shriver	
	d. Kathy Jordan, Elizabeth Sayers Smylie	5–7, 6–4, 6–2
1988	Gigi Fernandez, Robin White	
	d. Patty Fendick, Jill Hetherington	6–4, 6–1
1989	Hana Mandlikova, Martina Navratilova	
	d. Mary Joe Fernandez, Pam Shriver	5–7, 6–4, 6–4
1990	Gigi Fernandez, Martina Navratilova	
	d. Jana Novotna, Helena Sukova	6–2, 6–4
1991	Pam Shriver, Natasha Zvereva	
	d. Jana Novotha, Larisa Neiland	6–4, 4–6, 7–6 (5)
1992	Gigi Fernandez, Natasha Zvereva	
	d. Jana Novotna, Larisa Neiland	7–6 (4), 6–1
1993	Arantxa Sanchez-Vicario, Helena Sukova	
	d. Amanda Coetzer, Ines Gorrochategui	6–4, 6–2
1994	Arantxa Sanchez-Vicario, Jana Novotna	
	d. Katarina Maleeva, Robin White	6–3, 6–3
1995	Gigi Fernandez, Natasha Zvereva	
	d. Brenda Schultz McCarthy, Rennae Stubbs	7–5, 6–3
1996	Gigi Fernandez, Natasha Zvereva	
	d. Jana Novotna, Arantxa Sanchez-Vicario	1–6, 6–1, 6–4
1997	Jana Novotna, Lindsay Davenport	
	d. Gigi Fernandez, Natasha Zvereva	6–3, 6–4
1998	Martina Hingis, Jana Novotna	
	d. Lindsay Davenport, Natasha Zvereva	6–3, 6–3

Year	Final Round Results	Scores
1999	Venus Williams, Serena Williams	
	d. Larisa Neiland, Arantxa Sanchez-Vicario	4–6, 6–1, 6–4
2000	Julie Halard Decugis, Ai Sugiyama	
	d. Cara Black, Elena Likhovtseva	6–1, 1–6, 6–1
2001	Lisa Raymond, Rennae Stubbs	
	d. Kimberly Po-Messerli, Natalie Tauziat	6–2, 5–7, 7–5
2002	Virginia Ruano Pascual, Paola Suarez	
	d. Elena Dementieva, Janette Husarova	6–2, 6–1
2003	Virginia Ruano Pascual, Paola Suarez	
	d. Martina Navratilova, Svetlana Kuznetsova	6–2, 6–2
2004	Virginia Ruano Pascual, Paola Suarz	
	d. Elena Likhovtseva, Svetlana Kuznetsova	6–4, 7–5
2005	Lisa Raymond, Samantha Stosur	
	d. Elena Dementieva, Flavia Penetta	6–2, 5–7, 6–3
2006	Nathalie Dechy, Vera Zvonareva	
	d. Dinara Safina, Katarina Srebotnik	7–6 (5), 7–5
2007	Nathalie Dechy, Dinara Safina	
	d. Yung-Jan Chan, Chia-Jung Chuang	6–4, 6–2
2008	Cara Black, Liezel Huber	
	d. Lisa Raymond, Samantha Stosur	6–3, 7–6 (6)

Mixed Doubles

Year	Final Round Results	Scores
1892	Mabel Cahill, Clarence Hobart	
	d. Elisabeth Moore, Rod Beach	5–7, 6–1, 6–4
1893	Ellen Roosevelt, Clarence Hobart	
	d. Ethel Bankson, Robert Willson, Jr.	6–1, 4–6, 10–8, 6–1
1894	Juliette Atkinson, Edwin Fischer	
	d. Mrs. McFadden, Gustav Remack, Jr.	6–3, 6–2, 6–1
1895	Juliette Atkinson, Edwin Fischer	
	d. Amy Williams, Mantle Fielding	4–6, 8–6, 6–2
1896	Juliette Atkinson, Edwin Fischer	
	d. Amy Williams, Mantle Fielding	6–2, 6–3, 6–3
1897	Laura Henson, D. L. Magruder	
	d. Maud Banks, R. A. Griffin	6–4, 6–3, 7–5
1898	Carrie Neely, Edwin Fischer	
	d. Helen Chapman, J. A. Hill	6–2, 6–4, 8–6
1899	Elizabeth Rastall, Albert Hoskins	
	d. Jane Craven, James Gardner	6–4, 6–0, default
1900	Margaret Hunnewell, Alfred Codman	
	d. T. Shaw, George Atkinson	11–9, 6–3, 6–1
1901	Marion Jones, Raymond Little	
	d. Myrtle McAteer, Clyde Stevens	6–4, 6–4, 7–5
1902	Elisabeth Moore, Wylie Grant	
	d. Elizabeth Rastall, Albert Hoskins	6–2, 6–1
1903	Helen Chapman, Harry Allen	
	d. Carrie Neely, W. H. Rowland	6–4, 7–5
1904	Elisabeth Moore, Wylie Grant	
	d. May Sutton, Trevanion Dallas	6–2, 6–1

Year	Final Round Results	Scores
1905	Augusta Schultz Hobart, Clarence Hobart	
	d. Elisabeth Moore, Edward Dewhurst	6–2, 6–4
1906	Sarah Coffin, Edward Dewhurst	
	d. Margaret Johnson, Wallace Johnson	6–3, 7–5
1907	May Sayers, Wallace Johnson	
	d. Natalie Wildey, William Morris Tilden	6–1, 7–5
1908	Edith Rotch, Nat Niles	
	d. Louise Hammond, Raymond Little	6–4, 4–6, 6–4
1909	Hazel Hotchkiss, Wallace Johnson	
	d. Louise Hammond, Raymond Little	6–2, 6–0
1910	Hazel Hotchkiss, Joseph Carpenter, Jr.	
	d. Edna Wildey, Herbert M. Tilden	6–2, 6–2
1911	Hazel Hotchkiss, Wallace Johnson	
	d. Edna Wildey, Herbert M. Tilden	6–4, 6–4
1912	Mary K. Browne, Dick Williams	
	d. Eleonora Sears, Bill Clothier	6–4, 2–6, 11–9
1913	Mary K. Browne, Bill Tilden	
	d. Dorothy Green, C. S. Rogers	7–5, 7–5
1914	Mary K. Browne, Bill Tilden	
	d. Margarete Myers, J.R. Rowland	6–1, 6–4
1915	Hazel Hotchkiss Wightman, Harry Johnson	
	d. Molla Bjurstedt, Irving Wright	6–0, 6–1
1916	Eleonora Sears, Willis Davis	
	d. Florence Ballin, Bill Tilden	6–4, 7–5
1917	Molla Bjurstedt, Irving Wright	
	d. Florence Ballin, Bill Tilden	10–12, 6–1, 6–3
1918	Hazel Hotchkiss Wightman, Irving Wright	
	d. Molla Bjurstedt, Fred Alexander	6–2, 6–4
1919	Marion Zinderstein, Vincent Richards	
	d. Florence Ballin, Bill Tilden	2–6, 11–9, 6–2
1920	Hazel Hotchkiss Wightman, Wallace Johnson	
	d. Molla Bjurstedt Mallory, Craig Biddle	6–4, 6–3
1921	Mary K. Browne, Bill Johnston	
	d. Molla Bjurstedt Mallory, Bill Tilden	3–6, 6–4, 6–3
1922	Molla Bjurstedt Mallory, Bill Tilden	
	d. Helen Wills, Howard Kinsey	6–4, 6–3
1923	Molla Bjurstedt Mallory, Bill Tilden	
	d. Kitty McKane, John Hawkes	6–3, 2–6, 10–8
1924	Helen Wills, Vincent Richards	
	d. Molla Bjurstedt Mallory, Bill Tilden	6–8, 7–5, 6–0
1925	Kitty McKane, John Hawkes	
	d. Ermyntrude Harvey, Vincent Richards	6–2, 6–4
1926	Elizabeth Ryan, Jean Borotra	
	d. Hazel Hotchkiss Wightman, Rene Lacoste	6–4, 7–5
1927	Eileen Bennett, Henri Cochet	
	d. Hazel Hotchkiss Wightman, Rene Lacoste	2–6, 6–0, 6–2
1928	Helen Wills, John Hawkes d. Edith Cross, Gar Moon	6–1, 6–3
1929	Betty Nuthall, George Lott	
	d. Phyllis Covell, Henry Austin	6–3, 6–3

Year	Final Round Results	Scores
1930	Edith Cross, Wilmer Allison	
	d. Marjorie Morrill, Frank Shields	6–4, 6–4
1931	Betty Nuthall, George Lott	
	d. Anna McCune Harper, Wilmer Allison	6–3, 6–3
1932	Sarah Palfrey, Fred Perry	
	d. Helen Jacobs, Ellsworth Vines	6–3, 7–5
1933	Elizabeth Ryan, Ellsworth Vines	
	d. Sarah Palfrey, George Lott	11–9, 6–1
1934	Helen Jacobs, George Lott	
	d. Elizabeth Ryan, Les Stoefen	4–6, 13–11, 6–2
1935	Sarah Palfrey Fabyan, Enrique Maier	
	d. Kay Stammers, Roderic Menzel	6–3, 3–6, 6–4
1936	Alice Marble, Gene Mako	
	d. Sarah Palfrey Fabyan, Don Budge	6–3, 6–2
1937	Sarah Palfrey Fabyan, Don Budge	
	d. Sylvie Henrotin, Yvon Petra	6–2, 8–10, 6–0
1938	Alice Marble, Donald Budge	
	d. Thelma Coyne, John Bromwich	6–1, 6–2
1939	Alice Marble, Harry Hopman	
	d. Sarah Palfrey Fabyan, Elwood Cooke	9–7, 6–1
1940	Alice Marble, Bobby Riggs	
	d. Dorothy Bundy, Jack Kramer	9–7, 6–1
1941	Sarah Palfrey Cooke, Jack Kramer	
	d. Pauline Betz, Bobby Riggs	4–6, 6–4, 6–4
1942	Louise Brough, Ted Schroeder	
	d. Patricia Canning Todd, Alejo Russell	3–6, 6–1, 6–4
1943	Margaret Osborne, Bill Talbert	
	d. Pauline Betz, Francisco "Pancho" Segura	10–8, 6–4
1944	Margaret Osborne, Bill Talbert	
	d. Dorothy Bundy, Lt. Don McNeill	6–2, 6–3
1945	Margaret Osborne, Bill Talbert	
	d. Doris Hart, Bob Falkenburg	6–4, 6–4
1946	Margaret Osborne, Bill Talbert	
	d. Louise Brough, Robert Kimbrell	6–3, 6–4
1947	Louise Brough, John Bromwich	
	d. Gertrude Moran, Francisco "Pancho" Segura	6–3, 6–1
1948	Louise Brough, Tom Brown	
	d. Margaret Osborne duPont, Bill Talbert	6–4, 6–4
1949	Louise Brough, Eric Strugess	
	d. Margaret Osborne duPont, Bill Talbert	4–6, 6–3, 7–5
1950	Margaret Osborne duPont, Ken McGregor	
	d. Doris Hart, Frank Sedgman	6–4, 3–6, 6–3
1951	Doris Hart, Frank Sedgman	
	d. Shirley Fry, Mervyn Rose	6–3, 6–2
1952	Doris Hart, Frank Sedgman	
	d. Thelma Coyne Long, Lew Hoad	6–3, 7–5
1953	Doris Hart, Vic Seixas	
	d. Julia Sampson, Rex Hartwig	6–2, 4–6, 6–4

Year	Final Round Results	Scores
1954	Doris Hart, Vic Seixas	
	d. Margaret Osborne duPont, Ken Rosewall	4–6, 6–1, 6–1
1955	Doris Hart, Vic Seixas d. Shirley Fry, Gardnar Mulloy	7–5, 5–7, 6–2
1956	Margaret Osborne duPont, Ken Rosewall	
	d. Darlene Hard, Lew Hoad	9–7, 6–1
1957	Althea Gibson, Kurt Nielsen	
	d. Darlene Hard, Bob Howe	6–3, 9–7
1958	Margaret Osborne duPont, Neale Fraser	
	d. Maria Bueno, Alex Olmedo	6–4, 3–6, 9–7
1959	Margaret Osborne duPont, Neale Fraser	
	d. Janet Hopps, Bob Mark	7–5, 13–15, 6–2
1960	Margaret Osborne duPont, Neale Fraser	
	d. Maria Bueno, Antonio Palafox	6–3, 6–2
1961	Margaret Smith, Bob Mark	
	d. Darlene Hard, Dennis Ralston	default due to Ralston's suspension
1962	Margaret Smith, Fred Stolle	
	d. Lesley Turner, Frank Froehling III	7–5, 6–2
1963	Margaret Smith, Ken Fletcher	
	d. Judy Tegart, Ed Rubinoff	3–6, 8–6, 6–2
1964	Margaret Smith, John Newcombe	
	d. Judy Tegart, Ed Rubinoff	10–8, 4–6, 6–3
1965	Margaret Smith, Fred Stolle	
	d. Judy Tegart, Frank Froehling III	6–2, 6–2
1966	Donna Floyd Fales, Owen Davidson	
	d. Carol Hanks Aucamp, Ed Rubinoff	6–1, 6–3
1967	Billie Jean King, Owen Davidson	
	d. Rosemary Casals, Stan Smith	6–3, 6–2
1968	Mary Ann Eisel, Peter Curtis	
	d. Tory Ann Fretz, Robert Perry	6–4, 7–5
1969	Patti Hogan, Paul Sullivan	
	d. Kristy Pigeon, Terry Addison	6–4, 2–6, 12–10
	(U.S. Lawn Tennis Association Championship, amateur)	
1969	Margaret Smith Court, Marty Riessen	
	d. Francoise Durr, Dennis Ralston	7–5, 6–3
	(U.S. Open Championship, professional)	
1970	Margaret Smith Court, Marty Riessen	
	d. Judy Tegart Dalton, Frew McMillan	6–4, 6–4
1971	Billie Jean King, Owen Davidson	
	d. Betty Stove, Rob Maud	6–3, 7–5
1972	Margaret Smith Court, Marty Riessen	
	d. Rosemary Casals, Ilie Nastase	6–3, 7–5
1973	Billie Jean King, Owen Davidson	
	d. Margaret Smith Court, Marty Riessen	6–3, 3–6, 7–6
1974	Pam Teeguarden, Geoff Masters	
	d. Chris Evert, Jimmy Connors	6–1, 7–6
1975	Rosemary Casals, Dick Stockton	
	d. Billie Jean King, Fred Stolle	6–3, 7–6

Year	Final Round Results	Scores
1976	Billie Jean King, Phil Dent	
	d. Betty Stove, Frew McMillan	3–6, 6–2, 7–5
1977	Betty Stove, Frew McMillan	
	d. Billie Jean King, Vitas Gerulaitis	6–2, 3–6, 6–3
1978	Betty Stove, Frew McMillan	
	d. Billie Jean King, Ray Ruffels	6–3, 7–6
1979	Greer Stevens, Bob Hewitt	
	d. Betty Stove, Frew McMillan	6–3, 7–5
1980	Wendy Turnbull, Marty Riessen	
	d. Betty Stove, Frew McMillan	7–5, 6–2
1981	Anne Smith, Kevin Curren	
	d. JoAnne Russell, Steve Denton	6–4, 7–6 (4)
1982	Anne Smith, Kevin Curren	
	d. Barbara Potter, Ferdi Taygan	6–7, 7–6 (4), 7–6 (5)
1983	Elizabeth Sayers, John Fitzgerald	
	d. Barbara Potter, Ferdi Taygan	3–6, 6–3, 6–4
1984	Manuela Maleeva, Tom Gulikson	
	d. Elizabeth Sayers, John Fitzgerald	2–6, 7–5, 6–4
1985	Martina Navratilova, Heinz Gunthardt	
	d. Elizabeth Sayers Smylie, John Fitzgerald	6–3, 6–4
1986	Raffaella Reggi, Sergio Casal	
	d. Martina Navratilova, Peter Fleming	6–4, 6–4
1987	Martina Navratilova, Emilio Sanchez	
	d. Betsy Nagelson, Paul Annacone	6–4, 6–7 (6), 7–6 (2)
1988	Jana Novotna, Jim Pugh	
	d. Elizabeth Sayers Smylie, Patrick McEnroe	7–5, 6–3
1989	Robin White, Shelby Cannon	
	d. Meredith McGrath, Rick Leach	3–6, 6–2, 7–5
1990	Elizabeth Sayers Smylie, Todd Woodbridge	
	d. Natasha Zvereva, Jim Pugh	6–4, 6–2
1991	Manon Bollegraf, Tom Nijssen	
	d. Arantxa Sanchez-Vicario, Emilio Sanchez	6–2, 7–6 (2)
1992	Nicole Provis, Mark Woodforde	
	d. Helena Sukova, Tom Nijssen	4–6, 6–3, 6–3
1993	Helena Sukova, Todd Woodbridge	
	d. Martina Navratilova, Mark Woodforde	6–3, 7–6 (6)
1994	Elna Reinach, Patrick Galbraith	
	d. Jana Novotna, Todd Woodbridge	6–2, 6–4
1995	Meredith McGrath, Matt Lucena	
	d. Gigi Fernandez, Cyril Suk	6–4, 6–4
1996	Lisa Raymond, Patrick Galbraith	
	d. Manon Bollegraf, Rick Leach	7–6 (6), 7–6 (4)
1997	Manon Bollegraf, Rich Leach	
	d. Mercedes Paz, Pablo Albano	3–6, 7–5, 7–6 (3)
1998	Serena Williams, Max Mirnyi	
	d. Lisa Raymond, Patrick Galbraith	6–2, 6–2
1999	Ai Sugiyama, Mahesh Bhupathi	
	d. Kimberly Po, Donald Johnson	6–4, 6–4

Year	Final Round Results	Scores
2000	Arantxa Sanchez-Vicario, Jared Palmer	
	d. Anna Kournikova, Max Mirnyi	6–4, 6–3
2001	Rennae Stubbs, Todd Woodbridge	
	d. Lisa Raymond, Leander Paes	6–4, 5–7, 7–6 (7)
2002	Lisa Raymond, Bob Bryan	
	d. Kara Srebotnik Mike Bryan	7–6 (9), 7–6 (1)
2003	Katarina Srebotnik, Bob Bryan	
	d. Lina Krasnoroutskaya, Daniel Nestor	5–7, 7–5, 7–6 (5)
2004	Vera Zvonereva, Bob Bryan	
	d. Alicia Molik, Todd Woodbridge	6–3, 6–4
2005	Daniela Hantuchova, Mahesh Bhupathi	
	d. Katarina Srebotnik, Nenad Zimonjic	6–4, 6–2
2006	Martina Navratilova, Bob Bryan	
	d. Kveta Peschke, Martin Damm	6–2, 6–3
2007	Victoria Azarenka, Max Mirnyi	
	d. Meghann Shaughnessy, Leander Paes	6–4, 7–6 (6)
2008	Cara Black, Leander Paes	
	d. Liezel Huber, Jamie Murray	7–6 (6), 6–4

THE FED CUP

Hazel Hotchkiss Wightman's original concept for an international competition among women tennis players was rejected in 1919 when presented to the International Tennis Federation. Wightman responded by donating a silver trophy for an annual competition between the United States and Great Britain which began in 1923 known as The Wightman Cup. It was not until decades later that Wightman's dream of a true international competition of women tennis players was realized. With the help of Nell Hopman and Mary Hardwick Hare, the International Tennis Federation celebrated its 50th anniversary in 1963 with the inauguration of the Federation Cup. Competition was held at Queen's Club in London that first year when 16 countries participated. In the final round, the United States beat Australia 2–1 for the title.

From 1963 through 1994 the competition format remained the same. Each year the final teams met at one location in a single elimination tournament during a one week period. The number of players representing each team varied from between two to four. Team competition was comprised of three matches, two singles and one doubles. Each match was determined by playing the best two-of-three sets. Professionals were permitted to participate beginning in 1969. Prize money has been awarded since 1976 when Colgate became the Cup's first sponsor.

In 1995, the Federation Cup changed its name to the Fed Cup and adopted the Davis Cup format. The new format is comprised of the eight strongest nations playing in the World Group. Each country in this group competes in a single elimination tournament to determine the winner of the Cup. The next eight strongest nations play in Group One. The remaining nations participate in Regional Qualifying Events. First round losers in the World Group each year drop down to Regional play the following year. In recent years more than 100 nations have participated in Fed Cup play.

As in Davis Cup competition, a "tie" is played between two teams over a period of two days. On the first day, two singles matches are played. On the second day, reverse singles are played and a doubles match. The team winning three matches wins the tie. The host country has the right to choose the location and playing surface.

Year	Final Round Results
1963	United States defeated Australia 2–1 (Played on grass at Queen's Club, London, England). *Singles:* Margaret Smith (AUS) d. Darlene Hard (USA) 6–3, 6–0; Billie Jean King (USA) d. Lesley Turner (AUS) 5–7, 6–0, 6–3. *Doubles:* Darlene Hard, Billie Jean King (USA) d. Margaret Smith, Lesley Turner (AUS) 3–6, 13–11, 6–3

Year	*Final Round Results*

1964 Australia defeated United States 2–1 (Played on grass at Germantown Cricket Club, Philadelphia, Pennsylvania). *Singles:* Margaret Smith (AUS) d. Billie Jean King (USA) 6–2, 6–3; Lesley Turner (AUS) d. Nancy Richey (USA) 7–5, 6–1. *Doubles:* Billie Jean King, Karen Hantze Susman (USA) d. Margaret Smith, Lesley Turner (AUS) 4–6, 7–5, 6–1

1965 Australia defeated United States 2–1 (Played on grass at Kooyong Tennis Club, Melbourne, Australia). *Singles:* Lesley Turner (AUS) d. Carole Caldwell Graebner (USA) 6–3, 2–6, 6–3; Margaret Smith (AUS) d. Billie Jean King (USA) 6–4, 8–6. *Doubles:* Billie Jean King, Carole Caldwell Graebner (USA) d. Margaret Smith, Judy Tegart (AUS) 7–5, 4–6, 6–4

1966 United States defeated Germany 3–0 (Played on clay at Press Sporting Club, Turin, Italy). *Singles:* Julie Heldman (USA) d. Helga Niessen (GER) 4–6, 7–5, 6–1; Billie Jean King (USA) d. Edda Buding (GER) 6–3, 3–6, 6–1. *Doubles:* Carole Caldwell Graebner, Billie Jean King (USA) d. Helga Schultze, Edda Buding (GER) 6–4, 6–2

1967 United States defeated Great Britain 2–0 (Played on clay at Blau Weiss Club, Berlin, Germany). *Singles:* Rosie Casals (USA) d. Virginia Wade (GBR) 9–7, 8–6; Billie Jean King (USA) d. Ann Haydon Jones (GBR) 6–3, 6–4. *Doubles:* Doubles match suspended at a set-all

1968 Australia defeated Netherlands 3–0 (Played on clay at Stade Roland Garros, Paris, France). *Singles:* Kerry Melville (AUS) d. Marijke Jansen (NED) 4–6, 7–5, 6–3; Margaret Court (AUS) d. Astrid Suurbeek (NED) 6–1, 6–3. *Doubles:* Margaret Court, Kerry Melville (AUS) d. Astrid Suurbeek, Lidy Jansen Venneboer (NED) 6–3, 6–8, 7–5

1969 United States defeated Australia 2–1 (Played on clay at Athens Tennis Club, Athens, Greece). *Singles:* Nancy Richey (USA) d. Kerry Melville (AUS) 6–4, 6–3; Margaret Court (AUS) d. Julie Heldman (USA) 6–1, 8–6. *Doubles:* Jane "Peaches" Bartkowicz, Nancy Richey (USA) d. Margaret Court, Judy Tegart (AUS) 6–4, 6–4

1970 Australia defeated Germany 3–0 (Played on clay at Freiburg Tennis Club, Freiburg, West Germany). *Singles:* Karen Krantzcke (AUS) d. Helga Hoesel-Schultze (GER) 6–2, 6–3; Judy Tegart Dalton (AUS) d. Helga Niessen (GER) 4–6, 6–3, 6–3. *Doubles:* Karen Krantzcke, Judy Tegart Dalton (AUS) d. Helga Hoesel-Schultze, Helga Niessen (GER) 6–2, 7–5

1971 Australia defeated Great Britain 3–0 (Played on grass at Royal King's Park Tennis Club, Perth, Australia). *Singles:* Margaret Court (AUS) d. Ann Haydon Jones (GBR) 6–8, 6–3, 6–2 Evonne Goolagong (AUS) d. Virginia Wade (GBR) 6–4, 6–1. *Doubles:* Margaret Court, Lesley Hunt (AUS) d. Virginia Wade, Winnie Shaw (GBR) 6–4, 6–4

1972 South Africa defeated Great Britain 2–1 (Played on grass at Ellis Park, Johannesburg, South Africa). *Singles:* Virginia Wade (GBR) d. Pat Waldken Pretorius (RSA) 6–3, 6–2; Brenda Kirk (RSA) d. Winnie Shaw (GBR) 4–6, 7–5, 6–0. *Doubles:* Brenda Kirk, Pat Waldken Pretorius (RSA) d. Virginia Wade, Joyce Williams (GBR) 6–1, 7–5

1973 Australia defeated South Africa 3–0 (Played on clay at Bad Homburg Tennis Club, Bad Homburg, West Germany). *Singles:* Evonne Goolagong (AUS) d. Pat Waldken Pretorius (RSA) 6–0, 6–2; Pattie Coleman (AUS) d. Brenda Kirk (RSA) 10–8,

Year	*Final Round Results*

6–0. *Doubles:* Evonne Goolagong, Janet Young (AUS) d. Brenda Kirk, Pat Wald-ken Pretorius (RSA) 6–1, 6–2

1974   Australia defeated United States 2–1 (Played on clay at Tennis Club of Naples, Naples, Italy). *Singles:* Evonne Goolagong (AUS) d. Julie Heldman (USA) 6–1, 7–5; Jeanne Evert (USA) d. Dianne Fromholtz (AUS) 2–6, 7–5, 6–4. *Doubles:* Evonne Goolagong, Janet Young (AUS) d. Julie Heldman, Sharon Walsh (USA) 7–5, 8–6

1975   Czechoslovakia defeated Australia 3–0 (Played on clay at Aixoise Country Club, Aix-en-Provence, France). *Singles:* Martina Navratilova (CZE) d. Evonne Goola-gong (AUS) 6–3, 6–4; Renata Tomanova (CZE) d. Helen Gourlay (AUS) 6–4, 6–2. *Doubles:* Martina Navratilova, Renata Tomanova (CZE) d. Dianne Fromholtz, Helen Gourlay (AUS) 6–3, 6–1

1976   United States defeated Australia 2–1 (Played on carpet at The Spectrum, Philadel-phia, Pennsylvania). *Singles:* Kerry Melville Reid (AUS) d. Rosie Casals (USA) 1–6, 6–3, 7–5; Billie Jean King (USA) d. Evonne Goolagong (AUS) 7–6, 6–4. *Doubles:* Billie Jean King, Rosie Casals (USA) d. Evonne Goolagong, Kerry Melville Reid (AUS) 7–5, 6–3

1977   United States defeated Australia 2–1 (Played on grass at Devonshire Park, East-bourne, England). *Singles:* Billie Jean King (USA) d. Dianne Fromholtz (AUS) 6–1, 2–6, 6–2; Chris Evert (USA) d. Kerry Melville Reid (AUS) 7–5, 6–3. *Dou-bles:* Kerry Melville Reid, Wendy Turnbull (AUS) d. Chris Evert, Rosie Casals (USA) 6–3, 6–3

1978   United States defeated Australia 2–1 (Played on grass at Kooyong Stadium, Mel-bourne, Australia). *Singles:* Kerry Melville Reid (AUS) d. Tracy Austin (USA) 6–3, 6–3; Chris Evert (USA) d. Wendy Turnbull (AUS) 3–6, 6–1, 6–1. *Doubles:* Chris Evert, Billie Jean King (USA) d. Wendy Turnbull, Kerry Melville Reid (AUS) 4–6, 6–1, 6–4

1979   United States defeated Australia 3–0 (Played on clay at R.S.H.E. Club de Campo Madrid, Spain). *Singles:* Tracy Austin (USA) d. Kerry Melville Reid (AUS) 6–3, 6–0; Chris Evert (USA) d. Dianne Fromholtz (AUS) 2–6, 6–3, 8–6. *Doubles:* Billie Jean King, Rosie Casals (USA) d. Wendy Turnbull, Kerry Melville Reid (AUS) 3–6, 6–3, 8–6

1980   United States defeated Australia 3–0 (Played on clay at Rot-Weiss Tennis Club, Berlin, Germany). *Singles:* Chris Evert (USA) d. Dianne Fromholtz (AUS) 4–6, 6–1, 6–1; Tracy Austin (USA) d. Wendy Turnbull (AUS) 6–2, 6–3. *Doubles:* Rosie Casals, Kathy Jordan (USA) d. Dianne Fromholtz, Susan Leo (AUS) 2–6, 6–4, 6–4

1981   United States defeated Great Britain 3–0 (Played on clay at Tamagawa-en Racquet Club, Tokyo, Japan). *Singles:* Chris Evert (USA) d. Sue Barker (GBR) 6–2, 6–1; Andrea Jaeger (USA) d. Virginia Wade (GBR) 6–3, 6–1. *Doubles:* Kathy Jordan, Rosie Casals (USA) d. Sue Barker, Virginia Wade (GBR) 6–4, 7–5

1982   United States defeated Germany 3–0 (Played on hard courts at Decathlon Club, Santa Clara, California). *Singles:* Chris Evert (USA) d. Claudia Kohde-Kilsch (GER) 2–6, 6–1, 6–3; Martina Navratilova (USA) d. Bettina Bunge (GER) 6–4, 6–4. *Doubles:* Martina Navratilova, Chris Evert (USA) d. Claudia Kohde-Kilsch, Bettina Bunge (GER) 3–6, 6–1, 6–2

Year   *Final Round Results*

1983   Czechoslovakia defeated Germany 2–1 (Played at on clay at Albisgueti Tennis Complex, Zurich, Switzerland). *Singles:* Helena Sukova (CZE) d. Claudia Kohde-Kilsch (GER) 6–4, 2–6, 6–2; Hana Mandlikova (CZE) d. Bettina Bunge (GER) 6–2, 3–0 retired. *Doubles:* Claudia Kohde-Kilsch, Eva Pfaff (GER) d. Iva Budarova, Marcela Skuherska (CZE) 3–6, 6–2, 6–1

1984   Czechoslovakia defeated Australia 2–1 (Played on clay at Esporte Clube Pinheiros, Sao Paulo, Brazil). *Singles:* Anne Minter (AUS) d. Helena Sukova (CZE) 7–5, 7–5; Hana Mandlikova (CZE) d. Elizabeth Sayers (AUS) 6–1, 6–0. *Doubles:* Hana Mandlikova, Helena Sukova (CZE) d. Elizabeth Sayers, Wendy Turnbull (AUS) 6–2, 6–2

1985   Czechoslovakia defeated United States 2–1 (Played on hard courts at Nagoya Green Tennis Club, Nagoya, Japan). *Singles:* Hana Mandlikova (CZE) d. Kathy Jordan (USA) 7–5, 6–1; Helena Sukova (CZE) d. Elise Burgin (USA) 6–3, 6–7, 6–4. *Doubles:* Elise Burgin, Sharon Walsh (USA) d. Regina Marsikova, Andrea Holikova (CZE) 6–2, 6–3

1986   United States defeated Czechoslovakia 3–0 (Played on clay at Stvanice Stadium, Prague, Czechoslovakia). *Singles:* Chris Evert (USA) d. Helena Sukova (CZE) 7–5, 7–6; Martina Navratilova (USA) d. Hana Mandlikova (CZE) 7–5, 6–1. *Doubles:* Martina Navratilova, Pam Shriver (USA) d. Hana Mandlikova, Helena Sukova (CZE) 6–4, 6–2

1987   Germany defeated United States 2–1 (Played on hard courts at Hollyburn Country Club, Vancouver, Canada). *Singles:* Pam Shriver (USA) d. Claudia Kohde-Kilsch (GER) 6–0, 7–6; Steffi Graf (GER) d. Chris Evert (USA) 6–2, 6–1. *Doubles:* Steffi Graf, Claudia Kohde-Kilsch (GER) d. Chris Evert, Pam Shriver (USA) 1–6, 7–5, 6–4

1988   Czechoslovakia defeated Russia 2–1 (Played on hard courts at Flinders Park, Melbourne, Australia). *Singles:* Radka Zrubakova (CZE) d. Larisa Savchenko (RUS) 6–1, 7–6; Helena Sukova (CZE) d. Natasha Zvereva (RUS) 6–3, 6–4. *Doubles:* Larisa Savchenko, Natasha Zvereva (RUS) d. Jana Novotna, Jana Pospislova (CZE) 7–6, 7–5

1989   United States defeated Spain 3–0 (Played on hard courts at Ariake Tennis Centre, Tokyo, Japan). *Singles:* Chris Evert (USA) d. Conchita Martinez (ESP) 6–3, 6–2; Martina Navratilova (USA) d. Arantxa Sanchez-Vicario (ESP) 0–6, 6–3, 6–4. *Doubles:* Zina Garrison, Pam Shriver (USA) d. Conchita Martinez, Arantxa Sanchez-Vicario (ESP) 7–5, 6–1

1990   United States defeated Russia 2–1 (Played on hard courts at Peachtree World of Tennis, Atlanta, Georgia). *Singles:* Jennifer Capriati (USA) d. Leila Meskhi (RUS) 7–6, 6–2; Natasha Zvereva (RUS) d. Zina Garrison (USA) 4–6, 6–3, 6–3. *Doubles:* Zina Garrison, Gigi Fernandez (USA) d. Natasha Zvereva, Larisa Savchenko (RUS) 6–4, 6–3

1991   Spain defeated United States 2–1 (Played on hard courts at City of Nottingham Tennis Centre, Nottingham, England). *Singles:* Jennifer Capriati (USA) d. Conchita Martinez (ESP) 4–6, 7–6, 6–1; Arantxa Sanchez-Vicario (ESP) d. Mary Joe Fernandez (USA) 6–3, 6–4. *Doubles:* Conchita Martinez, Arantxa Sanchez-Vicario (ESP) d. Gigi Fernandez, Zina Garrison (USA) 3–6, 6–1, 6–1

1992   Germany defeated Spain 2–1 (Played on clay at Waldstadion, Frankfurt, Germany). *Singles:* Steffi Graf (GER) d. Arantxa Sanchez-Vicario (ESP) 6–4, 6–2;

Year	*Final Round Results*

Anke Huber (GER) d. Conchita Martinez (ESP) 6–3, 6–7, 6–1. *Doubles:* Arantxa Sanchez-Vicario, Conchita Martinez (ESP) d. Anke Huber, Barbara Rittner (GER) 6–1, 6–2

1993   Spain defeated Australia 3–0 (Played on clay at Waldstadion, Frankfurt, Germany). *Singles:* Conchita Martinez (ESP) d. Michelle Jaggard-Lai (AUS) 6–0, 6–2; Arantxa Sanchez-Vicario (ESP) d. Nicole Provis (AUS) 6–2, 6–3. *Doubles:* Conchita Martinez, Arantxa Sanchez-Vicario (ESP) d. Elizabeth Smylie, Rennae Stubbs (AUS) 3–6, 6–1, 6–3

1994   Spain defeated United States 3–0 (Played on clay at Waldstadion, Frankfurt, Germany). *Singles:* Conchita Martinez (ESP) d. Mary Joe Fernandez (USA) 6–2, 6–2; Aranxta Sanchez-Vicario (ESP) d. Lindsey Davenport (USA) 6–2, 6–1. *Doubles:* Conchita Martinez, Aranxta Sanchez-Vicario (ESP) d. Gigi Fernandez, Mary Joe Fernandez (USA) 6–3, 6–4

1995   Spain defeated United States 3–2 (Played on clay in Valencia, Spain). *Singles:* Conchita Martinez (ESP) d. Chanda Rubin (USA) 7–5, 7–6; Arantxa Sanchez-Vicario (ESP) d. Mary Joe Fernandez (USA) 6–3, 6–2; Conchita Martinez (ESP) d. Mary Joe Fernandez (USA) 6–3, 6–4; Chanda Rubin (USA) d. Arantxa Sanchez-Vicario (ESP) 1–6, 6–4, 6–4. *Doubles:* Lindsay Davenport, Gigi Fernandez (USA) d. Virginia Ruano-Pascual, Maria Antonia Sanchez Lorenzo (ESP) 6–3, 7–6

1996   United States defeated Spain 5–0 (Played on carpet at Atlantic City Convention Center, Atlantic City, New Jersey). *Singles:* Monica Seles (USA) d. Conchita Martinez (ESP) 6–2, 6–4; Lindsay Davenport (USA) d. Arantxa Sanchez-Vicario (ESP) 7–5, 6–1; Monica Seles (USA) d. Arantxa Sanchez-Vicario (ESP) 3–6, 6–3, 6–1; Lindsay Davenport (USA) d. Gala Leon (ESP) 7–5, 6–2. *Doubles:* Linda Wild, Mary Joe Fernandez (USA) d. Gala Leon, Virginia Ruano-Pascual (ESP) 6–1, 6–4

1997   France defeated The Netherlands 4–1 (Played on carpet at Brabant Hall, Den Bosch, The Netherlands). *Singles:* Sandrine Testud (FRA) d. Brenda Schultz-McCarthy (NED) 6–4, 4–6, 6–3; Mary Pierce (FRA) d. Miriam Oremans (NED) 6–4, 6–1; Sandrine Testud (FRA) d. Miriam Oremans (NED) 0–6, 6–3, 6–3; Brenda Schultz-McCarthy (NED) d. Mary Pierce (FRA) 4–6, 6–3, 6–4. *Doubles:* Alexandra Fusai, Nathalie Tauziat (FRA) d. Manon Bollegraf, Caroline Vis (NED) 6–3, 6–4

1998   Spain defeated Switzerland 3–2 (Played on greenset carpet at the Palexpo in Geneva, Switzerland). *Singles:* Martina Hingis (SUI) d. Arantxa Sanchez-Vicario (ESP) 7–6 (5), 6–3; Conchita Martinez (ESP) d. Patty Schnyder (SUI) 6–3, 2–6, 9–7; Martina Hingis (SUI) d. Conchita Martinez (ESP) 6–4, 6–4; Arantxa Sanchez-Vicario (ESP) d. Patty Schnyder (SUI) 6–1, 3–6, 6–2. *Doubles:* Arantxa Sanchez-Vicario, Conchita Martinez (ESP) d. Martina Hingis, Patty Schnyder (SUI) 6–0, 6–2

1999   United States defeated Russia 4–1 (Played on hard courts at Stanford University in Palo Alto, California). *Singles:* Lindsay Davenport (USA) d. Elena Dementieva (RUS) 6–4, 6–0; Venus Williams (USA) d. Elena Likhovtseva (RUS) 6–3, 6–4; Lindsay Davenport (USA) d. Elena Likhovtseva (RUS) 6–4, 6–4; Elena Dementieva (RUS) d. Venus Williams (USA) 6–1, 3–6, 7–5. *Doubles:* Venus Williams, Serena Williams (USA) d. Elena Dementieva, Elena Makarova (RUS) 6–2, 6–1

2000   United States defeated Spain 5–0 (Played on carpet at the Mandalay Bay Events Center in Las Vegas, Nevada). *Singles:* Lindsay Davenport (USA) d. Arantxa

Year	Final Round Results

Sanchez-Vicario (ESP) 6–2, 1–6, 6–3; Monica Seles (USA) d. Conchita Martinez (ESP) 6–2, 6–3; Lindsay Davenport (USA) d. Conchita Martinez (ESP) 6–1, 6–2; Jennifer Capriati (USA) d. Arantxa Sanchez-Vicario (ESP) 6–1, 1–0 retired. *Doubles:* Jennifer Capriati, Lisa Raymond (USA) d. Magui Serna, Virginia Ruano Pascual (ESP) 4–6, 6–4, 6–2

2001   Belgium defeated Russia 2–1 (Played at Parque Ferial Juan Carlos 1 in Madrid, Spain). *Singles:* Justine Henin (BEL) d. Nadia Petrova (RUS) 6–0, 6–3; Kim Clijsters (BEL) d. Elena Dementieva (RUS) 6–0, 6–4. *Doubles:* Elena Likhovtseva, Nadia Petrova (RUS) d. Els Callens, Laurence Courtois (BEL) 7–5, 7–6 (2)

2002   Slovakia defeated Spain 3–1 (Played at Palacio de Congresos de Maspalomas in Gran Canaria, Spain). *Singles:* Conchita Martinez (ESP) d. Janette Husarova (SVK) 6–4, 7–6 (6); Daniela Hantuchova (SVK) d. Magui Serna (ESP) 6–2, 6–1; Daniela Hantuchova (SVK) d. Conchita Martinez (ESP) 6–7 (8), 7–5, 6–4; Janette Husarova (SVK) d. Arantxa Sanchez-Vicario (ESP) 6–0, 6–2. *Doubles:* Daniela Hantuchova, Janette Husarova (SVK) vs. Virginia Ruano Pascual, Magui Serna (ESP) Not Played

2003   France defeated United States 4–1 (Played on carpet at Olympic Stadium in Moscow, Russia). *Singles:* Amelie Mauresmo (FRA) d. Lisa Raymond (USA) 6–4, 6–3; Mary Pierce (FRA) d. Meghann Shaughnessy (USA) 6–3, 3–6, 8–6; Amelie Mauresmo (FRA) d. Meghann Shaughnessy (USA) 6–2, 6–1; Emilie Loit (FRA) d. Alexandra Stevenson (USA) 6–4, 6–2. *Doubles:* Martina Navratilova, Lisa Raymond (USA) d. Stephanie Cohen-Aloro, Emilie Loit (FRA) 6–4, 6–0

2004   Russia defeated France 3–2 (Played on carpet at the Ice Stadium Krylatskoe in Moscow, Russia). *Singles:* Nathalie Dechy (FRA) d. Svetlana Kuznetsova (RUS) 3–6, 7–6 (4), 8–6; Anastasia Myskina (RUS) d. Tatiana Golovin (FRA) 6–4, 7–6 (5); Anastasia Myskina (RUS) d. Nathalie Dechy (FRA) 6–3, 6–4; Tatiana Golovin (FRA) d. Svetlana Kuznetsova (RUS) 6–4, 6–1. *Doubles:* Anastasia Myskina, Vera Zvonareva (RUS) d. Marion Bartoli, Emilie Loit (FRA) 7–6 (5), 7–5

2005   Russia defeated France 3–2 (Played on red clay at Roland Garros in Paris, France). *Singles:* Elena Dementieva (RUS) d. Mary Pierce (FRA) 7–6 (1), 2–6, 6–1; Amelie Mauresmo (FRA) d. Anastasia Myskina (RUS) 6–4, 6–2; Elena Dementieva (RUS) d. Amelie Mauresmo (FRA) 6–4, 4–6, 6–2; Mary Pierce (FRA) d. Anastasia Myskina (RUS) 4–6, 6–4, 6–2. *Doubles:* Elena Dementieva, Dinara Safina (RUS) d. Amelie Mauresmo, Mary Pierce (FRA) 6–4, 1–6, 6–3

2006   Italy defeated Belgium 3–2 (Played on indoor hard court at Spiroudome in Charleroi, Belgium). *Singles:* Francesca Schiavone (ITA) d. Kirsten Flipkens (BEL) 6–1, 6–3; Justine Henin (BEL) d. Flavia Pennetta (ITA) 6–4, 7–5; Justine Henin (BEL) d. Francesca Schiavone (ITA) 6–4, 7–5; Mara Santangelo (ITA) d. Kirsten Flipkens (BEL) 6–7(3), 6–3, 6–0. *Doubles:* Francesca Schiavone, Roberta Vinci (ITA) d. Justine Henin, Kirsten Flipkens (BEL) 3–6, 6–2, 2–0 retired

2007   Russia defeated Italy 4–0 (Played on indoor hard court at Small Sports Arena "Luzhniki" in Moscow, Russia). *Singles:* Anna Chakvetadze (RUS) d. Francesca Schiavone (ITA) 6–4, 4–6, 6–4; Svetlana Kuznetsova (RUS) d. Mara Santangelo (ITA) 6–1, 6–2; Svetlana Kuznetsova (RUS) d. Francesca Schiavone (ITA) 4–6, 7–6 (7), 7–5; Elena Vesnina (RUS) d. Mara Santangelo (ITA) 6–2, 6–4. *Doubles:* Nadia Petrova, Elena Vesnina (RUS) v. Mara Santangelo, Roberta Vinci (ITA) Not Played

Year   *Final Round Results*

2008   Russia defeated Spain 4–0 (Played on red clay at Club de Campo-Villa de Madrid,
                Madrid, Spain) *Singles:* Vera Zvonareva (RUS) d. Anabel Medina Garrigues (ESP)
                6–3, 6–4; Svetlana Kuznetsova (RUS) d. Carla Suarez Navarro (ESP) 6–3, 6–1; Svet-
                lana Kuznetsova (RUS) d. Anabel Medina Garrigues (ESP) 5–7, 6–3, 6–4; *Dou-
                bles:* Ekaterina Makarova, Elena Vesnina (RUS) d. Nuria Llagostera Vives, Carla
                Suarez Navarro (ESP) 6–2, 6–1

THE OLYMPIC GAMES

Tennis was played for the first time at the Olympic Games in Athens in 1896, although there was no women's competition until 1900. It continued as an Olympic sport through 1924, the year in which all the tennis events were won by Americans. Shortly after the 1924 Games, a rift developed between the Olympic Committee and the International Tennis Federation.

The disagreement concerned the definition of amateurism. Unfortunately, no consensus of opinion could be reached and tennis was dropped as an official Olympic sport. Tennis was played as a demonstration sport at the 1968 games in Mexico City and at the 1984 games in Los Angeles. In 1988, tennis was finally re-instated as an official sport of the Olympic Games.

Year	*Final Round Results*
1896	(Athens, Greece). No women's competition
1900	(Paris, France). Singles Medal Winners — *Gold:* Charlotte Cooper (Great Britain); *Silver:* Helene Prevost (France); *Bronze:* Marion Jones (United States); *Bronze:* Hedwig Rosenbaum (Bohemia/Czechoslovakia). Singles Final: Charlotte Cooper d. Helene Prevost 6–1, 6–4. Doubles: Not held. Mixed Doubles Medal Winners — *Gold:* Charlotte Cooper, Reginald Doherty (Great Britain); *Silver:* Helene Prevost (France), Harold Mahoney (Ireland); *Bronze:* Hedwig Rosenbaum (Bohemia/Czechoslovakia), Archibald Warden (Great Britain); *Bronze:* Marion Jones (United States), Hugh "Laurie" Doherty (Great Britain). Mixed Doubles Finals: Charlotte Cooper, Reginald Doherty d. Helene Prevost, Harold Mahoney, 6–2, 6–4
1904	(St. Louis, Missouri). No women's competition
1906	(Athens, Greece). Singles Medal Winners — *Gold:* Esmee Simiriotou (Greece); *Silver:* Sophia Marinou (Greece); *Bronze:* Euphrosine Paspati (Greece). Singles Finals: Esmee Simiriotou d. Sophia Marinou, 6–1, 6–4. Doubles: Not held. Mixed Doubles Medal Winners — *Gold:* Marie Decugis, Max Decugis (France); *Silver:* Sophia Marinou, Georgios Simiriotis (Greece); *Bronze:* Aspasia Matsa, Xenophon Kasdaglis (Greece). Mixed Doubles Finals: Marie Decugis, Max Decugis d. Sophia Marinou, Georgios Simiriotis 6–1, 6–2
1908	(London, England). Singles Medal Winners — *Gold:* Dorothea Lambert Chambers (Great Britain); *Silver:* Dorothy Boothby (Great Britain); *Bronze:* R. Joan Winch (Great Britain) Singles Finals: Dorothea Lambert Chambers d. Dorothy Boothby 6–1, 7–5
1908	(London, England; Indoors). Singles Medal Winners — *Gold:* Gwendoline Eastlake-Smith (Great Britain); *Silver:* Angela Greene (Great Britain); *Bronze:* Martha Adlerstrahle (Sweden). Singles Finals: Gwendoline Eastlake-Smith d. Angela

Year	*Final Round Results*
	Greene 6–2, 4–6, 6–0; 3rd Place: Martha Adlerstrahle d. Elsa Wallenberg (Sweden) 1–6, 6–3, 6–2
1912	(Stockholm, Sweden). Singles Medal Winners — *Gold:* Marguerite Broquedis (France); *Silver:* Dora Koring (Germany); *Bronze:* Anna "Molla" Bjurstedt (Norway). Singles Finals: Marguerite Broquedis d. Dora Koring 4–6, 6–3, 6–4; 3rd Place: Anna "Molla" Bjurstedt d. Edit Arnheim (Sweden) 6–2, 6–2. Doubles: Not held. Mixed Doubles Medal Winners — *Gold:* Dora Koring, Heinrich Schomburgk (Germany); *Silver:* Sigrid Fick, Gunnar Setterwall (Sweden); *Bronze:* Marguerite Broquedis, Albert Canet (France). Mixed Doubles Finals: Dora Koring, Heinrich Schomburgk d. Sigrid Fick, Gunnar Setterwall 6–4, 6–0
1912	(Stockholm, Sweden; Indoors). Singles Medal Winners — *Gold:* Edith Hannam (Great Britain); *Silver:* Thora Castenschiold (Denmark); *Bronze:* Mabel Parton (Great Britain). Singles Finals: Edith Hannam d. Thora Castenschiold 6–4, 6–3; 3rd Place: Mabel Parton d. Sigrid Fick 6–3, 6–3. Doubles: Not held. Mixed Doubles Medal Winners — *Gold:* Edith Hannam, Charles Percy Dixon (Great Britain); *Silver:* Helen Aitchison, Herbert Roper Barrett (Great Britain); *Bronze:* Sigrid Fick, Gunnar Setterwall (Sweden). Mixed Doubles Finals: Edith Hannam, Charles Percy Dixon d. Helen Aitchison, Herbert Roper Barrett 4–6, 6–3, 6–2; 3rd Place: Sigrid Fick, Gunnar Setterwall d. Margareta Cederschiold, Carl Kempe (Sweden) Walk Over
1920	(Antwerp, Belgium). Singles Medal Winners — *Gold:* Suzanne Lenglen (France); *Silver:* E. Dorothy Holman (Great Britain); *Bronze:* Kathleen "Kitty" McKane (Great Britain). Singles Finals: Suzanne Lenglen d. E. Dorothy Holman 6–3, 6–0; 3rd Place: Kathleen "Kitty" McKane d. Sigrid Fick (Sweden) 6–2, 6–0. Doubles Medal Winners — *Gold:* Winifred Margaret McNair, Kathleen "Kitty" McKane (Great Britain); *Silver:* W. Geraldine Beamish, E. Dorothy Holman (Great Britain); *Bronze:* Suzanne Lenglen, Elisabeth d'Ayen (France). Doubles Finals: Winifred Margaret McNair, Kathleen "Kitty" McKane d. Geraldine Beamish, E. Dorothy Holman 8–6, 6–4; 3rd Place: Suzanne Lenglen, Elisabeth d'Ayen d. Marie Storms, Fernande Arendt (Belgium) Walk Over. Mixed Doubles Medal Winners — *Gold:* Suzanne Lenglen, Max Decugis (France); *Silver:* Kathleen "Kitty" McKane, Max Woosnam (Great Britain); *Bronze:* Milada Skrbkova, Ladislav "Razny" Zemia (Czechoslovakia). Mixed Doubles Finals: Suzanne Lenglen, Max Decugis d. Kathleen "Kitty" McKane, Max Woosnam, 6–4, 6–2; 3rd Place: Milada Skrbkova, Ladislav "Razny" Zemia d. Amory Folmer-Hansen, Erik Tegner (Denmark), 8–6, 6–4
1924	(Paris, France). Singles Medal Winners — *Gold:* Helen Wills (United States); *Silver:* Julie "Diddie" Vlasto (France); *Bronze:* Kathleen "Kitty" McKane (Great Britain). Singles Finals: Helen Wills d. Julie "Diddie" Vlasto 6–2, 6–2; 3rd Place: Kathleen "Kitty" McKane d. Germaine Golding (France), 5–7, 6–3, 6–0. Doubles Medal Winners — *Gold:* Hazel Wightman, Helen Wills (United States); *Silver:* Phyllis Covell, Kathleen "Kitty" McKane (Great Britain); *Bronze:* Dorothy Shepherd-Barron, Evelyn Colyer (Great Britain). Doubles Finals: Hazel Wightman, Helen Wills d. Kathleen "Kitty" McKane, Phyllis Covell 7–5, 8–6; 3rd Place: Dorothy Shepherd-Barron, Evelyn Colyer d. Marguerite Billout, Yvonne Bourgeois (France) 6–1, 6–2. Mixed Doubles Medal Winners — *Gold:* Hazel Wightman, Richard Norris Williams (United States); *Silver:* Marion Jessup, Vincent Richards (United States); *Bronze:* Cornelia Bouman, Hendrik Timmer (Holland).

Year	Final Round Results

Mixed Doubles Finals: Hazel Wightman, Richard Norris Williams d. Marion Jessup, Vincent Richards, 6–2, 6–3; 3rd Place: Cornelia Bouman, Hendrik Timmer d. Kathleen "Kitty" McKane, John Gilbert (Great Britain) Walk Over

1928–1984 No women's competition

1988 (Seoul, Korea). Singles Medal Winners — *Gold:* Steffi Graf (Germany); *Silver:* Gabriela Sabatini (Argentina); *Bronze:* Zina Garrison (United States); *Bronze:* Manuela Maleeva (Bulgaria). Singles Finals: Steffi Graf d. Gabriela Sabatini 6–3, 6–3. Doubles Medal Winners — *Gold:* Zina Garrison, Pam Shriver (United States); *Silver:* Jana Novotna, Helena Sukova (Czechoslovakia); *Bronze:* Elizabeth Smylie, Wendy Turnbull (Australia); *Bronze:* Steffi Graf, Claudia Kohde-Kilsch (Germany). Doubles Finals: Zina Garrison, Pam Shriver d. Jana Novotna, Helena Sukova 4–6, 6–2, 10–8. Mixed Doubles: Not held

1992 (Barcelona, Spain). Singles Medal Winners — *Gold:* Jennifer Capriati (United States); *Silver:* Steffi Graf (Germany); *Bronze:* Mary Joe Fernandez (United States); *Bronze:* Arantxa Sanchez-Vicario (Spain). Singles Finals: Jennifer Capriati d. Steffi Graf 3–6, 6–3, 6–4. Doubles Medal Winners — *Gold:* Gigi Fernandez, Mary Joe Fernandez (United States); *Silver:* Conchita Martinez, Arantxa Sanchez-Vicario (Spain); *Bronze:* Rachel McQuillan, Nicole Provis (Australia); *Bronze:* Leila Meskhi, Natalia Zvereva (former Soviet Union). Doubles Finals: Gigi Fernandez, Mary Joe Fernandez d. Conchita Martinez, Arantxa Sanchez-Vicario, 7–5, 2–6, 6–2

1996 (Atlanta, Georgia). Singles Medal Winners — *Gold:* Lindsay Davenport (United States); *Silver:* Arantxa Sanchez-Vicario (Spain); *Bronze:* Jana Novotna (Czech Republic). Singles Finals: Lindsay Davenport d. Arantxa Sanchez-Vicario 7–6, 6–2; 3rd Place: Jana Novotna d. Mary Joe Fernandez 7–6, 6–4. Doubles Medal Winners — *Gold:* Gigi Fernandez, Mary Joe Fernandez (United States); *Silver:* Jana Novotna, Helena Sukova (Czech Republic); *Bronze:* Arantxa Sanchez-Vicario, Conchita Martinez (Spain). Doubles Finals: Gigi Fernandez, Mary Joe Fernandez d. Jana Novotna, Helena Sukova 7–6, 6–4; 3rd Place: Arantxa Sanchez-Vicario, Conchita Martinez d. Manon Bollegraf, Brenda Schultz-McCarthy (Netherlands) 6–1, 6–3

2000 (Sydney, Australia). Singles Medal Winners — *Gold:* Venus Williams (United States); *Silver:* Elena Dementieva (Russia); *Bronze:* Monica Seles (United States). Singles Finals: Venus Williams d. Elena Dementieva 6–2, 6–4; 3rd Place: Monica Seles d. Jelena Dokic (Australia) 6–1, 6–4. Doubles Medal Winners — *Gold:* Venus Williams, Serena Williams (United States); *Silver:* Kristie Boogert, Miriam Oremans (Netherlands); *Bronze:* Dominique Van Roost, Els Callens (Belgium). Doubles Finals: Venus Williams, Serena Williams d. Kristie Boogert, Miriam Oremans 6–1, 6–1; 3rd Place: Dominique Van Roost, Els Callens d. Olga Barabanschikova, Natasha Zvereva (Belarus) 4–6, 6–4, 6–1

2004 (Athens, Greece). Singles Medal Winners — *Gold:* Justine Henin (Belgium); *Silver:* Amelie Mauresmo (France); *Bronze:* Alicia Molik (Australia). Singles Finals: Justine Henin d. Amelie Mauresmo 6–3, 6–3; 3rd Place: Alicia Molik d. Anastasia Myskina (Russia) 6–3, 6–4. Doubles Medal Winners — *Gold:* Ting Li, Tiantian Sun (China); *Silver:* Conchita Martinez, Virginia Ruano Pascual (Spain); *Bronze:* Paola Suarez, Patricia Tarabini (Argentina). Doubles Finals: Ting Li, Tiantian Sun d. Conchita Martinez, Virginia Ruano Pascual 6–3, 6–3; 3rd Place: Paola Suarez, Patricia Tarabini d. Shinobu Asagoe, Ai Sugiyama (Japan) 6–3, 6–3

Year	*Final Round Results*
2008	(Beijing, China). Singles Medal Winners — *Gold:* Elena Dementieva (Russia); *Silver:* Dinara Safina (Russia); *Bronze:* Vera Zvonareva (Russia). Singles Finals: Elena Dementieva d. Dinara Safina 3–6, 7–5, 6–3; 3rd Place: Vera Zvonareva d. Li Na (China) 6–0, 7–5. Doubles Medal Winners — *Gold:* Serena Williams, Venus Williams (United States); *Silver:* Anabel Medina Garrigues, Virginia Ruano Pascual (Spain); *Bronze:* Zi Yan, Jie Zheng (China). Doubles Finals: Serena Williams, Venus Williams d. Anabel Medina Garrigues, Virginia Ruano Pascual 6–2, 6–0; 3rd Place: Zi Yan, Jie Zheng d. Alona Bondarenko, Kateryna Bondarenko (Ukraine) 6–2, 6–2

THE WIGHTMAN CUP

Wightman Cup competition began in 1923 when Hazel Hotchkiss Wightman donated a Silver trophy for an annual competition between the two great tennis playing nations of the time — the United States and Great Britain. Each year from 1923 to 1989 the teams played a best-of-seven match comprised of five singles and two doubles. The United States won 51 of the 61 team matches played.

Year	*Results*
1923	United States defeated Great Britain 7–0 (Played at West Side Tennis Club, Forest Hills, New York). *Singles:* Helen Wills d. Kitty McKane 6–2, 7–5; Molla Bjurstedt Mallory d. M. H. Davey Clayton 6–1, 8–6; Eleanor Goss d. Geraldine Beamish 6–2, 0–6, 7–5; Helen Wills d. M. H. Clayton 6–2, 6–3; Molla Bjurstedt Mallory d. Kitty McKane 6–2, 6–3. *Doubles:* Hazel Hotchkiss Wightman, Eleanor Goss d. Kitty McKane, Phyllis Covell 10–8, 5–7, 6–4; Molla Bjurstedt Mallory, Helen Wills Moody d. Geraldine Beamish, M. H. Davey Clayton 6–3, 6–2
1924	Great Britain defeated United States 6–1 (Played at Wimbledon, London, England). *Singles:* Phyllis Howkins Covell d. Helen Wills 6–2, 6–4; Kitty McKane d. Molla Bjurstedt Mallory 6–3, 6–3; Kitty McKane d. Helen Wills 6–2, 6–2; Phyllis Covell d. Molla Bjurstedt Mallory 6–2, 5–7, 6–3; Geraldine Beamish d. Eleanor Goss 6–1, 8–10, 6–3. *Doubles:* Phyllis Covell, Dorothy Shepherd Barron d. Marion Jessup, Eleanor Goss 6–2, 6–2; Hazel Hotchkiss Wightman, Helen Wills d. Kitty McKane, Evelyn Colyer 2–6, 6–2, 6–4
1925	Great Britain defeated United States 4–3 (Played at West Side Tennis Club, Forest Hills, New York). *Singles:* Kitty McKane d. Molla Bjurstedt Mallory 6–4, 5–7, 6–0; Helen Wills d. Joan Fry 6–0, 7–5; Dorothea Douglass Lambert Chambers d. Eleanor Goss 7–5, 3–6, 6–1; Helen Wills d. Kitty McKane 6–1, 1–6, 9–7; Molla Bjurstedt Mallory d. Joan Fry 6–3, 6–0. *Doubles:* Dorothea Douglass Lambert Chambers, Ermyntrude Harvey d. Molla Bjurstedt Mallory, May Sutton Bundy 10–8, 6–1; Kitty McKane, Evelyn Colyer d. Helen Wills, Mary K. Browne 6–0, 6–3
1926	United States defeated Great Britain 4–3 (Played at Wimbledon, London, England). *Singles:* Elizabeth Ryan d. Joan Fry 6–1, 6–3; Kitty McKane Godfree d. Mary K. Browne 6–1, 7–5; Joan Fry d. Mary K. Browne 3–6, 6–0, 6–4; Kitty McKane Godfree d. Elizabeth Ryan 6–1, 5–7, 6–4; Marion Z. Jessup d. Dorothy Shepherd-Barron 6–1, 5–7, 6–4. *Doubles:* Marion Z. Jessup, Eleanor Goss d. Dorothea Douglass Lambert Chambers Dorothy Shepherd-Barron 6–4, 6–2; Mary K. Browne, Elizabeth Ryan d. Kitty McKane Godfree, Evelyn Colyer 3–6, 6–2, 6–4

Year	Results
1927	United States defeated Great Britain 5–2 (Played at West Side Tennis Club, Forest Hills, New York). *Singles:* Helen Wills d. Joan Fry 6–2, 6–0; Molla Bjurstedt Mallory d. Kitty McKane Godfree 6–4, 6–2; Betty Nuthall d. Helen Jacobs 6–3, 2–6, 6–1; Helen Wills d. Kitty McKane Godfree 6–1, 6–1; Molla Bjurstedt Mallory d. Joan Fry 6–2, 11–9. *Doubles:* Gwendolyn Sterry, Betty Hill d. Eleanor Goss, Charlotte Hosmer Chapin 5–7, 7–5, 7–5; Helen Wills, Hazel Hotchkiss Wightman d. Kitty McKane Godfree, Ermyntrude Harvey 6–4, 4–6, 6–3
1928	Great Britain defeated United States 4–3 (Played at Wimbledon, London, England). *Singles:* Helen Wills d. Phoebe Watson 6–1, 6–2; Eileen Bennett d. Molla Bjurstedt Mallory 6–1, 6–3; Helen Wills d. Eileen Bennett 6–3, 6–2; Phoebe Watson d. Molla Bjurstedt Mallory 2–6, 6–1, 6–2; Helen Jacobs d. Betty Nuthall 6–3, 6–1. *Doubles:* Ermyntrude Harvey, Peggy Saunders d. Eleanor Goss, Helen Jacobs 6–4, 6–1; Eileen Bennett, Phoebe Watson d. Helen Wills, Penelope Anderson 6–2, 6–1
1929	United States defeated Great Britain 4–3 (Played at West Side Tennis Club, Forest Hills, New York). *Singles:* Helen Wills d. Phoebe Watson 6–1, 6–4; Helen Jacobs d. Betty Nuthall 7–5, 8–6; Phoebe Watson d. Helen Jacobs 6–3, 6–2; Edith Cross d. Peggy Saunders Michell 6–3, 3–6, 6–3; Helen Wills d. Betty Nuthall 8–6, 8–6. *Doubles:* Phoebe Watson, Peggy Michell d. Helen Wills, Edith Cross 6–4, 6–1; Phyllis Covell, Dorothy Shepherd-Barron d. Hazel Hotchkiss Wightman, Helen Jacobs 6–2, 6–1
1930	Great Britain defeated United States 4–3 (Played at Wimbledon, London, England). *Singles:* Helen Wills Moody d. Joan Fry 6–1, 6–1; Phoebe Watson d. Helen Jacobs 2–6, 6–2, 6–4; Helen Wills Moody d. Phoebe Watson 7–5, 6–1; Helen Jacobs d. Joan Fry 6–0, 6–3; Phyllis Mudford d. Sarah Palfrey 6–0, 6–2. *Doubles:* Joan Fry, Ermyntrude Harvey d. Sarah Palfrey, Edith Cross 2–6, 6–2, 6–4; Phoebe Watson, Kitty McKane Godfree d. Helen Wills Moody, Helen Jacobs 7–5, 1–6, 6–4
1931	United States defeated Great Britain 5–2 (Played at West Side Tennis Club, Forest Hills, New York). *Singles:* Helen Wills Moody d. Betty Nuthall 6–4, 6–2; Anna Harper d. Dorothy Round 6–3, 4–6, 9–7; Helen Jacobs d. Phyllis Mudford 6–4, 6–2; Helen Wills Moody d. Phyllis Mudford 6–1, 6–4; Helen Jacobs d. Betty Nuthall 8–6, 6–4. *Doubles:* Phyllis Mudford, Dorothy Shepherd-Barron d. Sarah Palfrey, Hazel Hotchkiss Wightman 6–4, 10–8; Betty Nuthall, Eileen Whittingstall d. Helen Wills Moody, Anna Harper 8–6, 5–7, 6–3
1932	United States defeated Great Britain 4–3 (Played at Wimbledon, London, England). *Singles:* Helen Jacobs d. Dorothy Round 6–4, 6–3; Helen Wills Moody d. Eileen Bennett Whittingstall 6–4, 6–2; Helen Moody d. Dorothy Round 6–2, 6–3; Eileen Bennett Whittingstall d. Helen Jacobs 6–4, 2–6, 6–1; Phyllis Mudford King d. Anna Harper 3–6, 6–3, 6–1. *Doubles:* Anna Harper, Helen Jacobs d. Peggy Saunders Michell, Dorothy Round 6–4, 6–1; Eileen Whittingstall, Betty Nuthall d. Helen Wills Moody, Sarah Palfrey 6–3, 1–6, 10–8
1933	United States defeated Great Britain 4–3 (Played at West Side Tennis Club, Forest Hills, New York). *Singles:* Helen Jacobs d. Dorothy Round 6–4, 6–2; Sarah Palfrey d. Margaret Scriven 6–3, 6–1; Betty Nuthall d. Carolin Babcock 1–6, 6–1, 6–3; Dorothy Round d. Sarah Palfrey 6–4, 10–8; Helen Jacobs d. Margaret Scriven 5–7, 6–2, 7–5. *Doubles:* Helen Jacobs, Sarah Palfrey d. Dorothy Round, Mary Heeley 6–4, 6–2; Betty Nuthall, Freda James d. Alice Marble, Marjorie Gladman Van Ryn 7–5, 6–2

Year	Results

1934   United States defeated Great Britain 5–2 (Played at Wimbledon, London, England). *Singles:* Sarah Palfrey d. Dorothy Round 6–3, 3–6, 8–6; Helen Jacobs d. Margaret Scriven 6–1, 6–1; Helen Jacobs d. Dorothy Round 6–4, 6–4; Sarah Palfrey d. Margaret Scriven 4–6, 6–2, 8–6; Betty Nuthall d. Carolin Babcock 5–7, 6–3, 6–4. *Doubles:* Nancy Lyle, Evelyn Dearman d. Carolin Babcock, Josephine Cruickshank 7–5, 7–5; Helen Jacobs, Sarah Palfrey d. Kitty McKane Godfree, Betty Nuthall 5–7, 6–3, 6–2

1935   United States defeated Great Britain 4–3 (Played at West Side Tennis Club, Forest Hills, New York). *Singles:* Kay Stammers d. Helen Jacobs 5–7, 6–1, 9–7; Dorothy Round d. Ethel B. Arnold 6–0, 6–3; Sarah Palfrey Fabyan d. Phyllis Mudford King 6–0, 6–3; Helen Jacobs d. Dorothy Round 6–3, 6–2; Ethel B. Arnold d. Kay Stammers 6–2, 1–6, 6–3. *Doubles:* Helen Jacobs, Sarah Palfrey Fabyan d. Kay Stammers, Freda James 6–3, 6–2; Nancy Lyle, Evelyn Dearman d. Dorothy Andrus, Carolin Babcock 3–6, 6–4, 6–1

1936   United States defeated Great Britain 4–3 (Played at Wimbledon, London, England). *Singles:* Kay Stammers d. Helen Jacobs 12–10, 6–1; Dorothy Round d. Sarah Palfrey Fabyan 6–3, 6–4; Sarah Palfrey Fabyan d. Kay Stammers 6–3, 6–4; Dorothy Round d. Helen Jacobs 6–3, 6–3; Carolin Babcock d. Mary Hardwick 6–4, 4–6, 6–2. *Doubles:* Carolin Babcock, Marjorie Gladman Van Ryn d. Evelyn Dearman, Nancy Lyle 6–2, 1–6, 6–3; Helen Jacobs, Sarah Palfrey Fabyan d. Kay Stammers, Freda James 1–6, 6–3, 7–5

1937   United States defeated Great Britain 6–1 (Played at West Side Tennis Club, Forest Hills, New York). *Singles:* Alice Marble d. Mary Hardwick 4–6, 6–2, 6–4; Helen Jacobs d. Kay Stammers 6–1, 4–6, 6–4; Helen Jacobs d. Mary Hardwick 2–6, 6–4, 6–2; Alice Marble d. Kay Stammers 6–3, 6–1; Sarah Palfrey Fabyan d. Margot Lumb 6–3, 6–1. *Doubles:* Alice Marble, Sarah Palfrey Fabyan d. Evelyn Dearman, Joan Ingram 6–3, 6–2; Kay Stammers, Freda James d. Marjorie Gladman Van Ryn, Dorothy Bundy 6–3, 10–8

1938   United States defeated Great Britain 5–2 (Played at Wimbledon, London, England). *Singles:* Kay Stammers d. Alice Marble 3–6, 7–5, 6–3; Helen Wills Moody d. Margaret Scriven 6–0, 7–5; Sarah Palfrey Fabyan d. Margot Lumb 5–7, 6–2, 6–3; Alice Marble d. Margaret Scriven 6–3, 3–6, 6–0; Helen Wills Moody d. Kay Stammers 6–2, 3–6, 6–3. *Doubles:* Alice Marble, Sarah Palfrey Fabyan d. Margot Lumb, Freda James 6–4, 6–2; Evelyn Dearman, Joan Ingram d. Helen Wills Moody, Dorothy Bundy 6–2, 7–5

1939   United States defeated Great Britain 5–2 (Played at West Side Tennis Club, Forest Hills, New York). *Singles:* Alice Marble d. Mary Hardwick 6–3, 6–4; Kay Stammers d. Helen Jacobs 6–2, 1–6, 6–3; Valerie Scott d. Sarah Palfrey Fabyan 6–3, 6–4; Alice Marble d. Kay Stammers 3–6, 6–3, 6–4; Helen Jacobs d. Mary Hardwick 6–2, 6–2. *Doubles:* Dorothy Bundy, Mary Arnold d. Betty Nuthall, Nina Brown 6–3, 6–1; Alice Marble, Sarah Palfrey Fabyan d. Kay Stammers, Freda James Hammersley 7–5, 6–2

1940–1945   Not held because of World War II

1946   United States defeated Great Britain 7–0 (Played at Wimbledon, London, England). *Singles:* Pauline Betz d. Jean Bostock 6–2, 6–4; Margaret Osborne d. Jean Bostock 6–1, 6–4; Margaret Osborne d. Kay Stammers Menzies 6–3, 6–2; Louise Brough d. Joan Curry 8–6, 6–3; Pauline Betz d. Kay Stammers Menzies 6–4, 6–4.

Year	Results

Doubles: Margaret Osborne, Louise Brough d. Jean Bostock, Mary Halford 6–2, 6–1; Pauline Betz, Doris Hart d. Betty Passingham, Molly Lincoln 6–1, 6–3

1947   United States defeated Great Britain 7–0 (Played at West Side Tennis Club, Forest Hills, New York). *Singles:* Margaret Osborne d. Jean Bostock 6–4, 2–6, 6–2; Louise Brough d. Kay Stammers Menzies 6–4, 6–2; Doris Hart d. Betty Hilton 4–6, 6–3, 7–5; Louise Brough d. Jean Bostock 6–4, 6–4; Margaret Osborne d. Kay Stammers Menzies 7–5, 6–2. *Doubles:* Doris Hart, Patricia C. Todd d. Joy Gannon, Jean Quertier 6–1, 6–2; Margaret Osborne, Louise Brough d. Jean Bostock, Betty Hilton 6–1, 6–4

1948   United States defeated Great Britain 6–1 (Played at Wimbledon, London, England). *Singles:* Margaret Osborne duPont d. Jean Bostock 6–4, 8–6; Louise Brough d. Betty Hilton 6–1, 6–1; Margaret Osborne duPont d. Betty Hilton 6–3, 6–4; Louise Brough d. Jean Bostock 6–2, 4–6, 7–5; Doris Hart d. Joy Gannon 6–1, 6–4. *Doubles:* Louise Brough, Margaret Osborne duPont d. Kay Stammers Menzies, Betty Hilton 6–2, 6–2; Jean Bostock, Molly Lincoln Blair d. Doris Hart, Patricia C. Todd 6–3, 6–4

1949   United States defeated Great Britain 7–0 (Played at Merion Cricket Club, Haverford, Pennsylvania). *Singles:* Doris Hart d. Jean Walker-Smith 6–3, 6–1; Margaret Osborne duPont d. Betty Hilton 6–1, 6–3; Doris Hart d. Betty Hilton 6–1, 6–3; Margaret Osborne duPont d. Jean Walker-Smith 6–4, 6–2; Beverly Baker d. Jean Quertier 6–4, 7–5. *Doubles:* Doris Hart, Shirley Fry d. Jean Quertier, Molly Lincoln Blair 6–1, 6–2; Gussy Moran, Patricia C. Todd d. Betty Hilton, Kay Tuckey 6–4, 8–6

1950   United States defeated Great Britain 7–0 (Played at Wimbledon, London, England). *Singles:* Margaret Osborne duPont d. Betty Hilton 6–3, 6–4; Doris Hart d. Joan Curry 6–2, 6–4; Louise Brough d. Betty Hilton 2–6, 6–2, 7–5; Margaret Osborne duPont d. Jean Walker-Smith 6–3, 6–2; Louise Brough d. Jean Walker-Smith 6–0, 6–0. *Doubles:* Patricia C. Todd, Doris Hart d. Jean Walker-Smith, Jean Quertier 6–2, 6–3; Louise Brough, Margaret Osborne duPont d. Betty Hilton, Kay Tuckey 6–2, 6–0

1951   United States defeated Great Britain 6–1 (Played at Longwood Cricket Club, Chestnut Hill, Massachusetts). *Singles:* Doris Hart d. Jean Quertier 6–4, 6–4; Shirley Fry d. Jean Walker-Smith 6–1, 6–4; Maureen Connolly d. Kay Tuckey 6–1, 6–3; Doris Hart d. Jean Walker-Smith 6–4, 2–6, 7–5; Jean Quertier d. Shirley Fry 6–3, 8–6. *Doubles:* Patricia C. Todd, Nancy Chaffee d. Pat Ward, Joy Gannon Mottram 7–5, 6–3; Shirley Fry, Doris Hart d. Jean Quertier, Kay Tuckey 6–3, 6–3

1952   United States defeated Great Britain 7–0 (Played at Wimbledon, London, England). *Singles:* Doris Hart d. Jean Quertier-Rinkel 6–3, 6–3; Maureen Connolly d. Jean Walker-Smith 3–6, 6–1, 7–5; Doris Hart d. Jean Walker-Smith 7–5, 6–2; Maureen Connolly d. Jean Quertier-Rinkel 9–7, 6–2; Shirley Fry d. Susan Partridge 6–0, 8–6. *Doubles:* Shirley Fry, Doris Hart d. Helen Fletcher, Jean Quertier-Rinkel 8–6, 6–4; Louise Brough, Maureen Connolly d. Joy Gannon Mottram, Pat Ward 6–0, 6–3

1953   United States defeated Great Britain 7–0 (Played at Westchester Country Club, Rye, New York). *Singles:* Maureen Connolly d. Angela Mortimer 6–1, 6–1; Doris Hart d. Helen Fletcher 6–4, 7–5; Shirley Fry d. Jean Quertier-Rinkel 6–2, 6–4; Maureen Connolly d. Helen Fletcher 6–1, 6–1; Doris Hart d. Angela Mortimer

Year	Results

6–1, 6–1. *Doubles:* Maureen Connolly, Louise Brough d. Angela Mortimer, Jacqueline Anne Shilcock 6–2, 6–3; Doris Hart, Shirley Fry d. Jean Quertier-Rinkel, Helen Fletcher 6–2, 6–1

1954   United States defeated Great Britain 6–0 (Played at Wimbledon, London, England). *Singles:* Maureen Connolly d. Helen Fletcher 6–1, 6–3; Doris Hart d. Jacqueline Anne Shilcock 6–4, 6–1; Doris Hart d. Helen Fletcher 6–1, 6–8, 6–2; Louise Brough d. Angela Buxton 8–6, 6–2; Maureen Connolly d. Jacqueline Anne Shilcock 6–2, 6–2. *Doubles:* Louise Brough, Margaret Osborne duPont d. Angela Buxton, Pat Hird 2–6, 6–4, 7–5; Helen Fletcher, Jacqueline Anne Shilcock vs. Shirley Fry, Doris Hart match was not played.

1955   United States defeated Great Britain 6–1 (Played at Westchester Country Club, Rye, New York). *Singles:* Angela Mortimer d. Doris Hart 6–4, 1–6, 7–5; Louise Brough d. Shirley Bloomer 6–2, 6–4; Louise Brough d. Angela Mortimer 6–0, 6–2; Dorothy H. Knode d. Angela Buxton 6–3, 6–3; Doris Hart d. Shirley Bloomer 7–5, 6–3. *Doubles:* Louise Brough, Margaret Osborne duPont d. Shirley Bloomer, Patricia Ward 6–3, 6–3; Doris Hart, Shirley Fry d. Angela Mortimer, Angela Buxton 3–6, 6–2, 7–5

1956   United States defeated Great Britain 5–2 (Played at Wimbledon, London, England). *Singles:* Louise Brough d. Angela Mortimer 3–6, 6–4, 7–5; Shirley Fry d. Angela Buxton 6–2, 6–8, 7–5; Louise Brough d. Angela Buxton 3–6, 6–3, 6–4; Shirley Bloomer d. Dorothy H. Knode 6–4, 6–4; Angela Mortimer d. Shirley Fry 6–4, 6–3. *Doubles:* Dorothy H. Knode, Beverly Baker Fleitz d. Shirley Bloomer, Patricia Ward 6–1, 6–4; Louise Brough, Shirley Fry d. Angela Buxton, Angela Mortimer 6–2, 6–2

1957   United States defeated Great Britain 6–1 (Played at Edgeworth Club, Sewickley, Pennsylvania). *Singles:* Althea Gibson d. Shirley Bloomer 6–4, 4–6, 6–2; Dorothy H. Knode d. Christine Truman 6–2, 11–9; Ann Haydon d. Darlene Hard 6–3, 3–6, 6–4; Dorothy H. Knode d. Shirley Bloomer 5–7, 6–1, 6–2; Althea Gibson d. Christine Truman 6–4, 6–2. *Doubles:* Althea Gibson, Darlene Hard d. Shirley Bloomer, Sheila Armstrong 6–3, 6–4; Louise Brough, Margaret Osborne duPont d. Jacqueline Anne Shilcock, Ann Haydon 6–4, 6–1

1958   Great Britain defeated United States 4–3 (Played at Wimbledon, London, England). *Singles:* Althea Gibson d. Shirley Bloomer 6–3, 6–4; Christine Truman d. Dorothy H. Knode 6–4, 6–4; Dorothy H. Knode d. Shirley Bloomer 6–4, 6–2; Christine Truman d. Althea Gibson 2–6, 6–3, 6–4; Ann Haydon d. Mimi Arnold 6–3, 5–7, 6–3. *Doubles:* Christine Truman, Shirley Bloomer d. Karol Fageros, Dorothy H. Knode 6–2, 6–3; Althea Gibson, Janet Hopps d. Jacqueline Anne Shilcock, Pat Ward 6–4, 3–6, 6–3

1959   United States defeated Great Britain 4–3 (Played at Edgeworth Club, Sewickley, Pennsylvania). *Singles:* Beverly B. Fleitz d. Angela Mortimer 6–2, 6–1; Christine Truman d. Darlene Hard 6–4, 2–6, 6–3; Darlene Hard d. Angela Mortimer 6–3, 6–8, 6–4; Beverly B. Fleitz d. Christine Truman 6–4, 6–4; Ann Haydon d. Sally Moore 6–1, 6–1. *Doubles:* Darlene Hard, Jeanne Arth d. Shirley Bloomer Brasher, Christine Truman 9–7, 9–7; Ann Haydon, Angela Mortimer d. Janet Hopps, Sally Moore 6–2, 6–4

1960   Great Britain defeated United States 4–3 (Played at Wimbledon, London, England). *Singles:* Ann Haydon d. Karen Hantze 2–6, 11–9, 6–1; Darlene Hard d.

Year   *Results*

Christine Truman 4–6, 6–3, 6–4; Darlene Hard d. Ann Haydon 5–7, 6–2, 6–1; Christine Truman d. Karen Hantze 7–5, 6–3; Angela Mortimer d. Janet Hopps 6–8, 6–4, 6–1. *Doubles:* Karen Hantze, Darlene Hard d. Ann Haydon, Angela Mortimer 6–0, 6–0; Christine Truman, Shirley Bloomer Brasher d. Janet Hopps, Dorothy H. Knode 6–4, 9–7

1961   United States defeated Great Britain 6–1 (Played at Saddle and Cycle Club, Chicago, Illinois). *Singles:* Karen Hantze d. Christine Truman 7–9, 6–1, 6–1; Billie Jean King d. Ann Haydon 6–4, 6–4; Karen Hantze d. Ann Haydon 6–1, 6–4; Christine Truman d. Billie Jean King 6–3, 6–2; Justina Bricka d. Angela Mortimer 10–8, 4–6, 6–3. *Doubles:* Karen Hantze, Billie Jean King d. Christine Truman, Deidre Catt 7–5, 6–2; Margaret Osborne duPont, Margaret Varner d. Angela Mortimer, Ann Haydon won by default.

1962   United States defeated Great Britain 4–3 (Played at Wimbledon, London, England). *Singles:* Darlene Hard d. Christine Truman 6–2, 6–2; Ann Haydon d. Karen H. Susman 10–8, 7–5; Deidre Catt d. Nancy Richey 6–1, 7–5; Darlene Hard d. Ann Haydon 6–3, 6–8, 6–4; Karen Susman d. Christine Truman 6–4, 7–5. *Doubles:* Margaret Osborne duPont, Margaret Varner d. Deidre Catt, Elizabeth Starkie 6–2, 3–6, 6–2; Christine Truman, Ann Haydon d. Darlene Hard, Billie Jean King 6–4, 6–3

1963   United States defeated Great Britain 6–1 (Played at Cleveland Skating Club, Cleveland, Ohio). *Singles:* Ann Haydon Jones d. Darlene Hard 6–1, 0–6, 8–6; Billie Jean King d. Christine Truman 6–4, 19–17; Nancy Richey d. Deidre Catt 14–12, 6–3; Darlene Hard d. Christine Truman 6–3, 6–0; Billie Jean King d. Ann Haydon Jones 6–4, 4–6, 6–3. *Doubles:* Darlene Hard, Billie Jean King d. Christine Truman, Ann Haydon Jones 4–6, 7–5, 6–2; Nancy Richey, Donna F. Fales d. Deidre Catt, Elizabeth Starkie 6–4, 6–8, 6–2

1964   United States defeated Great Britain 5–2 (Played at Wimbledon, London, England). *Singles:* Nancy Richey d. Deidre Catt 4–6, 6–4, 7–5; Billie Jean King d. Ann Haydon Jones 4–6, 6–2, 6–3; Carole Caldwell d. Elizabeth Starkie 6–4, 1–6, 6–3; Nancy Richey d. Ann Haydon Jones 7–5, 11–9; Billie Jean King d. Deidre Catt 6–3, 4–6, 6–3. *Doubles:* Deidre Catt, Ann Haydon Jones d. Carole Caldwell, Billie Jean King 6–2, 4–6, 6–0; Angela Mortimer, Elizabeth Starkie d. Nancy Richey, Donna F. Fales 2–6, 6–3, 6–4

1965   United States defeated Great Britain 5–2 (Played at Harold T. Clark Courts, Cleveland Heights, Ohio). *Singles:* Ann Haydon Jones d. Billie Jean King 6–2, 6–4; Nancy Richey d. Elizabeth Starkie 6–1, 6–0; Carole Caldwell Graebner d. Virginia Wade 3–6, 10–8, 6–4; Billie Jean King d. Elizabeth Starkie 6–3, 6–2; Ann Haydon Jones d. Nancy Richey 6–4, 8–6. *Doubles:* Carole Caldwell Graebner, Nancy Richey d. Nell Truman, Elizabeth Starkie 6–1, 6–0; Billie Jean King, Karen H. Susman d. Ann Haydon Jones, Virginia Wade 6–3, 8–6

1966   United States defeated Great Britain 4–3 (Played at Wimbledon, London, England). *Singles:* Ann Haydon Jones d. Nancy Richey 2–6, 6–4, 6–3; Billie Jean King d. Virginia Wade 6–2, 6–3; Winnie Shaw d. Mary Ann Eisel 6–3, 6–3; Nancy Richey d. Virginia Wade 2–6, 6–2, 7–5; Billie Jean King d. Ann Haydon Jones 5–7, 6–2, 6–3. *Doubles:* Ann Haydon Jones, Virginia Wade d. Billie Jean King, Jane Albert 7–5, 6–2; Nancy Richey, Mary Ann Eisel d. Rita Bentley, Elizabeth Starkie 6–1, 6–2

Year	Results

1967   United States defeated Great Britain 6–1 (Played at Harold T. Clark Courts, Cleveland Heights, Ohio). *Singles:* Billie Jean King d. Virginia Wade 6–3, 6–2; Nancy Richey d. Ann Haydon Jones 6–2, 6–2; Christine Truman d. Rosie Casals 3–6, 7–5, 6–1; Nancy Richey d. Virginia Wade 3–6, 8–6, 6–2; Billie Jean King d. Ann Haydon Jones 6–1, 6–2. *Doubles:* Rosie Casals, Billie Jean King d. Ann Haydon Jones, Virginia Wade 10–8, 6–4; Mary Ann Eisel, Carole Caldwell Graebner d. Winnie Shaw, Joyce Barclay Williams 8–6, 12–10

1968   Great Britain defeated United States 4–3 (Played at Wimbledon, London, England). *Singles:* Nancy Richey d. Christine Truman Janes 6–1, 8–6; Virginia Wade d. Mary Ann Eisel 6–0, 6–1; Jane "Peaches" Bartkowicz d. Winnie Shaw 7–5, 3–6, 6–4; Mary Ann Eisel d. Christine Truman Janes 6–4, 6–3; Virginia Wade d. Nancy Richey 6–4, 2–6, 6–3. *Doubles:* Virginia Wade, Winnie Shaw d. Nancy Richey, Mary Ann Eisel 5–7, 6–4, 6–3; Nell Truman, Christine Truman Janes d. Stephanie DeFina, Kathy Harter 6–3, 2–6, 6–3

1969   United States defeated Great Britain 5–2 (Played at Harold T. Clark Courts, Cleveland Heights, Ohio). *Singles:* Julie Heldman d. Virginia Wade 3–6, 6–1, 8–6; Nancy Richey d. Winnie Shaw 8–6, 6–2; Jane "Peaches" Bartkowicz d. Christine Truman Janes 8–6, 6–0; Virginia Wade d. Nancy Richey 6–3, 2–6, 6–4; Julie Heldman d. Winnie Shaw 6–3, 6–4. *Doubles:* Julie Heldman, Jane "Peaches" Bartkowicz d. Winnie Shaw, Virginia Wade 6–4, 6–2; Nell Truman, Christine Truman Janes d. Mary Ann Eisel Curtis, Valerie Ziegenfuss 6–1, 3–6, 6–4

1970   United States defeated Great Britain 4–3 (Played at Wimbledon, London, England). *Singles:* Billie Jean King d. Virginia Wade 8–6, 6–4; Ann Haydon Jones d. Nancy Richey 6–3, 6–3; Julie Heldman d. Joyce Barclay Williams 6–3, 6–2; Virginia Wade d. Nancy Richey 6–3, 6–2; Billie Jean King d. Ann Haydon Jones 6–4, 6–2. *Doubles:* Ann Haydon Jones, Joyce Barclay Williams d. Mary Ann Eisel Curtis, Julie Heldman 6–3, 6–2; Billie Jean King, Jane "Peaches" Bartkowicz d. Virginia Wade, Winnie Shaw 7–5, 6–8, 6–2

1971   United States defeated Great Britain 4–3 (Played at Harold T. Clark Courts, Cleveland Heights, Ohio). *Singles:* Chris Evert d. Winnie Shaw 6–0, 6–4; Virginia Wade d. Julie Heldman 7–5, 7–5; Joyce Barclay Williams d. Kristy Pigeon 7–5, 3–6, 6–4; Valerie Ziegenfuss d. Winnie Shaw 6–4, 4–6, 6–3; Chris Evert d. Virginia Wade 6–1, 6–1. *Doubles:* Mary Ann Eisel Curtis, Valerie Ziegenfuss d. Christine Truman Janes, Nell Truman 6–1, 6–4; Virginia Wade, Joyce Barclay Williams d. Carole Caldwell Graebner, Chris Evert 10–8, 4–6, 6–1

1972   United States defeated Great Britain 5–2 (Played at Wimbledon, London, England). *Singles:* Joyce Barclay Williams d. Wendy Overton 6–3, 3–6, 6–3; Chris Evert d. Virginia Wade 6–4, 6–4; Patti Hogan d. Corinne Molesworth 6–8, 6–4, 6–2; Chris Evert d. Joyce Williams 6–2, 6–3; Virginia Wade d. Wendy Overton 8–6, 7–5. *Doubles:* Valerie Ziegenfuss, Wendy Overton d. Virginia Wade, Joyce Barclay Willams 6–3, 6–3; Chris Evert, Patti Hogan d. Winnie Shaw, Nell Truman 7–5, 6–4

1973   United States defeated Great Britain 5–2 (Played at Longwood Cricket Club, Brookline, Massachusetts). *Singles:* Chris Evert d. Virginia Wade 6–4, 6–2; Patti Hogan d. Veronica Burton 6–4, 6–3; Linda Tuero d. Glynis Coles 7–5, 6–2; Chris Evert d. Veronica Burton 6–3, 6–0; Virginia Wade d. Patti Hogan 6–2, 6–2. *Doubles:* Patti Hogan, Jeanne Evert d. Lindsey Beaven, Lesley Charles 6–3, 4–6, 8–6; Virginia Wade, Glynis Coles d. Chris Evert, Marita Redondo 6–3, 6–4

Year	Results
1974	Great Britain defeated United States 6–1 (Played at Deeside Leisure Center, Queensferry, North Wales). *Singles:* Virginia Wade d. Julie Heldman 5–7, 9–7, 6–4; Glynis Coles d. Janet Newberry 4–6, 6–1, 6–3; Sue Barker d. Jeanne Evert 4–6, 6–4, 6–1; Glynis Coles d. Julie Heldman 6–0, 6–4; Virginia Wade d. Janet Newberry 6–1, 6–3. *Doubles:* Julie Heldman, Mona Schallau d. Virginia Wade, Glynis Coles 7–5, 6–4; Lesley Charles, Sue Barker d. Janet Newberry, Betsy Nagelsen 4–6, 6–2, 6–1
1975	Great Britain defeated United States 5–2 (Played at Public Auditorium, Cleveland, Ohio). *Singles:* Virginia Wade d. Mona Schallau 6–2, 6–2; Chris Evert d. Glynis Coles 6–4, 6–1; Sue Barker d. Janet Newberry 6–4, 7–5; Chris Evert d. Virginia Wade 6–3, 7–6; Glynis Coles d. Mona Schallau 6–3, 7–6. *Doubles:* Glynis Coles, Sue Barker d. Chris Evert, Mona Schallau 7–5, 6–4; Virginia Wade, Ann Haydon Jones d. Janet Newberry, Julie Anthony 6–2, 6–3
1976	United States defeated Great Britain 5–2 (Played at Wimbledon, London, England). *Singles:* Chris Evert d. Virginia Wade 6–2, 3–6, 6–3; Sue Barker d. Rosie Casals 1–6, 6–3, 6–2; Terry Holladay d. Glynis Coles 3–6, 6–1, 6–4; Virginia Wade d. Rosie Casals 3–6, 9–7, retired; Chris Evert d. Sue Barker 2–6, 6–2, 6–2. *Doubles:* Ann Kiyomura, Mona Schallau Guerrant d. Sue Mappin, Lesley Charles 6–2, 6–2; Chris Evert, Rosie Casals d. Virginia Wade, Sue Barker 6–0, 5–7, 6–1
1977	United States defeated Great Britain 7–0 (Played at Oakland Sports Areana, Oakland, California). *Singles:* Chris Evert d. Virginia Wade 7–5, 7–6; Billie Jean King d. Sue Barker 6–1, 6–4; Rosie Casals d. Michele Tyler 6–2, 3–6, 6–4; Billie Jean King d. Virginia Wade 6–4, 3–6, 8–6; Chris Evert d. Sue Barker 6–1, 6–2. *Doubles:* Chris Evert, Rosie Casals d. Virginia Wade, Sue Barker 6–2, 6–4; Billie Jean King, Jo Anne Russell d. Sue Mappin, Lesley Charles 6–0, 6–1
1978	Great Britain defeated United States 4–3 (Played at Albert Hall, London, England). *Singles:* Chris Evert d. Sue Barker 6–2, 6–1; Michele Tyler d. Pam Shriver 5–7, 6–3, 6–3; Virginia Wade d. Tracy Austin 3–6, 7–5, 6–3; Chris Evert d. Virginia Wade 6–0, 6–1; Sue Barker d. Tracy Austin 6–3, 3–6, 6–0. *Doubles:* Virginia Wade, Sue Barker d. Chris Evert, Pam Shriver 6–0, 5–7, 6–4; Billie Jean King, Tracy Austin d. Sue Mappin, Anne Hobbs 6–2, 4–6, 6–2
1979	United States defeated Great Britain 7–0 (Played at Wellington, West Palm Beach, Florida). *Singles:* Chris Evert d. Sue Barker 7–5, 6–2; Kathy Jordan d. Anne Hobbs 6–4, 6–7, 6–2; Tracy Austin d. Virginia Wade 6–1, 6–4; Tracy Austin d. Sue Barker 6–4, 6–2; Chris Evert d. Virginia Wade 6–1, 6–1. *Doubles:* Chris Evert, Rosie Casals d. Virginia Wade, Sue Barker 6–0, 6–1; Tracy Austin, Ann Kiyomura d. Jo Durie, Debbie Jevans 6–3, 6–1
1980	United States defeated Great Britain 5–2 (Played at Albert Hall, London, England). *Singles:* Chris Evert d. Sue Barker 6–1 6–2; Anne Hobbs d. Kathy Jordan 4–6, 6–4, 6–1; Andrea Jaeger d. Virginia Wade 3–6, 6–3, 6–2; Chris Evert d. Virginia Wade 7–5, 3–6, 7–5; Sue Barker d. Andrea Jaeger 5–7, 6–3, 6–3. *Doubles:* Kathy Jordan, Anne Smith d. Sue Barker, Virginia Wade 6–4, 7–5; Rosie Casals, Chris Evert d. Glynis Coles, Anne Hobbs 6–3, 6–3
1981	United States defeated Great Britain 7–0 (Played at International Amphitheatre, Chicago, Illinois). *Singles:* Tracy Austin d. Sue Barker 7–5, 6–3; Andrea Jaeger d. Anne Hobbs 6–0, 6–0; Chris Evert d. Virginia Wade 6–1, 6–3; Tracy Austin

Year   *Results*

d. Virginia Wade 6–3, 6–1; Chris Evert d. Sue Barker 6–3, 6–0; *Doubles:* Chris Evert, Rosie Casals d. Glynis Coles, Virginia Wade 6–3, 6–3; Andrea Jaeger, Pam Shriver d. Anne Hobbs, Jo Durie 6–1, 6–3

1982   United States defeated Great Britain 6–1 (Played at Albert Hall, London, England). *Singles:* Barbara Potter d. Sue Barker 6–2, 6–2; Anne Smith d. Virginia Wade 3–6, 7–5, 6–3; Chris Evert d. Jo Durie 6–2, 6–2; Barbara Potter d. Jo Durie 5–7, 7–6, 6–2; Chris Evert d. Sue Barker 6–4, 6–3. *Doubles:* Jo Durie, Anne Hobbs d. Rosie Casals, Anne Smith 6–3, 2–6, 6–2; Barbara Potter, Sharon Walsh d. Sue Barker, Virginia Wade 2–6, 6–4, 6–4

1983   United States defeated Great Britain 6–1 (Played at William and Mary Hall, Williamsburg, Virginia). *Singles:* Martina Navratilova d. Sue Barker 6–2, 6–0; Kathy Rinaldi d. Virginia Wade 6–2, 6–2; Pam Shriver d. Jo Durie 6–3, 6–2; Pam Shriver d. Sue Barker 6–0, 6–1; Martina Navratilova d. Jo Durie 6–3, 6–3. *Doubles:* Sue Barker, Virginia Wade d. Candy Reynolds, Paula Smith 7–5, 3–6, 6–1; Martina Navratilova, Pam Shriver d. Annabel Croft, Jo Durie 6–2, 6–1

1984   United States defeated Great Britain 5–2 (Played at Albert Hall, London, England). *Singles:* Chris Evert d. Anne Hobbs 6–2, 6–2; Annabel Croft d. Alycia Moulton 6–1, 5–7, 6–4; Jo Durie d. Barbara Potter 6–3, 7–6; Barbara Potter d. Anne Hobbs 6–1, 6–3; Chris Evert d. Jo Durie 7–6, 6–1. *Doubles:* Barbara Potter, Sharon Walsh d. Jo Durie, Anne Hobbs 7–6, 4–6, 9–7; Chris Evert, Alycia Moulton d. Virginia Wade, Amanda Brown 6–2, 6–2

1985   United States defeated Great Britain 7–0 (Played at William and Mary Hall, Williamsburg, Virginia). *Singles:* Chris Evert d. Jo Durie 6–2, 6–3; Kathy Rinaldi d. Anne Hobbs 7–5, 7–5; Pam Shriver d. Annabel Croft 6–0, 6–0; Pam Shriver d. Jo Durie 6–4, 6–4; Chris Evert d. Annabel Croft 6–3, 6–0. *Doubles:* Chris Evert, Pam Shriver d. Jo Durie, Anne Hobbs 6–3, 6–7, 6–2; Betsy Nagelsen, Anne White d. Annabel Croft, Virginia Wade 6–4, 6–1

1986   United States defeated Great Britain 7–0 (Played at Albert Hall, London, England). *Singles:* Kathy Rinaldi d. Sara Gomer 6–3, 7–6; Stephanie Rehe d. Annabel Croft 6–3, 6–1; Bonnie Gadusek d. Jo Durie 6–2, 6–4; Bonnie Gadusek d. Anne Hobbs 2–6, 6–4, 6–4; Kathy Rinaldi d. Jo Durie 6–4, 6–2. *Doubles:* Elise Burgin, Anne White d. Jo Durie, Anne Hobbs 7–6, 6–3; Bonnie Gadusek, Kathy Rinaldi d. Annabel Croft, Sara Gomer 6–3, 5–7, 6–3

1987   United States defeated Great Britain 5–2 (Played at William and Mary Hall, Williamsburg, Virginia). *Singles:* Zina Garrison d. Anne Hobbs 7–5, 6–2; Lori McNeil d. Sara Gomer 6–2, 6–1; Pam Shriver d. Jo Durie 6–1, 7–5; Pam Shriver d. Anne Hobbs 6–4, 6–3; Jo Durie d. Zina Garrison 7–6, 6–3. *Doubles:* Jo Durie, Anne Hobbs d. Zina Garrison, Lori McNeil 0–6, 6–4, 7–5; Gigi Fernandez, Robin White d. Sara Gomer, Clare Wood 6–4, 6–1

1988   United States defeated Great Britain 7–0 (Played at Albert Hall, London, England). *Singles:* Zina Garrison d. Jo Durie 6–2, 6–4; Patty Fendick d. Monique Javer 6–2, 6–1; Lori McNeil d. Sara Gomer 6–7, 6–4, 6–4; Zina Garrison d. Claire Wood 6–3, 6–2; Lori McNeil d. Jo Durie 6–1, 6–2. *Doubles:* Gigi Fernandez, Zina Garrison d. Jo Durie, Clare Wood 6–1, 6–3; Lori McNeil, Betsy Nagelsen d. Sara Gomer, Julie Salmon 6–3, 6–2

1989   United States defeated Great Britain 7–0 (Played at William and Mary Hall, Williamsburg, Virginia). *Singles:* Lori McNeil d. Jo Durie 7–5, 6–1; Jennifer Capriati

Year   *Results*

d. Clare Wood 6–0, 6–0; Mary Joe Fernandez d. Sara Gomer 6–1, 6–2; Lori Mc-Neil d. Sara Gomer 6–4, 6–2; Mary Joe Fernandez d. Jo Durie 6–1, 7–5. *Doubles:* Patty Fendick, Lori McNeil d. Jo Durie, Anne Hobbs 6–3, 6–3; Mary Joe Fernandez, Betsy Nagelsen d. Sara Gomer, Clare Wood 6–2, 7–6

THE HOPMAN CUP

The Hopman Cup is named in honor of Harry Hopman, one of Australia's greatest players and coaches. He was born on August 12, 1906, in Glebe, New South Wales, and died on December 27, 1985. Hopman captained the Aussie Davis Cup team to 15 championships from 1938 to 1969. Even though Hopman is best remembered as a coach, he was also a world-class tennis player. He won seven Grand Slam doubles and mixed doubles titles and reached the men's singles finals of the Australian Open three times.

The Hopman Cup, under the aegis of the International Tennis Federation since 1997, is played each year in Perth, Australia. The first Hopman Cup match was played on December 28, 1988. The match marked the return of international tennis to Perth since the mid–1970s. The unique format is the best-of-three matches — women's singles, men's singles, and mixed doubles.

Year	Final Round Results
1989	Czechoslovakia defeated Australia 2–0 (Played Dec. 28, 1988–Jan. 1, 1989). *Singles:* Helena Sukova (CZE) d. Hana Mandlikova (AUS) 6–4, 6–3. *Doubles:* Helena Sukova, Miloslav Mecir (CZE) d. Hana Mandlikova, Pat Cash (AUS) 6–2, 6–4
1990	Spain defeated United States 2–1 (Played Dec. 26, 1989–Jan. 1, 1990). *Singles:* Arantxa Sanchez-Vicario (ESP) d. Pam Shriver (USA) 6–3, 6–3; Emilio Sanchez (ESP) d. John McEnroe (USA) 5–7, 7–5, 7–5. *Doubles:* Pam Shriver, John McEnroe (USA) d. Arantxa Sanchez-Vicario, Emilio Sanchez (ESP) 6–3, 6–2
1991	Yugoslavia defeated United States 3–0 (Played Dec. 27, 1990–Jan. 4, 1991). *Singles:* Monica Seles (YUG) d. Zina Garrison (USA) 6–1, 6–1; Goran Prpic (YUG) d. David Wheaton (USA) 4–6, 6–3, 7–5. *Doubles:* Monica Seles, Goran Prpic d. Zina Garrison, David Wheaton (USA) 8–3
1992	Switzerland defeated Czechoslovakia 2–1 (Played Dec. 27, 1991–Jan. 3, 1992). *Singles:* Manuela Maleeva-Fragniere (SUI) d. Helena Sukova (CZE) 6–2, 6–4; Jakob Hlasek (SUI) d. Karel Novacek (CZE) 6–4, 6–4. *Doubles:* Helena Sukova, Karel Novacek (CZE) d. Manuela Maleeva-Fragniere, Jakob Hlasek (SUI) 8–4
1993	Germany defeated Spain 2–1 (Played Jan. 2, 1993–Jan. 8, 1993). *Singles:* Steffi Graf (GER) d. Arantxa Sanchez-Vicario (ESP) 6–4, 6–3; Michael Stich (GER) d. Emilio Sanchez (ESP) 7–5, 6–3. *Doubles:* Arantxa Sanchez-Vicario, Emilio Sanchez (ESP) d. Steffi Graf, Michael Stich (GER) Walk Over
1994	Czech Republic defeated Germany 2–1 (Played Dec. 31, 1993–Jan. 7, 1994). *Singles:* Jana Novotna (CZE) d. Anke Huber (GER) 1–6, 6–4, 6–3; Petr Korda (CZE) d. Bernd Karbacher (GER) 6–3, 6–3. *Doubles:* Anke Huber, Bernd Karbacher (GER) d. Jana Novotna, Petr Korda (CZE) 8–3

Year	*Final Round Results*
1995	Germany defeated Ukraine 3–0 (Played Dec. 31, 1994–Jan. 7, 1995). *Singles:* Anke Huber (GER) d. Natalia Medvedeva (UKR) 6–4, 3–6, 6–4; Boris Becker (GER) d. Andrei Medvedev (UKR) 6–3, 6–7 (7–3), 6–3. *Doubles:* Anke Huber, Boris Becker (GER) d. Natalia Medvedeva, Andre Medvedev (UKR) Walk Over
1996	Croatia defeated Switzerland 2–1 (Played Dec. 31, 1995–Jan. 6, 1996). *Singles:* Martina Hingis (SUI) d. Iva Majoli (HRV) 6–3, 6–0; Goran Ivanisevec (HRV) d. Marc Rosset (SUI) 7–6, 7–5. *Doubles:* Iva Majoli, Goran Ivanisevec (HRV) d. Martina Hingis, Marc Rosset (SUI) 3–6, 7–6, 5–5 Retired
1997	United States defeated South Africa 2–1 (Played Dec. 29, 1996–Jan. 4, 1997). *Singles:* Chanda Rubin (USA) d. Amanda Coetzer (RSA) 7–5, 6–2; Wayne Ferreira (RSA) d. Justin Gimelstob (USA) 6–4, 7–6 (7–4). *Doubles:* Chanda Rubin, Justin Gimelstob (USA) d. Amanda Coetzer, Wayne Ferreira (RSA) 3–6, 6–2, 7–5
1998	Slovak Republic defeated France 2–1 (Played Jan. 4, 1998–Jan. 10, 1998). *Singles:* Mary Pierce (FRA) d. Karina Habsudova (SVK) 6–4, 7–5; Karol Kucera (SVK) d. Cedric Pioline (FRA) 7–6 (9–7), 6–4. *Doubles:* Karina Habsudova, Karol Kucera (SVK) d. Mary Pierce, Cedric Pioline (FRA) 6–3, 6–4
1999	Australia defeated Sweden 2–1 (Played Jan. 2, 1999–Jan. 9, 1999). *Singles:* Jelena Dokic (AUS) d. Asa Carlsson (SWE) 6–2, 7–6 (10–8); Mark Philippousis (AUS) d. Jonas Bjorkman (SWE) 6–3, 7–6 (8–6). *Doubles:* Asa Carlsson, Jonas Bjorkman (SWE) d. Jelena Dokic, Mark Philippousis (AUS) 8–6
2000	South Africa defeated Thailand 3–0 (Played Jan. 1, 2000–Jan. 8, 2000). *Singles:* Amanda Coetzer (RSA) d. Tamarine Tanasugarn (THA) 3–6, 6–4, 6–4; Wayne Ferreira (RSA) d. Paradorn Srichaphan (THA) 7–6, 6–3. *Doubles:* Amanda Coetzer, Wayne Ferreira (RSA) d. Tamarine Tanasugarn, Paradorn Srichaphan (THA) 8–1
2001	Switzerland defeated United States 2–1 (Played Dec. 30, 2000–Jan. 6, 2001). *Singles:* Martina Hingis (SUI) d. Monica Seles (USA) 7–5, 6–4; Roger Federer (SUI) d. Jan Michael Gambill (USA) 6–4, 6–3. *Doubles:* Monica Seles, Jan Michael Gambill (USA) d. Martina Hingis, Roger Federer (SUI) 2–6, 6–4, 7–6
2002	Spain defeated United States 2–1 (Played Dec. 29, 2001–Jan. 5, 2002). *Singles:* Monica Seles (USA) d. Arantxa Sanchez Vicario (ESP) 6–1, 7–6; Tommy Robredo (ESP) d. Jan Michael Gambill (USA) 6–3, 2–6, 7–6 (7–2). *Doubles:* Arantxa Sanchez-Vicario, Tommy Robredo (ESP) d. Monica Seles, Jan Michael Gambill (USA) 6–4, 6–2
2003	United States defeated Australia 3–0 (Played Dec. 28, 2002–Jan. 4, 2003). *Singles:* Serena Williams (USA) d. Alicia Molik (AUS) 6–2, 6–3; James Blake (USA) d. Lleyton Hewitt (AUS) 6–3, 6–4. *Doubles:* Serena Williams, James Blake (USA) d. Alicia Molik, Lleyton Hewitt (AUS) 6–3, 6–2
2004	United States defeated Slovak Republic 2–1 (Played Jan. 3, 2004–Jan.10, 2004). *Singles:* Lindsay Davenport (USA) d. Daniela Hantuchova (SVK) 6–3, 6–1; Karol Kucera (SVK) d. James Blake (USA) 4–6, 6–4, 7–6 (7–5). *Doubles:* Lindsay Davenport, James Blake (USA) d. Daniela Hantuchova, Karol Kucera (SVK) 6–2, 6–3
2005	Slovak Republic defeated Argentina 3–0 (Played Jan. 1, 2005–Jan. 8, 2005). *Singles:* Daniela Hantuchova (SVK) d. Gisela Dulko (ARG) 1–6, 6–4, 6–4; Dominik Hrbaty (SVK) d. Guillermo Coria (ARG) 6–4, 6–1. *Doubles:* Daniela Hantuchova, Dominik Hrbaty (SVK) d. Gisela Dulko, Guillermo Coria (ARG) Walk Over

Year	Final Round Results
2006	United States defeated Netherlands 2–1 (Played Dec. 30, 2005–Jan. 6, 2006). *Singles:* Michaella Krajicek (NED) d. Lisa Raymond (USA) 6–4, 7–6 (4); Taylor Dent (USA) d. Peter Wessels (NED) 6–1, 6–4. *Doubles:* Lisa Raymond, Taylor Dent (USA) d. Michaella Krajicek, Peter Wessels (NED) 4–6, 6–2, 7–6 (7)
2007	Russia defeated Spain 2–0 (Played Dec. 30, 2006–Jan. 5, 2007). *Singles:* Nadia Petrova (RUS) d. Anabel Medina Garrigues (ESP) 6–0, 6–4; Dmitry Tursunov (RUS) d. Tommy Robredo (ESP) 6–4, 7–5. *Doubles:* Not Played
2008	United States defeated Serbia 2–1 (Played Dec. 29, 2007–Jan. 4, 2008). *Singles:* Serena Williams (USA) d. Jelena Jankovic (SER) 6–0, 6–0 Walk Over; Novak Djokovic (SER) d. Mardy Fish (USA) 6–2, 6–7 (4), 7–6 (4). *Doubles:* Serena Williams, Mardy Fish (USA) d. Jelena Jankovic, Novak Djokovic (SER) 7–6 (4), 6–2

III
RANKINGS

USTA TOP 10 WOMEN'S SINGLES RANKINGS

Each year the United States Tennis Association ranks the top female tennis players residing in the United States. These rankings included only amateur players through the year 1971. Beginning in 1972, the rankings include all players. Annual rankings are based on each player's performance in officially sponsored tournaments during the year.

1913

1. Mary K. Browne
2. Ethel Sutton Bruce
3. Florence Sutton
4. Helen Homans McLean
5. Louise Riddell Williams
6. Marie Wagner
7. Dorothy Green Briggs
8. Edith Rotch
9. Anita Myers
10. Gwendolyn Rees

1914

1. Mary K. Browne
2. Florence Sutton
3. Marie Wagner
4. Louise Hammond Raymond
5. Edith Rotch
6. Eleonora Sears
7. Louise Riddell Williams
8. Sarita Van Vliet Wood
9. Mrs. H. Niemeyer
10. Sara Livingston

1915

1. Molla Bjurstedt
2. Hazel Hotchkiss Wightman
3. Helen Homans McLean

4. Florence Sutton
5. Maud Barger Wallach
6. Marie Wagner
7. Anita Myers
8. Sara Livingston
9. Clare Cassel
10. Eleonora Sears

1916

1. Molla Bjurstedt
2. Louise Hammond Raymond
3. Evelyn Sears
4. Anita Myers
5. Sara Livingston
6. Marie Wagner
7. Adelaide Browning Green
8. Martha Guthrie
9. Eleonora Sears
10. Maud Barger Wallach

1917

No Rankings

1918

1. Molla Bjurstedt
2. Hazel Hotchkiss Wightman
3. Adelaide Browning Green
4. Eleanor Goss

5. Marie Wagner
6. Carrie Neely
7. Corinne Gould
8. Helene Pollak
9. Edith Handy
10. Clare Cassel

1919

1. Hazel Hotchkiss Wightman
2. Eleanor Goss
3. Molla Bjurstedt Mallory
4. Marion Zinderstein
5. Helen Baker
6. Louise Hammond Raymond
7. Helen Gilleaudeau
8. Marie Wagner
9. Corinne Gould
10. Helene Pollak

1920

1. Molla Bjurstedt Mallory
2. Marion Zinderstein
3. Eleanor Tennant
4. Helen Baker
5. Eleanor Goss
6. Louise Hammond Raymond
7. Helene Pollak Falk
8. Edith Sigourney
9. Florence Ballin
10. Marie Wagner

1921

1. Molla Bjurstedt Mallory
2. Mary K. Browne
3. Marion Zinderstein Jessup
4. May Sutton Bundy
5. Eleanor Goss
6. Helen Gilleaudeau
7. Anne Sheafe Cole
8. Leslie Bancroft
9. Louise Hammond Raymond
10. Margaret Grove

1922

1. Molla Bjurstedt Mallory
2. Leslie Bancroft
3. Helen Wills
4. Marion Zinderstein Jessup

5. May Sutton Bundy
6. Martha Bayard
7. Helen Gilleaudeau
8. Mary Dixon Thayer
9. Marie Wagner
10. Florence Ballin

1923

1. Helen Wills
2. Molla Bjurstedt Mallory
3. Eleanor Goss
4. Lillian Scharman
4. Helen Gilleaudeau Lockhorn
6. Mayme MacDonald
7. Edith Sigourney
8. Leslie Bancroft
9. Martha Bayard
10. Helen Hooker

1924

1. Helen Wills
2. Mary K. Browne
3. Molla Bjurstedt Mallory
4. Eleanor Goss
5. Marion Zinderstein Jessup
6. Martha Bayard
7. Mayme MacDonald
8. Anne Sheafe Cole
9. Mary Dixon Thayer
10. Leslie Bancroft

1925

1. Helen Wills
2. Elizabeth Ryan
3. Molla Bjurstedt Mallory
4. Marion Zinderstein Jessup
5. Eleanor Goss
6. Mary K. Browne
7. Martha Bayard
8. May Sutton Bundy
9. Charlotte Hosmer
10. Edith Sigourney

1926

1. Molla Bjurstedt Mallory
2. Elizabeth Ryan
3. Eleanor Goss
4. Martha Bayard

5. Charlotte Hosmer Chapin
6. Betty Corbiere
7. Margaret Blake
8. Penelope Anderson
9. Edna Hauslett Roeser
10. Mrs. Ellis Endicott

1927

1. Helen Wills
2. Molla Bjurstedt Mallory
3. Charlotte Hosmer Chapin
4. Helen Jacobs
5. Eleanor Goss
6. Betty Corbiere
7. Penelope Anderson
8. Margaret Blake
9. Edna Roeser
10. Alice Francis

1928

1. Helen Wills
2. Helen Jacobs
3. Edith Cross
4. Molla Bjurstedt Mallory
5. May Sutton Bundy
6. Marjorie Morrill
7. Marjorie Gladman
8. Anna McCune Harper
9. Charlotte Hosmer Chapin
10. Betty Corbiere

1929

1. Helen Wills Moody
2. Helen Jacobs
3. Edith Cross
4. Sarah Palfrey
5. Anna McCune Harper
6. Mary Greef
7. Eleanor Goss
8. Ethel Burkhardt
9. Marjorie Gladman
10. Josephine Cruickshank

1930

1. Anna McCune Harper
2. Marjorie Morrill
3. Dorothy Weisel
4. Virginia Hilleary

5. Josephine Cruickshank
6. Ethel Burkhardt
7. Marjorie Gladman Van Ryn
8. Sarah Palfrey
9. Mary Greef
10. Edith Cross

1931

1. Helen Wills Moody
2. Helen Jacobs
3. Anna McCune Harper
4. Marion Zinderstein Jessup
5. Mary Greef
6. Marjorie Morrill
7. Sarah Palfrey
8. Marjorie Gladman Van Ryn
9. Virginia Hilleary
10. Dorothy Andrus Burke

1932

1. Helen Jacobs
2. Anna McCune Harper
3. Carolin Babcock
4. Marjorie Morrill Painter
5. Josephine Cruickshank
6. Virginia Hilleary
7. Alice Marble
8. Marjorie Gladman Van Ryan
9. Virginia Rice
10. Marjorie Sachs

1933

1. Helen Jacobs
2. Helen Wills Moody
3. Alice Marble
4. Sarah Palfrey
5. Carolin Babcock
6. Josephine Cruickshank
7. Maud Rosenbaum Levi
8. Marjorie Gladman Van Ryn
9. Virginia Rice
10. Agnes Sherwood Lamme

1934

1. Helen Jacobs
2. Sarah Palfrey Fabyan
3. Carolin Babcock
4. Dorothy Andrus

5. Maude Rosenbaum Levi
6. Jane Sharp
7. Marjorie Morrill Painter
8. Mary Greef Harris
9. Marjorie Sachs
10. Catherine Wolf

1935

1. Helen Jacobs
2. Ethel Burkhardt Arnold
3. Sarah Palfrey Fabyan
4. Carolin Babcock
5. Marjorie Gladman Van Ryn
6. Gracyn Wheeler
7. Mary Greef Harris
8. Agnes Lamme
9. Dorothy Andrus
10. Catherine Wolf

1936

1. Alice Marble
2. Helen Jacobs
3. Sarah Palfrey Fabyan
4. Gracyn Wheeler
5. Carolin Babcock
6. Helen Pedersen
7. Marjorie Gladman Van Ryn
8. Dorothy Bundy
9. Katherine Winthrop
10. Mary Greef Harris

1937

1. Alice Marble
2. Helen Jacobs
3. Dorothy Bundy
4. Marjorie Gladman Van Ryn
5. Gracyn Wheeler
6. Sarah Palfrey Fabyan
7. Dorothy Burke Andrus
8. Helen Pedersen
9. Carolin Babcock Stark
10. Katherine Winthrop

1938

1. Alice Marble
2. Sarah Palfrey Fabyan
3. Dorothy Bundy
4. Barbara Winslow

5. Gracyn Wheeler
6. Dorothy Workman
7. Margaret Osborne
8. Helen Pedersen
9. Virginia Wolfenden
10. Katherine Winthrop

1939

1. Alice Marble
2. Helen Jacobs
3. Sarah Palfrey Fabyan
4. Helen Bernhard
5. Virginia Wolfenden
6. Dorothy Bundy
7. Dorothy Workman
8. Pauline Betz
9. Katherine Winthrop
10. Mary Arnold

1940

1. Alice Marble
2. Helen Jacobs
3. Pauline Betz
4. Dorothy Bundy
5. Gracyn Wheeler Kelleher
6. Sarah Palfrey Cooke
7. Virginia Wolfenden
8. Helen Bernhard
9. Mary Arnold
10. Hope Knowles

1941

1. Sarah Palfrey Cooke
2. Pauline Betz
3. Dorothy Bundy
4. Margaret Osborne
5. Helen Jacobs
6. Helen Bernhard
7. Hope Knowles
8. Mary Arnold
9. Virginia Wolfenden Kovacs
10. Louise Brough

1942

1. Pauline Betz
2. Louise Brough
3. Margaret Osborne
4. Helen Bernhard

5. Mary Arnold
6. Doris Hart
7. Patricia Canning Todd
8. Helen Pedersen Rihbany
9. Madge Harshaw Vosters
10. Katherine Winthrop

1943

1. Pauline Betz
2. Louise Brough
3. Doris Hart
4. Margaret Osborne
5. Dorothy Bundy
6. Mary Arnold
7. Dorothy Head
8. Helen Bernhard
9. Helen Pedersen Rihbany
10. Katherine Winthrop

1944

1. Pauline Betz
2. Margaret Osborne
3. Louise Brough
4. Dorothy Bundy
5. Mary Arnold
6. Doris Hart
7. Virginia Wolfenden Kovacs
8. Shirley Fry
9. Patricia Canning Todd
10. Dorothy Head

1945

1. Sarah Palfrey Cooke
2. Pauline Betz
3. Margaret Osborne
4. Louise Brough
5. Patricia Canning Todd
6. Doris Hart
7. Shirley Fry
8. Mary Arnold Prentiss
9. Dorothy Bundy
10. Helen Pedersen Rihbany

1946

1. Pauline Betz
2. Margaret Osborne
3. Louise Brough
4. Doris Hart

5. Patricia Canning Todd
6. Dorothy Bundy Cheney
7. Shirley Fry
8. Mary Arnold Prentiss
9. Virginia Wolfenden Kovacs
10. Dorothy Head

1947

1. Louise Brough
2. Margaret Osborne duPont
3. Doris Hart
4. Patricia Canning Todd
5. Shirley Fry
6. Barbara Krase
7. Dorothy Head
8. Mary Arnold Prentiss
9. Gertrude "Gussy" Moran
10. Helen Pedersen Rihbany

1948

1. Margaret Osborne duPont
2. Louise Brough
3. Doris Hart
4. Gertrude "Gussy" Moran
5. Beverly Baker
6. Patricia Canning Todd
7. Shirley Fry
8. Helen Pastall Perez
9. Virginia Wolfenden Kovacs
10. Helen Pedersen Rihbany

1949

1. Margaret Osborne duPont
2. Louise Brough
3. Doris Hart
4. Patricia Canning Todd
5. Helen Pastall Perez
6. Shirley Fry
7. Gertrude "Gussy" Moran
8. Beverly Baker Beckett
9. Dorothy Head
10. Barbara Scofield

1950

1. Margaret Osborne duPont
2. Doris Hart
3. Louise Brough
4. Beverly Baker

5. Patricia Canning Todd
6. Nancy Chaffee
7. Barbara Scofield
8. Shirley Fry
9. Helen Pastall Perez
10. Maureen Connolly

1951

1. Maureen Connolly
2. Doris Hart
3. Shirley Fry
4. Nancy Chaffee Kiner
5. Patricia Canning Todd
6. Beverly Baker Fleitz
7. Dorothy Head
8. Betty Rosenquest Pratt
9. Magda Rurac
10. Baba Madden Lewis

1952

1. Maureen Connolly
2. Doris Hart
3. Shirley Fry
4. Louise Brough
5. Nancy Chaffee Kiner
6. Anita Kanter
7. Patricia Canning Todd
8. Baba Madden Lewis
9. Althea Gibson
10. Julia Ann Sampson

1953

1. Maureen Connolly
2. Doris Hart
3. Shirley Fry
4. Louise Brough
5. Margaret Osborne duPont
6. Helen Pastall Perez
7. Althea Gibson
8. Mercedes "Baba" Madden Lewis
9. Anita Kanter
10. Julie Sampson

1954

1. Doris Hart
2. Louise Brough
3. Beverly Baker Fleitz
4. Shirley Fry

5. Betty Rosenquest Pratt
6. Barbara Breit
7. Darlene Hard
8. Lois Felix
9. Helen Pastall Perez
10. Barbara Scofield Davidson

1955

1. Doris Hart
2. Shirley Fry
3. Louise Brough
4. Dorothy Head Knode
5. Beverly Baker Fleitz
6. Barbara Scofield Davidson
7. Barbara Breit
8. Althea Gibson
9. Darlene Hard
10. Dorothy Bundy Cheney

1956

1. Shirley Fry
2. Althea Gibson
3. Louise Brough
4. Margaret Osborne duPont
5. Betty Rosenquest Pratt
6. Dorothy Head Knode
7. Darlene Hard
8. Karol Fageros
9. Janet Hopps
10. Miriam Arnold

1957

1. Althea Gibson
2. Louise Brough
3. Dorothy Head Knode
4. Darlene Hard
5. Karol Fageros
6. Miriam Arnold
7. Jeanne Arth
8. Sally Moore
9. Janet Hopps
10. Mary Ann Mitchell

1958

1. Althea Gibson
2. Beverly Baker Fleitz
3. Darlene Hard
4. Dorothy Head Knode

5. Margaret Osborne duPont
6. Jeanne Arth
7. Janet Hopps
8. Sally Moore
9. Gwyneth Thomas
10. Mary Ann Mitchell

1959

1. Beverly Baker Fleitz
2. Darlene Hard
3. Dorothy Head Knode
4. Sally Moore
5. Janet Hopps
6. Karen Hantze
7. Barbara Green Weigandt
8. Karol Fageros
9. Miriam Arnold
10. Lois Felix

1960

1. Darlene Hard
2. Karen Hantze
3. Nancy Richey
4. Billie Jean King
5. Donna Floyd
6. Janet Hopps
7. Gwyneth Thomas
8. Victoria Palmer
9. Kathy Chabot
10. Carol Hanks

1961

1. Darlene Hard
2. Karen Hantze
3. Billie Jean King
4. Kathy Chabot
5. Justina Bricka
6. Gwyneth Thomas
7. Marilyn Montgomery
8. Judy Alvarez
9. Carole Caldwell
10. Donna Floyd

1962

1. Darlene Hard
2. Karen Hantze Susman
3. Billie Jean King
4. Carole Caldwell

5. Donna Floyd Fales
6. Nancy Richey
7. Victoria Palmer
8. Gwyneth Thomas
9. Justina Bricka
10. Judy Alvarez

1963

1. Darlene Hard
2. Billie Jean King
3. Nancy Richey
4. Carole Caldwell
5. Gwyneth Thomas
6. Judy Alvarez
7. Carol Hanks
8. Tory Fretz
9. Donna Floyd Fales
10. Julie Heldman

1964

1. Nancy Richey
2. Billie Jean King
3. Carole Caldwell Graebner
4. Karen Hantze Susman
5. Carol Hanks Aucamp
6. Jane Albert
7. Julie Heldman
8. Justina Bricka
9. Tory Fretz
10. Mary Ann Eisel

1965

1. Billie Jean King (tie)
1. Nancy Richey (tie)
3. Carole Caldwell Graebner
4. Jane Albert
5. Mary Ann Eisel
6. Carol Hanks Aucamp
7. Kathleen Harter
8. Julie Heldman
9. Tory Fretz
10. Donna Floyd Fales

1966

1. Billie Jean King
2. Nancy Richey
3. Rosie Casals
4. Tory Fretz

5. Jane "Peaches" Bartkowicz
6. Mary Ann Eisel
7. Donna Floyd Fales
8. Carol Hand Aucamp
9. Stephanie DeFina
10. Fern Kellmeyer

1967

1. Billie Jean King
2. Nancy Richey
3. Mary Ann Eisel
4. Jane "Peaches" Bartkowicz
5. Rosie Casals
6. Carole Caldwell Graebner
7. Stephanie DeFina
8. Kathleen Harter
9. Lynne Abbes
10. Vicky Rogers

1968

1. Nancy Richey
2. Julie Heldman
3. Vicky Rogers
4. Mary Ann Eisel
5. Kathleen Harter
6. Kristy Pigeon
7. Jane "Peaches" Bartkowicz
8. Linda Tuero
9. Stephanie DeFina
10. Patti Hogan

1969

1. Nancy Richey
2. Julie Heldman
3. Mary Ann Eisel Curtis
4. Jane "Peaches" Bartkowicz
5. Patti Hogan
6. Kristy Pigeon
7. Betty Ann Grubb
8. Denise Carter
9. Valerie Ziegenfuss
10. Linda Tuero

1970

1. Billie Jean King
2. Rosie Casals
3. Nancy Richey Gunter
4. Mary Ann Eisel Curtis

5. Patti Hogan
6. Jane "Peaches" Bartkowicz
7. Valerie Ziegenfuss
8. Kristy Pigeon
9. Stephanie DeFina Johnson
10. Denise Carter Triolo

1971

1. Billie Jean King
2. Rosie Casals
3. Chris Evert
4. Nancy Richey Gunter
5. Mary Ann Eisel
6. Julie Heldman
7. Jane "Peaches" Bartkowicz
8. Linda Tuero
9. Patti Hogan
10. Denise Carter Triolo

1972

1. Billie Jean King
2. Nancy Richey Gunter
3. Chris Evert
4. Rosie Casals
5. Wendy Overton
6. Patti Hogan
7. Linda Tuero
8. Julie Heldman
9. Pam Teeguarden
10. Janet Newberry

1973

1. Billie Jean King
2. Chris Evert
3. Rosie Casals
4. Nancy Richey Gunter
5. Julie Heldman
6. Pam Teeguarden
7. Kristien Kemmer
8. Janet Newberry
9. Valerie Ziegenfuss
10. Wendy Overton

1974

1. Chris Evert
2. Billie Jean King
3. Rosie Casals
4. Nancy Richey Gunter

5. Julie Heldman
6. Kathy Kuykendall
7. Pam Teeguarden
8. Valerie Ziegenfuss
9. Jeanne Evert
10. Marcelyn Louie

1975

1. Chris Evert
2. Nancy Richey Gunter
3. Julie Heldman
4. Wendy Overton
5. Marcelyn Louie
6. Mona Schallau
7. Kathy Kuykendall
8. Janet Newberry
9. Terry Holladay
10. Rosie Casals

1976

1. Chris Evert
2. Rosie Casals
3. Nancy Richey Gunter
4. Terry Holladay
5. Marita Redondo
6. Mona Schallau Guerrant
7. Kathy May
8. JoAnne Russell
9. Janet Newberry
10. Kathy Kuykendall

1977

1. Chris Evert
2. Billie Jean King
3. Rosie Casals
4. Tracy Austin
5. JoAnne Russell
6. Kathy May
7. Terry Holladay
8. Kristien Kemmer Shaw
9. Janet Newberry
10. Laura DuPont

1978

1. Chris Evert
2. Billie Jean King
3. Tracy Austin
4. Rosie Casals

5. Pam Shriver
6. Marita Redondo
7. Kathy May Teacher
8. Anne Smith
9. JoAnne Russell
10. Jeanne DuVall

1979

1. Martina Navratilova
2. Chris Evert
3. Tracy Austin
4. Billie Jean King
5. Kathy Jordan
6. Ann Kiyomura
7. Caroline Stoll
8. Kathy May Teacher
9. Kate Latham
10. Terry Holladay

1980

1. Tracy Austin
2. Chris Evert
3. Martina Navratilova
4. Andrea Jaeger
5. Billie Jean King
6. Pam Shriver
7. Kathy Jordan
8. Bettina Bunge
9. Terry Holladay
10. Mary Lou Piatek

1981

1. Chris Evert
2. Tracy Austin
3. Martina Navratilova
4. Andrea Jaeger
5. Pam Shriver
6. Barbara Potter
7. Bettina Bunge
8. Kathy Jordan
9. Mary Lou Piatek
10. Pam Casale

1982

1. Martina Navratilova
2. Chris Evert
3. Andrea Jaeger
4. Tracy Austin

5. Pam Shriver
6. Barbara Potter
7. Billie Jean King
8. Anne Smith
9. Zina Garrison
10. Kathy Rinaldi

1983

1. Martina Navratilova
2. Chris Evert
3. Andrea Jaeger
4. Pam Shriver
5. Tracy Austin
6. Zina Garrison
7. Kathy Jordan
8. Kathy Rinaldi
9. Kathy Horvath
10. Bonnie Gadusek

1984

1. Martina Navratilova
2. Chris Evert
3. Pam Shriver
4. Kathy Jordan
5. Zina Garrison
6. Bonnie Gadusek
7. Barbara Potter
8. Pam Casale
9. Lisa Bonder
10. Kathy Rinaldi

1985

1. Martina Navratilova
2. Chris Evert
3. Pam Shriver
4. Bonnie Gadusek
5. Zina Garrison
6. Kathy Rinaldi
7. Kathy Jordan
8. Barbara Potter
9. Stephanie Rehe
10. Mareen Louie

1986

1. Martina Navratilova
2. Chris Evert
3. Pam Shriver
4. Kathy Rinaldi

5. Zina Garrison
6. Kathy Jordan
7. Bonnie Gadusek
8. Stephanie Rehe
9. Lori McNeil
10. Robin White

1987

1. Martina Navratilova
2. Chris Evert
3. Pam Shriver
4. Zina Garrison
5. Lori McNeil
6. Mary Joe Fernandez
7. Barbara Potter
8. Kate Gompert
9. Elly Hakami
10. Kathy Jordan

1988

1. Martina Navratilova
2. Chris Evert
3. Pam Shriver
4. Zina Garrison
5. Mary Joe Fernandez
6. Lori McNeil
7. Barbara Potter
8. Stephanie Rehe
9. Patty Fendick
10. Susan Sloane

1989

1. Martina Navratilova
2. Zina Garrison
9. Chris Evert
4. Mary Joe Fernandez
5. Pam Shriver
6. Gretchen Rush Magers
7. Patty Fendick
8. Gigi Fernandez
9. Amy Frazier
10. Susan Sloane

1990

1. Martina Navratilova
2. Mary Joe Fernandez
3. Jennifer Capriati
4. Zina Garrison

5. Amy Frazier
6. Meredith McGrath
7. Gretchen Rush Magers
8. Patty Fendick
9. Gigi Fernandez
10. Susan Sloane

1991

1. Martina Navratilova
2. Jennifer Capriati
3. Mary Joe Fernandez
4. Zina Garrison
5. Amy Frazier
6. Lori McNeil
7. Gigi Fernandez
8. Mary Pierce
9. Pam Shriver
10. Marianne Werdel

1992

1. Martina Navratilova
2. Jennifer Capriati
3. Mary Joe Fernandez
4. Lori McNeil
5. Amy Frazier
6. Zina Garrison Jackson
7. Gigi Fernandez
8. Pam Shriver
9. Patty Fendick
10. Ann Grossman

1993

1. Martina Navratilova
2. Jennifer Capriati
3. Mary Joe Fernandez
4. Zina Garrison Jackson
5. Lindsay Davenport
6. Lori McNeil
7. Patty Fendick
8. Pam Shriver
9. Kimberly Po
10. Ann Grossman

1994

1. Lindsay Davenport
2. Martina Navratilova
3. Chanda Rubin
4. Amy Frasier

5. Ginger Helgeson
6. Zina Garrison Jackson
7. Lori McNeil
8. Ann Grossman
9. Gigi Fernandez
10. Marianne Werdel

1995

1. Mary Joe Fernandez
2. Lindsay Davenport
3. Chanda Rubin
4. Amy Frazier
5. Lisa Raymond
6. Zina Garrison Jackson
7. Marianne Werdel Witmeyer
8. Lori McNeil
9. Lindsay Lee
10. Patty Fendick

1996

1. Monica Seles
2. Lindsay Davenport
3. Chanda Rubin
4. Mary Joe Fernandez
5. Meredith McGrath
6. Jennifer Capriati
7. Kimberly Po
8. Amy Frazier
9. Linda Wild
10. Lisa Raymond

1997

1. Lindsay Davenport
2. Monica Seles
3. Mary Joe Fernandez
4. Lisa Raymond
5. Venus Williams
6. Kimberly Po
7. Chanda Rubin
8. Amy Frazier
9. Sandra Cacic
10. Corina Morariu

1998

1. Lindsay Davenport
2. Venus Williams
3. Monica Seles
4. Serena Williams

5. Lisa Raymond
6. Corina Morariu
7. Tara Snyder
8. Chanda Rubin
9. Amy Frazier
10. Annie Miller

1999

1. Lindsay Davenport
2. Venus Williams
3. Serena Williams
4. Monica Seles
5. Amy Frazier
6. Chanda Rubin
7. Jennifer Capriati
8. Lisa Raymond
9. Corina Morariu
10. Mary Joe Fernandez

2000

1. Lindsay Davenport
2. Venus Williams
3. Monica Seles
4. Serena Williams
5. Chanda Rubin
6. Jennifer Capriati
7. Amy Frazier
8. Kristina Brandi
9. Lisa Raymond
10. Meghann Shaughnessy

2001

1. Lindsay Davenport
2. Jennifer Capriati
3. Venus Williams
4. Serena Williams
5. Monica Seles
6. Meghann Shaughnessy
7. Lisa Raymond
8. Meilen Tu
9. Amy Frazier
10. Chanda Rubin

2002

1. Serena Williams
2. Venus Williams
3. Jennifer Capriati

4. Monica Seles
5. Lindsay Davenport
6. Chanda Rubin
7. Alexandra Stevenson
8. Lisa Raymond
9. Meghann Shaughnessy
10. Amy Frazier

2003

1. Serena Williams
2. Lindsay Davenport
3. Jennifer Capriati
4. Chanda Rubin
5. Venus Williams
6. Meghann Shaughnessy
7. Lisa Raymond
8. Laura Granville
9. Ashley Harkleroad
10. Monica Seles

2004

1. Lindsay Davenport
2. Serena Williams
3. Venus Williams
4. Jennifer Capriati
5. Amy Frazier
6. Lisa Raymond
7. Meghann Shaughnessy
8. Chanda Rubin
9. Mashona Washington
10. Jill Craybas

2005

1. Lindsay Davenport
2. Venus Williams
3. Serena Williams
4. Jill Craybas
5. Amy Frazier
6. Laura Granville
7. Meghann Shaughnessy
8. Mashona Washington
9. Lisa Raymond
10. Jamea Jackson

2006

1. Lindsay Davenport
2. Meghann Shaughnessy

3. Shenay Perry
4. Jamea Jackson
5. Venus Williams
6. Vania King
7. Laura Granville
8. Jill Craybas
9. Ashley Harkleroad
10. Meilen Tu

3. Meilen Tuy
4. Meghann Shaughnessy
5. Laura Granville
6. Lindsay Davenport
7. Ashley Harkleroad
8. Jill Craybas
9. Julie Ditty
10. Lilia Osterloh

2007

1. Serena Williams
2. Venus Williams

WTA Season-Ending Top 10 Singles Rankings

Throughout the year the Women's Tennis Association ranks players according to a scientifically designed, state-of-the-art computer ranking system. The ranking system reflects both a player's performance in tournament play as well as her record against other players. The rankings database is updated after each event. New rankings are released every Monday except for the middle Monday during two-week tournaments.

1975

1. Chris Evert
2. Virginia Wade
3. Martina Navratilova
4. Billie Jean King
5. Evonne Goolagong Cawley
6. Margaret Smith Court
7. Olga Morozova
8. Nancy Richey Gunter
9. Francoise Durr
10. Kerry Melville

1976

1. Chris Evert
2. Evonne Goolagong Cawley
3. Virginia Wade
4. Martina Navratilova
5. Dianne Fromholtz
6. Rosie Casals
7. Betty Stove
8. Kerry Melville
9. Olga Morozova
10. Sue Barker

1977

1. Chris Evert
2. Billie Jean King
3. Martina Navratilova
4. Virginia Wade
5. Sue Barker
6. Rosie Casals
7. Betty Stove
8. Dianne Fromholtz
9. Wendy Turnbull
10. Kerry Reid

1978

1. Martina Navratilova
2. Chris Evert
3. Evonne Goolagong Cawley
4. Virgina Wade
5. Billie Jean King
6. Tracy Austin
7. Wendy Turnbull
8. Kerry Reid
9. Betty Stove
10. Dianne Fromholtz

1979

1. Martina Navratilova
2. Chris Evert
3. Tracy Austin
4. Evonne Goolagong Cawley
5. Billie Jean King
6. Dianne Fromholtz
7. Wendy Turnbull
8. Virginia Wade
9. Kerry Reid
10. Sue Barker

1980

1. Chris Evert
2. Tracy Austin
3. Martina Navratilova
4. Hana Mandlikova
5. Evonne Goolagong Cawley
6. Billie Jean King
7. Andrea Jaeger
8. Wendy Turnbull
9. Pam Shriver
10. Greer Stevens

1981

1. Chris Evert
2. Tracy Austin
3. Martina Navratilova
4. Andrea Jaeger
5. Hana Mandlikova
6. Sylvia Hanika
7. Pam Shriver
8. Wendy Turnbull
9. Bettina Bunge
10. Barbara Potter

1982

1. Martina Navratilova
2. Chris Evert
3. Andrea Jaeger
4. Tracy Austin
5. Wendy Turnbull
6. Pam Shriver
7. Hana Mandlikova
8. Barbara Potter
9. Bettina Bunge
10. Sylvia Hanika

1983

1. Martina Navratilova
2. Chris Evert
3. Andrea Jaeger
4. Pam Shriver
5. Sylvia Hanika
6. Jo Durie
7. Bettina Bunge
8. Wendy Turnbull
9. Tracy Austin
10. Zina Garrison

1984

1. Martina Navratilova
2. Chris Evert
3. Hana Mandlikova
4. Pam Shriver
5. Wendy Turnbull
6. Manuela Maleeva
7. Helena Sukova
8. Claudia Kohde-Kilsch
9. Zina Garrison
10. Kathy Jordan

1985

1. Martina Navratilova
2. Chris Evert
3. Hana Mandlikova
4. Pam Shriver
5. Claudia Kohde-Kilsch
6. Steffi Graf
7. Manuela Maleeva
8. Zina Garrison
9. Helena Sukova
10. Bonnie Gadusek

1986

1. Martina Navratilova
2. Chris Evert
3. Steffi Graf
4. Hana Mandlikova
5. Helena Sukova
6. Pam Shriver
7. Claudia Kohde-Kilsch
8. Manuela Maleeva
9. Kathy Rinaldi
10. Gabriela Sabatini

1987

1. Steffi Graf
2. Martina Navratilova
3. Chris Evert
4. Pam Shriver
5. Hana Mandlikova
6. Gabriela Sabatini
7. Helena Sukova
8. Manuela Maleeva-Fragniere
9. Zina Garrison
10. Claudia Kohde-Kilsch

1988

1. Steffi Graf
2. Martina Navratilova
3. Chris Evert
4. Gabriela Sabatini
5. Pam Shriver
6. Manuela Maleeva-Fragniere
7. Natasha Zvereva
8. Helena Sukova
9. Zina Garrison
10. Barbara Potter

1989

1. Steffi Graf
2. Martina Navratilova
3. Gabriela Sabatini
4. Zina Garrison Jackson
5. Arantxa Sanchez-Vicario
6. Monica Seles
7. Conchita Martinez
8. Helena Sukova
9. Manuela Maleeva-Fragniere
10. Chris Evert

1990

1. Steffi Graf
2. Monica Seles
3. Martina Navratilova
4. Mary Joe Fernandez
5. Gabriela Sabatini
6. Katerina Maleeva
7. Arantxa Sanchez-Vicario
8. Jennifer Capriati
9. Manuela Maleeva-Fragniere
10. Zina Garrison Jackson

1991

1. Monica Seles
2. Steffi Graf
3. Gabriela Sabatini
4. Martina Navratilova
5. Arantxa Sanchez-Vicario
6. Jennifer Capriati
7. Jana Novotna
8. Mary Joe Fernandez
9. Conchita Martinez
10. Manuela Maleeva-Fragniere

1992

1. Monica Seles
2. Steffi Graf
3. Gabriela Sabatini
4. Arantxa Sanchez-Vicario
5. Martina Navratilova
6. Mary Joe Fernandez
7. Jennifer Capriati
8. Conchita Martinez
9. Manuela Maleeva-Fragniere
10. Jana Novotna

1993

1. Steffi Graf
2. Arantxa Sanchez-Vicario
3. Martina Navratilova
4. Conchita Martinez
5. Gabriela Sabatini
6. Jana Novotna
7. Mary Joe Fernandez
8. Monica Seles
9. Jennifer Capriati
10. Anke Huber

1994

1. Steffi Graf
2. Arantxa Sanchez-Vicario
3. Conchita Martinez
4. Jana Novotna
5. Mary Pierce
6. Lindsay Davenport
7. Gabriela Sabatini
8. Martina Navratilova
9. Kimiko Date
10. Natasha Zvereva

1995

1. Steffi Graf (tie)
1. Monica Seles (tie)
2. Conchita Martinez
3. Arantxa Sanchez-Vicario
4. Kimiko Date
5. Mary Pierce
6. Magdalena Maleeva
7. Gabriela Sabatini
8. Mary Joe Fernandez
9. Iva Majoli
10. Anke Huber

1996

1. Steffi Graf
2. Monica Seles (tie)
2. Arantxa Sanchez-Vicario (tie)
3. Jana Novotna
4. Martina Hingis
5. Conchita Martinez
6. Anke Huber
7. Iva Majoli
8. Kimiko Date
9. Lindsay Davenport
10. Barbara Paulus

1997

1. Martina Hingis
2. Jana Novotna
3. Lindsay Davenport
4. Amanda Coetzer
5. Monica Seles
6. Iva Majoli
7. Mary Pierce
8. Irina Spirlea
9. Arantxa Sanchez-Vicario
10. Mary Joe Fernandez

1998

1. Lindsay Davenport
2. Martina Hingis
3. Jana Novotna
4. Arantxa Sanchez-Vicario
5. Venus Williams
6. Monica Seles
7. Mary Pierce
8. Conchita Martinez
9. Steffi Graf
10. Nathalie Tauziat

1999

1. Martina Hingis
2. Lindsay Davenport
3. Venus Williams
4. Serena Williams
5. Mary Pierce
6. Monica Seles
7. Nathalie Tauziat
8. Barbara Schett
9. Julie Halard Decugis
10. Amelie Mauresmo

2000

1. Martina Hingis
2. Lindsay Davenport
3. Venus Williams
4. Monica Seles
5. Conchita Martinez
6. Serena Williams
7. Mary Pierce
8. Anna Kournikova
9. Arantxa Sanchez-Vicario
10. Nathalie Tauziat

2001

1. Lindsay Davenport
2. Jennifer Capriati
3. Venus Williams
4. Martina Hingis
5. Kim Clijsters
6. Serena Williams
7. Justine Henin
8. Jelena Dokic
9. Amelie Mauresmo
10. Monica Seles

2002

1. Serena Williams
2. Venus Williams
3. Jennifer Capriati
4. Kim Clijsters
5. Justine Henin
6. Amelie Mauresmo
7. Monica Seles
8. Daniela Hantuchova

9. Jelena Dokic
10. Martina Hingis

2003

1. Justine Henin
2. Kim Clijsters
3. Serena Williams
4. Amelie Mauresmo
5. Lindsay Davenport
6. Jennifer Capriati
7. Anastasia Myskina
8. Elena Dementieva
9. Chanda Rubin
10. Ai Sugiyama

2004

1. Lindsay Davenport
2. Amelie Mauresmo
3. Anastasia Myskina
4. Maria Sharapova
5. Svetlana Kuznetsova
6. Elena Dementieva
7. Serena Williams
8. Justine Henin
9. Venus Williams
10. Jennifer Capriati

2005

1. Lindsay Davenport
2. Kim Clijsters
3. Amelie Mauresmo
4. Maria Sharapova
5. Mary Pierce
6. Justine Henin
7. Patty Schnyder
8. Elena Dementieva
9. Nadia Petrova
10. Venus Williams

2006

1. Justine Henin
2. Maria Sharapova
3. Amelie Maursemo
4. Svetlana Kuznetsova
5. Kim Clijsters
6. Nadia Petrova
7. Martina Hingis
8. Elena Dementieva
9. Patty Schnyder
10. Nicole Vaidsova

2007

1. Justine Henin
2. Svetlana Kuznetsova
3. Jelena Jankovic
4. Ana Ivanovic
5. Maria Sharapova
6. Anna Chakvetadze
7. Serena Williams
8. Venus Williams
9. Daniela Hantuchova
10. Marion Bartoli

2008

1. Jelena Jankovic
2. Serena Williams
3. Dinara Safina
4. Elena Dementieva
5. Ana Ivanovic
6. Venus Williams
7. Vera Zvonareva
8. Svetlana Kuznetsova
9. Maria Sharapova
10. Agnieszka Radwanska

WORLD RANKINGS

There is no official international ranking of tennis players. Each country's annual rankings include only players from that particular country. Since 1921 there have been unofficial women's rankings based on the opinions of respected tennis journalists. These journalists have included Wallis Myers (1921–1938), John Olliff (1939–1951), Lance Tingay (1952–1967) of the London *Daily Telegraph*, Bud Collins of the *Boston Globe* and *NBC* (1968–1996, 2002–2007), and John Barrett, editor of *World of Tennis* (1997–2001). The rankings ended in 2001.

1921

1. Suzanne Lenglen, France
2. Molla Bjurstedt Mallory, USA
3. Mary K. Browne, USA
4. Elizabeth Ryan, USA
5. Kitty McKane, England
6. May Sutton Bundy, USA
7. Irene Peacock, India
8. Winifred Beamish, England
9. Eleanor Goss, USA
10. Marion Zinderstein Jessup, USA

1922

1. Suzanne Lenglen, France
2. Molla Bjurstedt Mallory, USA
3. Helen Wills, USA
4. Kitty McKane, England
5. Geraldine Beamish, England
6. Irene Peacock, India
7. Elizabeth Ryan, USA
8. Marion Zinderstein Jessup, USA
9. May Sutton Bundy, USA
10. Margaret Molesworth, Australia

1923

1. Suzanne Lenglen, France
2. Kitty McKane, England
3. Helen Wills, USA
4. Geraldine Beamish, England
5. Molla Bjurstedt Mallory, USA
6. Eleanor Goss, USA
7. Elizabeth Ryan, USA
8. Didi Vlasto, France
9. Leslie Bancroft, USA
10. Margaret Molesworth, Australia

1924

1. Suzanne Lenglen, France
2. Kitty McKane, England
3. Helen Wills, USA
4. Molla Bjurstedt Mallory, USA
5. Mary K. Browne, USA
6. Eleanor Goss, USA
7. Elizabeth Ryan, USA
8. Phyllis Satterthwaite, England
9. Marion Zinderstein Jessup, USA
10. Sylvia Lance, Australia

1925

1. Suzanne Lenglen, France
2. Helen Wills, USA
3. Kitty McKane, England
4. Elizabeth Ryan, USA
5. Molla Bjurstedt Mallory, USA

6. Eleanor Goss, USA
7. Dorothea Douglass Lambert Chambers, England
8. Joan Fry, England
9. Marguerite Billout, France
10. Marion Zinderstein Jessup, USA

1926

1. Suzanne Lenglen, France
2. Kitty McKane Godfree, England
3. Lili de Alvarez, Spain
4. Molla Bjurstedt Mallory, USA
5. Elizabeth Ryan, USA
6. Mary K. Browne, USA
7. Joan Fry, England
8. Phoebe Holcroft Watson, England
9. Marion Zinderstein Jessup, USA
10. Didi Vlasto, France

1927

1. Helen Wills, USA
2. Lili de Alvarez, Spain
3. Elizabeth Ryan, USA
4. Molla Bjurstedt Mallory, USA
5. Kitty McKane Godfree, England
6. Betty Nuthall, England
7. Esther "Bobbie" Heine, South Africa
8. Joan Fry, England
9. Kea Bouman, Holland
10. Charlotte Hosmer Chapin, USA

1928

1. Helen Wills, USA
2. Lili de Alvarez, Spain
3. Daphne Akhurst, Australia
4. Eileen Bennett, England
5. Phoebe Holcroft Watson, England
6. Elizabeth Ryan, USA
7. Cilly Aussem, Germany
8. Kea Bouman, Holland
9. Helen Jacobs, USA
10. Esna Boyd, Australia

1929

1. Helen Wills Moody, USA
2. Phoebe Holcroft Watson, England
3. Helen Jacobs, USA
4. Betty Nuthall, England

5. Esther "Bobby" Heine, South Africa
6. Simone Passemard Mathieu, France
7. Eileen Bennett, England
8. Paula von Reznicek, Germany
9. Peggy Saunders Michell, England
10. Elsie Goldsack, England

1930

1. Helen Wills Moody, USA
2. Cilly Aussem, Germany
3. Phoebe Holcroft Watson, England
4. Elizabeth Ryan, USA
5. Simone Passemard Mathieu, France
6. Helen Jacobs, USA
7. Phyllis Mudford, England
8. Lili de Alvarez, Spain
9. Betty Nuthall, England
10. Hilde Krahwinkel, Germany

1931

1. Helen Wills Moody, USA
2. Cilly Aussem, Germany
3. Eileen Bennett Whittingstall, England
4. Helen Jacobs, USA
5. Betty Nuthall, England
6. Hilde Krahwinkel, Germany
7. Simone Passemard Mathieu, France
8. Lili de Alvarez, Spain
9. Phyllis Mudford, England
10. Elsie Goldsack Pittman, England

1932

1. Helen Wills Moody, USA
2. Helen Jacobs, USA
3. Simone Passemard Mathieu, France
4. Lolette Payot, Switzerland
5. Hilde Krahwinkel, Germany
6. Mary Heeley, England
7. Eileen Bennett Whittingstall, England
8. Marie Louise Horn, Germany
9. Kay Stammers, England
10. Josane Sigart, Belgium

1933

1. Helen Wills Moody, USA
2. Helen Jacobs, USA
3. Dorothy Round, England
4. Hilde Krahwinkel, Germany

5. Margaret Scriven, England
6. Simone Passemard Mathieu, France
7. Sarah Palfrey, USA
8. Betty Nuthall, England
9. Lolette Payot, Switzerland
10. Alice Marble, USA

1934

1. Dorothy Round, England
2. Helen Jacobs, USA
3. Hilde Krahwinkel Sperling, Germany
4. Sarah Palfrey, USA
5. Margaret Scriven, England
6. Simone Passemard Mathieu, France
7. Lolette Payot, Switzerland
8. Joan Hartigan, Australia
9. Cilly Aussem, Germany
10. Carolin Babcock, USA

1935

1. Helen Wills Moody, USA
2. Helen Jacobs, USA
3. Kay Stammers, England
4. Hilde Krahwinkel Sperling, Germany
5. Sarah Palfrey Fabyan, USA
6. Dorothy Round, England
7. Mary Arnold, USA
8. Simone Passemard Mathieu, France
9. Joan Hartigan, Australia
10. Margaret Scriven, England

1936

1. Helen Jacobs, USA
2. Hilde Krahwinkel Sperling, Germany
3. Dorothy Round, England
4. Alice Marble, USA
5. Simone Passemard Mathieu, France
6. Jadwiga Jedrzejowska, Poland
7. Kay Stammers, England
8. Anita Lizana, Chile
9. Sarah Palfrey Fabyan, USA
10. Carolin Babcock, USA

1937

1. Anita Lizana, Chile
2. Dorothy Round Little, England
3. Jadwiga Jedrzejowska, Poland
4. Hilde Krahwinkel Sperling, Germany

5. Simone Passemard Mathieu, France
6. Helen Jacobs, USA
7. Alice Marble, USA
8. Mary Louise Horn, Germany
9. Mary Hardwick, England
10. Dorothy Bundy, USA

1938

1. Helen Wills Moody, USA
2. Helen Jacobs, USA
3. Alice Marble, USA
4. Hilde Krahwinkel Sperling, Germany
5. Simone Passemard Mathieu, France
6. Jadwiga Jedrzejowska, Poland
7. Sarah Palfrey Fabyan, USA
8. Esther "Bobbie" Heine Miller, South Africa
9. Kay Stammers, England
10. Nancye Wynne, Australia

1939

1. Alice Marble, USA
2. Kay Stammers, England
3. Helen Jacobs, USA
4. Hilde Krahwinkel Sperling, Germany
5. Simone Passemard Mathieu, France
6. Sarah Palfrey Fabyan, USA
7. Jadwiga Jerdzejowska, Poland
8. Mary Hardwick, England
9. Valerie Scott, England
10. Virginia Wolfenden, USA

1940–1945 No World Rankings

1946

1. Pauline Betz, USA
2. Margaret Osborne, USA
3. Louise Brough, USA
4. Doris Hart, USA
5. Pat Canning Todd, USA
6. Dorothy Bundy, USA
7. Nelly Adamson Landry, France
8. Kay Stammers Menzies, England
9. Shirley Fry, USA
10. Virginia Wolfenden Kovacs, USA

1947

1. Margaret Osborne duPont, USA
2. Louise Brough, USA
3. Doris Hart, USA
4. Nancye Wynne Bolton, Australia
5. Pat Canning Todd, USA
6. Sheila Piercey Summers, South Africa
7. Jean Bostock, England
8. Barbara Krase, USA
9. Betty Hilton, England
10. Magda Rurac, Romania

1948

1. Margaret Osborne duPont, USA
2. Louise Brough, USA
3. Doris Hart, USA
4. Nancye Wynne Bolton, Australia
5. Pat Canning Todd, USA
6. Jean Bostock, England
7. Sheila Piercey Summers, South Africa
8. Shirley Fry, USA
9. Magda Rurac, Romania
10. Nelly Adamson Landry, France

1949

1. Margaret Osborne duPont, USA
2. Louise Brough, USA
3. Doris Hart, USA
4. Nancye Wynne Bolton, Australia
5. Pat Canning Todd, USA
6. Betty Hilton, England
7. Sheila Summers, South Africa
8. Anna Bossi, Italy
9. Joan Curry, England
10. Jean Walker Smith, England

1950

1. Margaret Osborne duPont, USA
2. Louise Brough, USA
3. Doris Hart, USA
4. Pat Canning Todd, USA
5. Barbara Scofield, USA
6. Nancy Chaffee, USA
7. Beverly Baker, USA
8. Shirley Fry, USA
9. Anna Bossi, Italy
10. Maria Weiss, Argentina

1951

1. Doris Hart, USA
2. Maureen Connolly, USA
3. Shirley Fry, USA
4. Nancy Chaffee Kiner, USA
5. Jean Walker Smith, England
6. Jean Quertier, England
7. Louise Brough, USA
8. Beverly Baker Fleitz, USA
9. Pat Canning Todd, USA
10. Kay Tuckey Maule, England

1952

1. Maureen Connolly, USA
2. Doris Hart, USA
3. Louise Brough, USA
4. Shirley Fry, USA
5. Pat Canning Todd, USA
6. Nancy Chaffee Kiner, USA
7. Thelma Coyne Long, Australia
8. Jean Walker Smith, England
9. Jean Quertier Rinkel, USA
10. Dorothy Head Knode, USA

1953

1. Maureen Connolly, USA
2. Doris Hart, USA
3. Louise Brough, USA
4. Shirley Fry, USA
5. Margaret Osborne duPont, USA
6. Dorothy Head Knode, USA
7. Suzi Kormoczi, Hungary
8. Angela Mortimer, England
9. Helen Fletcher, England
10. Jean Quertier Rinkel, England

1954

1. Maureen Connolly, USA
2. Doris Hart, USA
3. Beverly Baker Fleitz, USA
4. Louise Brough, USA
5. Margaret Osborne duPont, USA
6. Shirley Fry, USA
7. Betty Rosenquest Pratt, USA
8. Helen Fletcher, England
9. Angela Mortimer, England
10. Ginette Bucaille, France (tie)
10. Thelma Coyne Long, Australia (tie)

1955

1. Louise Brough, USA
2. Doris Hart, USA
3. Beverly Baker Fleitz, USA
4. Angela Mortimer, England
5. Dorothy Head Knode, USA
6. Barbara Breit, USA
7. Darlene Hard, USA
8. Beryl Penrose, Australia
9. Pat Ward, England
10. Suzi Kormoczi, Hungary (tie)
10. Shirley Fry, USA (tie)

1956

1. Shirley Fry, USA
2. Althea Gibson, USA
3. Louise Brough, USA
4. Angela Mortimer, England
5. Suzi Kormoczi, Hungary
6. Angela Buxton, England
7. Shirley Bloomer, England
8. Pat Ward, England
9. Betty Rosenquest Pratt, Jamaica
10. Margaret Osborne duPont, USA (tie)
10. Darlene Hard, USA (tie)

1957

1. Althea Gibson, USA
2. Darlene Hard, USA
3. Shirley Bloomer, England
4. Louise Brough, USA
5. Dorothy Head Knode, USA
6. Vera Puzejova, Czechoslovakia
7. Ann Haydon, England
8. Yola Ramirez, Mexico
9. Christine Truman, England
10. Margaret Osborne duPont, USA

1958

1. Althea Gibson, USA
2. Suzi Kormoczi, Hungary
3. Beverly Baker Fleitz, USA
4. Darlene Hard, USA
5. Shirley Bloomer, England
6. Christine Truman, England
7. Angela Mortimer, England
8. Ann Haydon, England
9. Maria Bueno, Brazil
10. Dorothy Head Knode, USA

1959

1. Maria Bueno, Brazil
2. Christine Truman, England
3. Darlene Hard, USA
4. Beverly Baker Fleitz, USA
5. Sandra Reynolds, South Africa
6. Angela Mortimer, England
7. Ann Haydon, England
8. Suzi Kormoczi, Hungary
9. Sally Moore, USA
10. Yola Ramirez, Mexico

1960

1. Maria Bueno, Brazil
2. Darlene Hard, USA
3. Sandra Reynolds, South Africa
4. Christine Truman, England
5. Suzi Kormoczi, Hungary
6. Ann Haydon, England
7. Angela Mortimer, England
8. Jan Lehane, Australia
9. Yola Ramirez, Mexico
10. Renee Schuurman, South Africa

1961

1. Angela Mortimer, England
2. Darlene Hard, USA
3. Ann Haydon, England
4. Margaret Smith, Australia
5. Sandra Reynolds, South Africa
6. Yola Ramirez, Mexico
7. Christine Truman, England
8. Suzi Kormoczi, Hungary
9. Renee Schuurman, South Africa
10. Karen Hantze, USA

1962

1. Margaret Smith, Australia
2. Maria Bueno, Brazil
3. Darlene Hard, USA
4. Karen Hantze Susman, USA
5. Vera Puzejova Sukova, Czechoslovakia
6. Sandra Reynolds Price, South Africa
7. Lesley Turner, Australia
8. Ann Haydon, England
9. Renee Schuurman, South Africa
10. Angela Mortimer, England

1963

1. Margaret Smith, Australia
2. Lesley Turner, Australia
3. Maria Bueno, Brazil
4. Billie Jean King, USA
5. Ann Haydon Jones, England
6. Darlene Hard, USA
7. Jan Lehane, Australia
8. Renee Schuurman, South Africa
9. Nancy Richey, USA
10. Vera Puzejova Sukova, Czechoslovakia

1964

1. Margaret Smith, Australia
2. Maria Bueno, Brazil
3. Lesley Turner, Australia
4. Carole Caldwell Graebner, USA
5. Helga Schultze, Germany
6. Nancy Richey, USA
7. Billie Jean King, USA
8. Karen Hantze Susman, USA
9. Robyn Ebbern, Australia
10. Jan Lehane, Australia

1965

1. Margaret Smith, Australia
2. Maria Bueno, Brazil
3. Lesley Turner, Australia
4. Billie Jean King, USA
5. Ann Haydon Jones, England
6. Annette Van Zyl, South Africa
7. Christine Truman, England
8. Nancy Richey, USA
9. Carole Caldwell Graebner, USA
10. Francoise Durr, France

1966

1. Billie Jean King, USA
2. Margaret Smith, Australia
3. Maria Bueno, Brazil
4. Ann Haydon Jones, England
5. Nancy Richey, USA
6. Annette Van Zyl, South Africa
7. Norma Baylon, Argentina
8. Francoise Durr, France
9. Rosie Casals, USA
10. Kerry Melville, Australia

1967

1. Billie Jean King, USA
2. Ann Haydon Jones, England
3. Francoise Durr, France
4. Nancy Richey, USA
5. Lesley Turner, Australia
6. Rosie Casals, USA
7. Maria Bueno, Brazil
8. Virginia Wade, England
9. Kerry Melville, Australia
10. Judy Tegart, Australia

1968

1. Billie Jean King, USA
2. Virginia Wade, England
3. Nancy Richey, USA
4. Margaret Smith Court, Australia
5. Maria Bueno, Brazil
6. Ann Haydon Jones, England
7. Judy Tegart, Australia
8. Lesley Turner Bowrey, Australia
9. Annette Van Zyl duPlooy, South Africa
10. Rosie Casals, USA

1969

1. Margaret Smith Court, Australia
2. Ann Haydon Jones, England
3. Billie Jean King, USA
4. Nancy Richey, USA
5. Julie Heldman, USA
6. Rosie Casals, USA
7. Kerry Melville, Australia
8. Mary Ann Eisel, USA
9. Virginia Wade, England
10. Lesley Turner Bowrey, Australia

1970

1. Margaret Smith Court, Australia
2. Billie Jean King, USA
3. Rosie Casals, USA
4. Nancy Richey, USA
5. Virginia Wade, England
6. Helga Niessen Masthoff, Germany
7. Ann Haydon Jones, England
8. Kerry Melville, Australia
9. Karen Krantzcke, Australia
10. Francoise Durr, France

1971

1. Billie Jean King, USA
2. Evonne Goolagong, Australia
3. Margaret Smith Court, Australia
4. Rosie Casals, USA
5. Kerry Melville, Australia
6. Francoise Durr, France
7. Virginia Wade, England
8. Helga Niessen Masthoff, Germany
9. Judy Tegart, Australia
10. Chris Evert, USA

1972

1. Billie Jean King, USA
2. Margaret Court, Australia
3. Nancy Richey Gunter, USA
4. Chris Evert, USA
5. Virginia Wade, England
6. Evonne Goolagong, Australia
7. Rosie Casals, USA
8. Kerry Melville, Australia
9. Francoise Durr, France
10. Olga Morozova, Russia

1973

1. Margaret Smith Court, Australia
2. Billie Jean King, USA
3. Evonne Goolagong, Australia
4. Chris Evert, USA
5. Rosie Casals, USA
6. Virginia Wade, England
7. Kerry Melville, Australia
8. Nancy Richey Gunter, USA
9. Julie Heldman, USA
10. Helga Niessen Masthoff, Germany

1974

1. Billie Jean King, USA
2. Evonne Goolagong, Australia
3. Chris Evert, USA
4. Virginia Wade, England
5. Julie Heldman, USA
6. Rosie Casals, USA
7. Kerry Melville, Australia
8. Olga Morozova, Russia
9. Lesley Hunt, Australia
10. Francoise Durr, France

1975

1. Chris Evert, USA
2. Billie Jean King, USA
3. Evonne Goolagong, Australia
4. Martina Navratilova, Czechoslovakia
5. Virginia Wade, England
6. Margaret Smith Court, Australia
7. Olga Morozova, Russia
8. Nancy Richey Gunter, USA
9. Francoise Durr, France
10. Rosie Casals, USA

1976

1. Chris Evert, USA
2. Evonne Goolagong, Australia
3. Virginia Wade, England
4. Martina Navratilova, Czechoslovakia
5. Sue Barker, England
6. Betty Stove, Netherlands
7. Dianne Fromholtz, Australia
8. Mima Jausovec, Yugoslavia
9. Rosie Casals, USA
10. Francoise Durr, France

1977

1. Chris Evert, USA
2. Billie Jean King, USA
3. Virginia Wade, England
4. Martina Navratilova, Czechoslovakia
5. Sue Barker, England
6. Wendy Turnbull, Australia
7. Betty Stove, Netherlands
8. Rosie Casals, USA
9. Dianne Fromholtz, Australia
10. Kerry Melville Reid, USA

1978

1. Martina Navratilova, Czechoslovakia
2. Chris Evert, USA
3. Evonne Goolagong, Australia
4. Virginia Wade, England
5. Billie Jean King, USA
6. Tracy Austin, USA
7. Pam Shriver, USA
8. Virginia Ruzici, Romania
9. Wendy Turnbull, Australia
10. Kerry Melville Reid, Australia

1979

1. Martina Navratilova, USA
2. Tracy Austin, USA
3. Chris Evert, USA
4. Evonne Goolagong, Australia
5. Billie Jean King, USA
6. Wendy Turnbull, Australia
7. Dianne Fromholtz, Australia
8. Kerry Melville Reid, Australia
9. Virginia Wade, England
10. Regina Marsikova, Czechoslovakia

1980

1. Chris Evert, USA
2. Tracy Austin, USA
3. Martina Navratilova, USA
4. Hana Mandlikova, Czechoslovakia
5. Andrea Jaeger, USA
6. Evonne Goolagong, Australia
7. Billie Jean King, USA
8. Wendy Turnbull, Australia
9. Pam Shriver, USA
10. Virginia Ruzici, Romania

1981

1. Tracy Austin, USA
2. Martina Navratilova, USA
3. Chris Evert, USA
4. Hana Mandlikova, Czechoslovakia
5. Pam Shriver, USA
6. Andrea Jaeger, USA
7. Sylvia Hanika, Germany
8. Mima Jausovec, Yugoslavia
9. Barbara Potter, USA
10. Virginia Ruzici, Romania

1982

1. Martina Navratilova, USA
2. Chris Evert, USA
3. Andrea Jaeger, USA
4. Barbara Potter, USA
5. Hana Mandlikova, Czechoslovakia
6. Tracy Austin, USA
7. Wendy Turnbull, Australia
8. Sylvia Hanika, Germany
9. Pam Shriver, USA
10. Bettina Bunge, Germany

1983

1. Martina Navratilova, USA
2. Chris Evert, USA
3. Pam Shriver, USA
4. Andrea Jaeger, USA
5. Jo Durie, England
6. Wendy Turnbull, Australia
7. Hana Mandlikova, Czechoslovakia
8. Andrea Temesvari, Hungary
9. Sylvia Hanika, Germany
10. Kathy Jordan, USA

1984

1. Martina Navratilova, USA
2. Chris Evert, USA
3. Hana Mandlikova, Czechoslovakia
4. Helena Sukova, Czechoslovakia
5. Manuela Maleeva, Bulgaria
6. Pam Shriver, USA
7. Claudia Kohde-Kilsch, Germany
8. Zina Garrison, USA
9. Wendy Turnbull, Australia
10. Carling Bassett, Canada

1985

1. Martina Navratilova, USA
2. Chris Evert, USA
3. Hana Mandlikova, Czechoslovakia
4. Claudia Kohde-Kilsch, Germany
5. Pam Shriver, USA
6. Zina Garrison, USA
7. Helena Sukova, Czechoslovakia
8. Steffi Graf, Germany
9. Kathy Rinaldi, USA
10. Gabriela Sabatini, Argentina

1986

1. Martina Navratilova, USA
2. Chris Evert, USA
3. Steffi Graf, Germany
4. Helena Sukova, Czechoslovakia
5. Pam Shriver, USA
6. Hana Mandlikova, Czechoslovakia
7. Claudia Kohde-Kilsch, Germany
8. Gabriela Sabatini, Argentina
9. Lori McNeil, USA
10. Manuela Maleeva, Bulgaria

1987

1. Steffi Graf, Germany
2. Martina Navratilova, USA
3. Chris Evert, USA
4. Pam Shriver, USA
5. Hana Mandlikova, Czechoslovakia
6. Gabriela Sabatini, Argentina
7. Helena Sukova, Czechoslovakia
8. Manuela Maleeva, Bulgaria
9. Lori McNeil, USA
10. Zina Garrison, USA

1988

1. Steffi Graf, Germany
2. Martina Navratilova, USA
3. Gabriela Sabatini, Argentina
4. Chris Evert, USA
5. Pam Shriver, USA
6. Natalia Zvereva, Russia
7. Manuela Maleeva, Bulgaria
8. Helena Sukova, Czechoslovakia
9. Zina Garrison, USA
10. Katerina Maleeva, Bulgaria

1989

1. Steffi Graf, Germany
2. Martina Navratilova, USA
3. Arantxa Sanchez-Vicario, Spain
4. Gabriela Sabatini, Argentina
5. Monica Seles, Yugoslavia
6. Zina Garrison, USA
7. Chris Evert, USA
8. Helena Sukova, Czechoslovakia
9. Manuela Maleeva, Bulgaria
10. Mary Joe Fernandez, USA

1990

1. Monica Seles, Yugoslavia
2. Gabriela Sabatini, Argentina
3. Steffi Graf, Germany
4. Martina Navratilova, USA
5. Jennifer Capriati, USA
6. Arantxa Sanchez-Vicario, Spain
7. Mary Joe Fernandez, USA
8. Katerina Maleeva, Bulgaria
9. Manuela Maleeva Fragniere, Bulgaria
10. Zina Garrison, USA

1991

1. Monica Seles, Yugoslavia
2. Steffi Graf, Germany
3. Gabriela Sabatini, Argentina
4. Martina Navratilova, USA
5. Jennifer Capriati, USA
6. Arantxa Sanchez-Vicario, Spain
7. Jana Novotna, Czechoslovakia
8. Mary Joe Fernandez, USA
9. Manuela Maleeva Fragniere, Bulgaria
10. Conchita Martinez, Spain

1992

1. Monica Seles, Yugoslavia
2. Steffi Graf, Germany
3. Arantxa Sanchez-Vicario, Spain
4. Jennifer Capriati, USA
5. Martina Navratilova, USA
6. Gabriela Sabatini, Argentina
7. Mary Joe Fernandez, USA
8. Conchita Martinez, Spain
9. Manuela Maleeva Fragniere, Bulgaria
10. Anke Huber, Germany

1993

1. Steffi Graf, Germany
2. Arantxa Sanchez-Vicario, Spain
3. Martina Navratilova, USA
4. Monica Seles, Yugoslavia
5. Jana Novotna, Czechoslovakia
6. Conchita Martinez, Spain
7. Mary Joe Fernandez, USA
8. Gabriela Sabatini, Argentina
9. Jennifer Capriati, USA
10. Anke Huber, Germany

1994

1. Arantxa Sanchez-Vicario, Spain
2. Steffi Graf, Germany
3. Conchita Martinez, Spain
4. Martina Navratilova, USA
5. Mary Pierce, France
6. Gabriela Sabatini, Argentina
7. Lindsay Davenport, USA
8. Kimiko Date, Japan
9. Jana Novotna, Czechoslovakia
10. Anke Huber, Germany

1995

1. Steffi Graf, Germany
2. Arantxa Sanchez-Vicario, Spain
3. Conchita Martinez, Spain
4. Mary Pierce, France
5. Kimiko Date, Japan
6. Monica Seles, USA
7. Mary Joe Fernandez, USA
8. Magdalena Maleeva, Bulgaria
9. Jana Novotna, Czech Republic
10. Gabriela Sabatini, Argentina

1996

1. Steffi Graf, Germany
2. Monica Seles, USA
3. Arantxa Sanchez-Vicario, Spain
4. Conchita Martinez, Spain
5. Lindsay Davenport, USA
6. Jana Novotna, Czech Republic
7. Kimiko Date, Japan
8. Martina Hingis, Switzerland
9. Anke Huber, Germany
10. Chanda Rubin, USA

1997

1. Martina Hingis, Switzerland
2. Jana Novotna, Czech Republic
3. Lindsay Davenport, USA
4. Monica Seles, USA
5. Iva Majoli, Croatia
6. Mary Pierce, France
7. Amanda Coetzer, South Africa
8. Arantxa Sanchez-Vicario, Spain
9. Irina Spirlea, Romania
10. Mary Joe Fernandez, USA

1998

1. Lindsay Davenport, USA
2. Martina Hingis, Switzerland,
3. Jana Novotna, Czech Republic
4. Arantxa Sanchez-Vicario, Spain
5. Venus Williams, USA
6. Monica Seles, USA
7. Mary Pierce, France
8. Conchita Martinez, Spain
9. Steffi Graf, Germany
10. Nathalie Tauziat, France (tie)
10. Patty Schnyder, Switzerland (tie)

1999

1. Martina Hingis, Switzerland
2. Lindsay Davenport, USA
3. Serena Williams, USA
4. Venus Williams, USA
5. Steffi Graf, Germany
6. Mary Pierce, France
7. Monica Seles, USA
8. Nathalie Tauziat, France
9. Barbara Schett, Austria
10. Julie Halard Decugis, France

2000

1. Martina Hingis, Switzerland
2. Lindsay Davenport, USA
3. Venus Williams, USA
4. Monica Seles, USA
5. Conchita Martinez, Spain
6. Serena Williams, USA
7. Mary Pierce, France
8. Anna Kournikova, Russia
9. Arantxa Sanchez-Vicario, Spain
10. Nathalie Tauziat, France

2001

1. Lindsay Davenport, USA
2. Jennifer Capriati, USA
3. Venus Williams, USA
4. Martina Hingis, Switzerland
5. Kim Clijsters, Belgium
6. Serena Williams, USA
7. Justine Henin, Belgium
8. Jelena Dokic, Yugoslavia
9. Amelie Mauresmo, France
10. Monica Seles, USA

2002

1. Serena Williams, USA
2. Venus Williams, USA
3. Jennifer Capriati, USA
4. Kim Clijsters, Belgium
5. Justine Henin, Belgium
6. Amelie Mauresmo, France
7. Monica Seles, USA
8. Daniela Hantuchova, Slovakia
9. Jelena Dokic, Yugoslavia
10. Martina Hingis, Switzerland

2003

1. Justine Henin, Belgium
2. Kim Clijsters, Belgium
3. Serena Williams, USA
4. Amelie Mauresmo, France
5. Lindsay Davenport, USA
6. Jennifer Capriati, USA
7. Anastasia Myskina, Russia
8. Elena Dementieva, Russia
9. Chanda Rubin, USA
10. Ai Sugiyama, Japan

2004

1. Lindsay Davenport, USA
2. Amelie Mauresmo, France
3. Anastasia, Myskina, Russia
4. Maria Sharapova, Russia
5. Svetlana Kuznetsova, Russia
6. Elena Dementieva, Russia
7. Serena Williams, USA
8. Justine Henin, Belgium
9. Venus Williams, USA
10. Jennifer Capriati, USA

2005

1. Lindsay Davenport, USA
2. Kim Clijsters, Belgium
3. Amelie Mauresmo, France
4. Maria Sharapova, Russia
5. Mary Pierce, France

6. Justine Henin, Belgium
7. Patty Schnyder, Switzerland
8. Elena Dementieva, Russia
9. Nadia Petrova, Russia
10. Venus Williams, USA

2006

1. Justine Henin, Belgium
2. Maria Sharapova, Russia
3. Amelie Mauresmo, France
4. Svetlana Kuznetsova, Russia
5. Kim Clijsters, Belgium
6. Nadia Petrova, Russia
7. Martina Hingis, Switzerland
8. Elena Dementieva, Russia
9. Patty Schnyder, Switzerland
10. Nicole Vaidisova, Czech Republic

2007

1. Justine Henin, Belgium
2. Jelena Jankovic, Serbia
3. Svetlana Kuznetsova, Russia
4. Ana Ivanovic, Serbia
5. Serena Williams, USA
6. Anna Chakvetadze, Russia
7. Venus Williams, USA
8. Daniela Hantuchova, Slovakia
9. Maria Sharapova, Russia
10. Marion Bartoli, France

Appendices

A. Career Earnings of Women Tennis Stars

Figures represent total prize money earned as of August 2008

Lindsay Davenport $22,087,173

Steffi Graf $21,895,277

Martina Navratilova $21,626,089

Venus Williams $20,288,478

Serena Williams $20,274,846

Martina Hingis $20,130,657

Justine Henin $19,461,375

Arantxa Sanchez-Vicario $16,942,640

Monica Seles $14,891,762

Jana Novotna $11,249,284

Chris Evert $8,896,195

Hana Mandlikova $3,340,959

Tracy Austin $1,992,380

Billie Jean King $1,966,487

Virginia Wade $1,542,278

Evonne Goolagong Cawley $1,385,814

B. Open Era Player Records of Women Tennis Stars

*Won-loss records cover matches played since 1968
through November 2006 unless otherwise noted*

	Won	Lost	Winning Percent
Martina Navratilova	1442	219	.868
Chris Evert	1304	144	.901
Steffi Graf	902	115	.887
Virginia Wade	839	329	.718
Arantxa Sanchez-Vicario	759	295	.720
Lindsay Davenport	716	188	.792
Evonne Goolagong Cawley	704	165	.810
Billie Jean King	695	155	.818
Monica Seles	595	122	.830
Margaret Smith Court*	593	56	.914
Jana Novotna	568	223	.717
Hana Mandlikova	567	195	.744
Martina Hingis	524	120	.814
Venus Williams	425	100	.810
Justine Henin	414	99	.807
Tracy Austin	335	90	.788
Serena Williams	320	67	.827

*Includes matches played before 1968.

C. Chronology of Women Tennis Stars by Year of Birth

Player	Year of Birth	Player	Year of Birth
Lottie Dod	1871	Margaret Smith	1942
Dorothea Douglass	1878	Billie Jean King	1943
Molla Bjurstedt	1884	Virginia Wade	1945
May Sutton	1886 (Sept.)	Evonne Goolagong	1951
Hazel Hotchkiss	1886 (Dec.)	Chris Evert	1954
Suzanne Lenglen	1899	Martina Navratilova	1956
Helen Wills	1905	Hana Mandlikova	1962 (Feb.)
Helen Jacobs	1908	Tracy Austin	1962 (Dec.)
Alice Marble	1913	Jana Novotna	1968
Margaret Osborne	1918	Steffi Graf	1969
Pauline Betz	1919	Arantxa Sanchez	1971
Louise Brough	1923	Monica Seles	1973
Doris Hart	1925	Lindsay Davenport	1976
Shirley Fry	1927 (June)	Venus Williams	1980 (June)
Althea Gibson	1927 (Aug.)	Martina Hingis	1980 (Sept.)
Maureen Connolly	1934	Serena Williams	1981
Darlene Hard	1936	Justine Henin	1982
Maria Bueno	1939		

D. ITF World Champions*

Justine Henin (BEL)	2006	Monica Seles (YUG)	1991
Kim Clijsters (BEL)	2005	Steffi Graf (GER)	1990
Anastasia Myskina (RUS)	2004	Steffi Graf (GER)	1989
Justine Henin (BEL)	2003	Steffi Graf (GER)	1988
Serena Williams (USA)	2002	Steffi Graf (GER)	1987
Jennifer Capriati (USA)	2001	Martina Navratilova (USA)	1986
Martina Hingis (SUI)	2000	Martina Navratilova (USA)	1985
Martina Hingis (SUI)	1999	Martina Navratilova (USA)	1984
Lindsay Davenport (USA)	1998	Martina Navratilova (USA)	1983
Martina Hingis (SUI)	1997	Martina Navratilova (USA)	1982
Steffi Graf (GER)	1996	Chris Evert (USA)	1981
Steffi Graf (GER)	1995	Chris Evert (USA)	1980
Arantxa Sanchez-Vicario (ESP)	1994	Martina Navratilova (CZE)	1979
Steffi Graf (GER)	1993	Chris Evert (USA)	1978
Monica Seles (YUG)	1992		

*The ITF World Champion is an honor bestowed upon a player each year by the International Tennis Federation based on a player's performance in Grand Slam tournaments, the Fed Cup, the Olympic Games (if played that year), and other competitions.

E. Women Tennis Stars Inducted into the International Tennis Hall of Fame by Year

May Sutton Bundy	1956	Suzanne Lenglen	1978
Hazel Hotchkiss Wightman	1957	Margaret Smith	1979
Molla Mallory	1958	Dorothea Douglass	1981
Helen Jacobs	1962	Charlotte Dod	1983
Alice Marble	1964	Billie Jean King	1987
Pauline Betz Addie	1965	Evonne Goolagong	1988
Louise Brough	1967	Virginia Wade	1989
Margaret Osborne DuPont	1967	Tracy Austin	1992
Maureen Connolly	1968	Hana Mandlikova	1994
Doris Hart	1969	Chris Evert	1995
Helen Wills	1969	Martina Navratilova	2000
Shirley Fry	1970	Steffi Graf	2004
Althea Gibson	1971	Jana Novotna	2005
Darlene Hard	1973	Arantxa Sanchez-Vicario	2007
Maria Bueno	1978		

F. A Brief History of Women's Tennis Fashion

Introduction

When Major Walter Clopton Wingfield invented the game of lawn tennis in 1873, the sport was enthusiastically embraced by the upper class. England's newest pastime, however, was only modestly popular with Victorian women. Society deemed that the fairer sex engage in more genteel pursuits. The importance of sport to physical well-being was a relatively new concept. Some ladies dressed for garden parties in all their finery, picked up heavy, loosely strung racquets and moved onto the court for an afternoon's activity. The first ladies' championship lawn tennis tournament in the world was held in Dublin, Ireland, in 1879.

Perusing the fashion prevalent during that era is like opening a window into both culture and community. Well-bred British ladies behaved and dressed conservatively. Those mores also dictated the tennis fashion of the period. Consequently, early tennis ensembles included long skirts and dresses, bustles, ties, hats and veils, steel-boned corsets, stockings, petticoats and gloves. Heavy fabrics such as flannel and serge, and accessories including scarves and fur, contributed to the discomfort experienced by the pioneering women of the sport.

These restrictive outfits became outmoded by the onset of the twentieth century. Heavy textiles morphed into lighter, more pliant fabrics, although the color white remained the norm. Today's tennis apparel encompasses short, brilliantly colored form-fitting outfits designed for comfort. Plunging bodices no longer shock and jewelry is commonplace.

1870s–1910s

Tennis was considered a man's sport in the 19th century. When women ventured into the game as competitors, they faced resistance from the males who dominated the courts. There was considerable debate as to whether women should be allowed to participate. Many believed the sport to be too strenuous for females. Some feared that it would jeopardize their femininity. Others felt that serious athletic competition among women was inappropriate, even ill-advised.

One of the first adaptations in apparel for the tennis court was India rubber-soled shoes. They were black so that grass stains weren't apparent. Often they were tied with pink or blue ribbons. These shoes were worn as early as 1878.

Women such as Maud Watson developed into competitive athletes despite the uncomfortable and restrictive clothing required by the All-England Croquet and Lawn Tennis Club. In 1884, she won the inaugural Wimbledon Ladies' Singles Championship in a grueling three-set match dressed in an all-white, ankle-length dress. Many tennis historians believe that white was the color of choice primarily because it masked any signs of perspiration.

Tennis prodigy Charlotte "Lottie" Dod circumvented convention by wearing calf-length skirts during her Wimbledon matches in the late 1800s. The teen sensation was actually wearing part of her school uniform, so officials gave her a pass on fashion protocol. In the early 1900s, women's matches began to require more player mobility and physical exertion. Both hats and bustles had virtually disappeared. Tennis aprons were worn prior to the addition of pockets in women's fashion. The bloomer outfit, initiated by Amelia Bloomer, was worn for tennis, but was not thought to be particularly flattering or feminine. Many women opted for stiff collars which presented a rather masculine look.

Elisabeth Moore, the U.S. champion at the beginning of the new century, appeared in a white lawn dress, leg-o'-mutton sleeves, sailor hat, and ornamental tennis shoes. This was a refreshing change from the dark skirts, big blouses and felt hats worn in the late 1800s.

In 1905, Californian May Sutton became

the first American man or woman to win Wimbledon. She created tennis history by rolling up her sleeves during the match, claiming that she was hot. A trendsetter in women's tennis fashion, Sutton played a match in a dress that was calf-length and sleeveless. Her risqué attire was considered indecent by many tennis officials and spectators. Sutton again shocked the tennis world by donning one of her father's shirts during a match, commenting that it allowed her more freedom to move about the court.

As a child Hazel Hotchkiss Wightman and her brothers would arrive at the Berkeley, California, tennis courts at 6 A.M., since females were not permitted to play after 8 A.M. Her mother created short-sleeved cotton dimity dresses for her. The skirts were about 4 inches off the ground and were worn along with a corset, stockings, high sneakers and a hat. The heavy boning which reinforced the corsets often gouged the players. There was a rack in the Wimbledon dressing room as late as 1914 where the blood-stained corsets could be hung to dry.

1920s–1940s

Early women tennis players caused only a minor ripple compared to the splash that tennis player Suzanne Lenglen, sometimes referred to as "the French hussy," generated in the 1920s. Her fame could be equated to that of current rock stars and Hollywood celebrities. Lenglen's emphasis on "spectacle" helped to popularize the sport. The Compiegne born right-hander was raised in Nice and began competing in her teens. Her unorthodox behavior on and off the court made her a magnet for gossip, while her choice of clothing shocked the tennis world. Lenglen sometimes took her shiny white stockings and rolled them to the knee.

In 1919, Lenglen played a tennis match minus stockings and a petticoat. The absence of stockings in tennis apparel had a surprising effect on the fashion of the sport. When the tops of stockings no longer determined the length of the garment, designers were free to experiment with the length of the skirts. The following year she appeared without a corset. Con-

ventional standards required that all of these articles be worn by the ladies of the court.

Lenglen made headlines with her designer apparel created by French couturier Jean Patou again in 1922. Her low cut, sleeveless, calf-length dresses were made of delicate silk, clingy and filmy — more like a ballet costume than athletic wear. Even in the heat of summer, Lenglen topped her beautiful ensembles with a fur coat.

Lenglen introduced brightly colored cardigan sweaters to the sport. In lieu of hats she wore matching turbans. This type of headband, also called a hair bandeau, was comprised of a two-yard length of silk wrapped around her head and fastened with a jeweled pin. It was very popular with the spectators. History records that in 1923 the public began betting on the bandeau color that the French superstar would wear in her next match. This fashion accessory soon became a wardrobe staple among the players. Lenglen's close friend and fellow player, Elizabeth Ryan, commented that, "All women players should go on their knees in thankfulness to Suzanne for delivering them from the tyranny of corsets." Women worldwide lauded the advent of appropriate sportswear thanks to the courage of this six-time Wimbledon champion.

Helen Wills preferred the golf-style visor or eyeshade. She never played without one. This functional accessory served to protect her skin from sun and weather, and became a trend among the players. As a teen Wills often wore knee-length pleated skirts of cotton broadcloth and her stockings were held up with garters at the knees. Wills blamed trailing hemlines for women's incompetence at the net. As she matured, her signature pigtails were shorn and her hair was styled into a bob. She typically wore a sweater, always red and preferably slightly frayed. She felt that this item of clothing gave her additional confidence. Wills wore two pairs of socks to protect her feet from blisters. She applied an extra layer of face powder so that drops of perspiration would not roll into her eyes.

Tennis fashion generally emulated trends in the apparel industry. When hemlines were raised in the early 1920s, tennis skirts got shorter. When skirts returned to a longer length at the end of the decade, however, women's style of play had progressed to the point that shorter attire was more practical. The refusal of women players to follow the general fashion trend was significant.

In 1929, Billie Tapscott became the first player at Wimbledon not to wear stockings. This South African raised a few British eyebrows by playing bare legged. Once the stockings were abandoned, shorts became the reasonable evolution in women's tennis attire. The conservative, albeit masculine, trend in tennis fashion was continued by Helen Hull Jacobs. In 1933, Jacobs became the first woman to break with tradition by wearing man-tailored shorts at Wimbledon. Long and baggy, the Bermuda length shorts had a dark stripe on the side. Shorts and crewneck t-shirts were commonplace and gender neutral during the late 1920s and 1930s.

American champion Alice Marble created controversy when she appeared on the court wearing shorter boyish shorts instead of a skirt. This clothing permitted her to develop an aggressive serve and volley game and contributed to her success on the court. Marble introduced the jockey cap as a fashion accessory. She felt strongly that the clothes a player wore affected their morale and spectator reaction.

There was little activity in the tennis world during World War II. The few matches that were played were mostly for exhibition with proceeds going toward the war effort. There were restrictions on the amount of yardage that could be used in clothing. Pauline Betz reported problems in purchasing tennis clothing in both the U.S. and Great Britain during wartime.

Couturier Theodore Tinling, born in Britain in 1910, grew up on the French Riviera. He was employed as master of ceremonies at Wimbledon in 1927 and continued in that position until 1949. Tinling wore many hats in the sport of tennis. His most famous role, that of designer for the top female players of the "Golden Age of Tennis," overshadowed his contributions as a player, umpire, commentator and historian of the game. Tinling experimented with fabric, color and form while out-

fitting the most glamorous figures in women's tennis. He designed a dress with a colored border for Joy Gannon to debut in 1947 at Wimbledon. This clearly violated the all-white dress rule and created a stir.

A combination of short skirts and lace panties designed for California native Gertrude "Gussy" Moran in 1949 resulted in Tinling's being banned from the game. He was accused of putting vulgarity and sin into tennis. Following the incident, lace became a fashion staple in every aspect of sport. Although Tinling was shunned by officials at Wimbledon for 33 years because of his flamboyant designs and use of color, he was ultimately reinstated as a liaison to the players at this venue. He went on to administer an annual budget in excess of $500,000 as the official designer for the Virginia Slims Tour. His intimate knowledge of the game and, in particular, his contribution to its fashion revolution, made him a highly influential force in the history of tennis.

1950s–Present

When Gussie Moran turned professional in 1950 she began designing some of her own clothing. The clothing was made by a dressmaker for exhibition matches on the tour. She wore a self-designed white piqué dress trimmed with gold braid on opening night of the tour, held at Madison Square Garden. Although not usually a fashion icon in the sport, Pauline Betz chose a gold lamé tunic and apricot fur panties to wear for the same event.

In the early 1950s, following Gussy Moran's lead, Italian tennis star Lea Pericoli sported a short skirt and frilly panties in a match held in the United Kingdom. This tough clay court player pushed the envelope once again in 1954 by wearing a body-hugging sleeveless top during the International Championship of Tennis held at Foro Italico in Rome. Her tight, skimpy attire was noted by fans and press alike.

Highly ranked player Nancy Chaffee honed her tennis skills as a member of the varsity men's team at the University of California, since no women's team existed. Chaffee introduced sharkskin to the world of tennis fashion in the early 1950s. Her most publicized outfit, however, was a dress made by Edith Sullivan for the National Doubles at Longwood, Massachusetts. The press called the ensemble the "Proper Bostonian." It was made of white bird's eye piqué with a 114 inch circular skirt, a row of Viennese lace around the edge, and a high Peter Pan collar with buttons down to the waist. Under that was a pink taffeta slip with contrasting pink panties. Chaffee often wore divided skirts, or culottes. They could be quite short yet remained relatively modest, making them a popular choice among women players of the day. Althea Gibson preferred shorts but took Tinling's advice and compromised by wearing the divided skirt.

By mid-century a greater variety of tennis designs and new fabrics were introduced. Although Argentinean Mary Weiss debuted the first lace tennis dress and Britain's Pat Ward wore the first nylon dress that same year, neither became a real fashion trend. Newly developed polyester knits and stretch woven fabrics provided much comfort for the athletes and were embraced by the players.

Former tennis champion turned stylist Fred Perry created a line of tennis fashions that included simple and functional short-sleeved knitted shirts, kilted skirts, and tailored shorts that were worn exclusively at the Wimbledon finals from 1961 to 1970. Perry Jones, the president of the Southern California Tennis Association from the 1950s to the early 1970s, envisioned women in proper clothes. This did not include t-shirts or shorts. Jones once gave Maureen Connolly's mother fifty dollars to buy something suitable when he saw her playing in shorts. Maureen Connolly devised a system for the perfect outfit for a finals match. She wore different dresses for each match, and then decided which features she preferred from each. Ted Tinling would then create the dress with her specifications with just hours to spare.

Louise Brough felt there was too much emphasis on women's clothing in the sport. She once played in an accordion pleated skirt which blew up over her head during windy conditions. She preferred more tailored clothes and would pair wool shorts made by the Izod Company with Fred Perry's shirts. Brough and her doubles partner Margaret Osborne duPont were known for their big topcoats called "steamer coats." Made of brightly colored gabardine, they were worn when walking to and from the courts as well as over street clothes. Many players traveled with only about five or six changes of clothing. Laundry had to be done on tour with regularity, since the grass and clay quickly stained the fabrics. Ironing was required. Players could hang their wardrobe to dry, but the wool socks inevitably required additional drying time.

Ambidextrous Californian Beverly Baker brought a feminine look to the courts in the mid– to late 1950s. She was the first player to wear a different dress for each round of her matches at Wimbledon. One of her dresses was made of organdy with thirty yards of trellis ruffles, all topped with a duster styled coat.

Tinling dressed the top female players as long as they were performing well. It was considered an honor to have clothing created by him. Not only were the styles attractive and comfortable, they were beautifully constructed. Many dresses were embroidered with designs significant to the player or the venue where they would be worn. Doris Hart's clothing featured heart shaped trims. Darlene Hard's outfits by Tinling typically had a stripe of red on the shoulder and red underlining on the dress, topped with a red velveteen jacket. Maria Bueno was a Tinling favorite. She received twenty to thirty dresses each year during her prime, far more than the other players.

Warm-up suits made their appearance in the mid–1960s. Prior to that, there was no way to keep the legs warm before playing. Short socks were introduced about the same time but it took a while before they were popular. Many players felt the longer socks were more practical when playing on clay, as they prevented the soil from lodging between the foot and sock.

When tennis matches began to be broadcast on television, colorful attire on the court became more fashionable. White clothing tended to create a glare on the screen. Shadows made the clothing appeared wrinkled. Designers worked around these technical problems. The first totally pastel outfits were worn at Forest Hills in 1972. Commentary was made easier by the addition of color in tennis wardrobes.

Margaret Smith Court found Tinling's designs too frilly. She asked that he create more tailored outfits for her, but he refused. This created friction in their relationship and she began wearing Fred Perry designs. Court enjoyed fashion and designed a line of clothing in the early 1970s. Evonne Goolagong was the first to wear rhinestones on a dress designed by Tinling in 1971. The next year, however, she signed to represent an American clothing company.

Chris Evert primarily wore Mondessa clothes, which included geometrics, florals and brilliant colors. However, Tinling designed a one-shoulder, sarong style dress for her to wear in the World Team Tennis League in the late 1970s. She also wore the halter style tennis dress during that decade. It was primarily Chris Evert's famous two-handed backhand that created the need for pockets in tennis apparel as a place to store the second ball when serving. In 1972, renegade Rosie Casals was sent back to the dressing room at Wimbledon when an official found her dress with a large purple design to be inappropriate. Her trademark headband was adapted the year prior.

In 1973, Billie Jean King and Bobby Riggs engaged in a tennis competition nicknamed the "Battle of the Sexes." She declined to wear the actual dress designed for this match, as the fabric felt different from her normal attire, and she thought that it would be a distraction. King wore the stand-by dress Tinling had created instead. She was carried out like royalty onto the court of the Houston Astrodome atop a gold Egyptian litter wearing a white dress with blue trim, rhinestones and sequins, a blue headband and matching tennis shoes. Her contract with Adidas stated that she wear royal blue tennis shoes, so all of Tinling's ensembles for King had to include that color. King's outfit reflected the glitzy styles popular throughout the decade.

In 1979, Linda Siegel's skimpy backless tank top resulted in an unfortunate wardrobe malfunction for which she later apologized. Several years later American Anne White wore an opalescent, skin-tight lycra body suit during her first round at Wimbledon. Made of white lycra, which adhered to the venue's color code, the outfit was ruled unsuitable by the Wimbledon authorities. Her competitor, Pam Shriver, complained that the garment had distracted her. With the score tied at one set all, the match was postponed overnight. White was ordered to wear a more conventional ensemble the following day when the match resumed. Although she lost the match, the press coverage at the All England Tennis and Croquet Club did wonders for White's self-confidence. Cat suits, body suits and even cocktail dresses have been occasionally worn by players ever since.

Venus and Serena Williams, well known for their fashion sense, have had the greatest impact on the fashion of tennis during the 1990s and the early 2000s. In the 1999 Australian Open, Venus Williams was penalized at a break point because her white hair beads flew onto the court. These baubles were her signature style. They became even more popular with her fans after she became the first unseeded finalist since 1968 at the U.S. Open.

Seventeen-year-old Serena Williams was dressed to kill in a body-hugging, black lycra cat suit at the 2002 U.S. Open. The "second skin," designed by Puma, left little to the imagination and received a lot of press attention. Serena once sported a tight fitting, black jacket with her name emblazoned in shimmering silver across the back. Under that was a studded black tank top that showed off her diamond belly ring. Serena commented that wearing bold fashions actually had given her more confidence on the court. The sisters also introduced short shorts, denim bodysuits and knee high boots, and, in doing so, have pushed tennis clothing to the limit. Their interest in fashion and design has led each of them to develop a line of clothing that includes active wear intended for competition.

The 2007 U.S. Open saw one tennis player wearing a metallic gold dress and later a leopard print ensemble. Defending champ Maria Sharapova became the first player to call a news conference to announce her tennis wardrobe prior to the Grand Slam event. A Nike designer, Colleen Sandieson, created separate outfits for day and night sessions. They were unveiled in dramatic fashion on the rooftop of

Rockefeller Center. Anything Sharapova endorsed translated into sales for the manufacturer. The red evening dress was a tennis first. The color was in honor of the Big Apple and the dress was constructed with a unique no-sew technique. The sleek garment was made of a breathable, microfiber lycra, wicking jersey. The seams were bonded with heat and silicone instead of thread. There were more than 600 Swarovski crystals sewn into the design. A graphic of the New York cityscape adorned the chest. A similar dress, sans crystals and in black and white, was worn during the day. The USTA acknowledged that some purists may not appreciate the emphasis on tennis fashion; however, with fewer superstars on the horizon, any publicity for the sport is positive.

Radical changes such as wars, struggles for civil rights, and clashes over new political ideologies often result in transformation in fashion. This is certainly true with regard to the evolution of fashion in the sport of tennis. These changes were largely the result of innovations within the fabric industry coupled with imaginative designers and audacious players who were willing to test the limits of the tennis establishment. Today, the women's designer tennis apparel industry is a multimillion dollar business.

Index